JEREMY DRISCOLL, O.S.B.

Theology at the Eucharistic Table

*Master Themes
in the Theological Tradition*

GRACEWING

First published jointly in 2003 by:
Centro Studi S. Anselmo
Piazza Cavalieri di Malta, 5
00153 Roma
Italia

Gracewing Publishing
2 Southern Avenue, Leominster
Herefordshire HR6 0QF
United Kingdom

This Gracewing edition published 2005

© 2003 Centro Studi S. Anselmo
© 2005 Gracewing Ltd

ISBN 0 85244 469 9

TABLE OF CONTENTS

Introduction 9

CHAPTER 1
Eucharist and Master Themes in the Theological Tradition. . . . 13

CHAPTER 2
Deepening the Theological Dimensions of Liturgical Studies . . . 29

Introduction 29
Vernacular 31
Sacred Music and Art 32
Music and Language Together 34
Lex Orandi, Lex Credendi 36
Christian Faith's Unique Understanding of History and the
   Celebration of the Paschal Mystery 38
Conclusion 42

CHAPTER 3
Discerning the Dynamic *Lex Orandi-Lex Credendi* in the Anaphora of
The Apostolic Tradition of Hippolytus 45

Introduction 45
1. The Anaphora of *The Apostolic Tradition of Hippolytus* . . . 48
   1.1. Structure 50
2. The Anaphora Shaped by Easter Homilies 52
   2.1. Overview of the First Part of the Anaphora 55
   2.2. Details in the First Part from the Easter Homilies . . . 57
3. The Second Part of the Anaphora: Anamnesis, Offering and
   Giving Thanks for the Present Moment 70
4. The Third Part of the Anaphora: Epiclesis 73
   4.1. The Spirit and the Cup 75
   4.2. The Petition for Unity. 76
Conclusion 80

CHAPTER 4
Uncovering the Dynamic *Lex Orandi-Lex Credendi* in the Trinitarian
Theology of Origen 83

The Dialogue with Heraclides. 84
The Treatise on Prayer 88
Homily 13 on Leviticus. 92
Conclusion 97

CHAPTER 5
Liturgy and Fundamental Theology: Frameworks for a Dialogue . .   99

   Salvatore Marsili   101
   Rino Fisichella   105
   Ghislain Lafont   112
   Hans Urs von Balthasar   118
   Conclusion   126

CHAPTER 6
The Eucharist and Fundamental Theology   129

   Parameters for the Present Discussion   130
   Basic Principles of Word and Sacrament in Dynamic Relation   .   132
   1. The Event Character of the Proclamation of the Word . . .   134
   2. The Bringing of the Gifts to the Altar, The Fruits of Creation
     and History   139
   3. The Transformation of the Gifts   143
   4. The Communion   148
   Conclusion   154

CHAPTER 7
Anamnesis, Epiclesis and Fundamental Theology   157

   Introduction   157
   1. Anamnesis and Epiclesis   160
     1.1. Anamnesis   160
     1.2. Epiclesis   165
   2. Anamnesis and Epiclesis Directed Toward Fundamental
     Theology   171
     2.1. Time, The Burden of History and Freedom   174
     2.2. Truth and History   177
     2.3. Hope for the Future   179
   Conclusion   183

CHAPTER 8
The Manifestation of the Trinitarian Mystery in the Eucharistic
Assembly   185

CHAPTER 9
Liturgy, Sacrament and Catechesis in the *General Directory for
Catechesis*   197

   Introduction   197
   1. Ecclesial Life and the Foundational Role of Liturgy   198
   2. Liturgy as Catechesis   201
   3. The Liturgical Face of the Catechetical Task   205

CHAPTER 10
Preaching in the Context of the Eucharist: A Patristic Perspective . 215

Introduction 215
1. A Theological Description of the Foundations of Preaching . . 217
2. A Theological Framework within which Preaching Unfolds . . 219
3. Specific Theological Content 223
4. Style and Tone. 231
Conclusion 234

CHAPTER 11
Adoration of the Blessed Sacrament 237

Introduction 237
Historical Notes 238
Theological Reflections 242

Reference to Original Publications 245

Index of Names 247

INTRODUCTION

For virtually all of my life as a monk and a theologian, and already from the time when I was a student, I have found ongoing inspiration for my work in the regular celebration of the eucharist. To come back to it again and again, no matter from what particular theme I may have been studying, was to enter a context in which whatever I had learned was secured and deepened at a new level, a context in which I could enter into the adoration that helped me to express my love for what I was learning. To celebrate eucharist often confirmed what I had learned — not directly but by means of signs, symbols, ritual action, and a different kind of language. Yet all these just as often indicated to me things I may have overlooked and further dimensions to pursue in my studies. Gradually I became aware of the fact that this power of the eucharist to shape my way of doing theology was becoming an actual method for me. I developed the habit of regularly coordinating my theological reflection with my regular celebration of the eucharist. I relied on the shape of the rite to give a shape to my theological projects and to indicate the proportions and relations of their various themes.

Naturally, what helped me in my own study of theology was what I would share with students when I found myself in the position of teaching. Through the years I have taught in varied contexts and been gladly assigned to teach any number of subjects. I have had time to write and pursue theological research. Also in my work as a priest and in the preaching and teaching that this entails, I more and more instinctively found that I let the eucharist shape whatever I tried to offer to others.

The present book gathers into one place a number of studies that I have produced during the years in these various settings. Eucharist is the thread that unites them all. Some chapters are the result of course work and have hopefully been refined by the experience of working with students on these themes over the years. Others are the results of invitations I have received either to speak at a conference or to contribute in writing something for a particular project. I have in part reworked all these and arranged them here in an order that follows a certain logic, though each chapter can stand on its own as a separate piece.

To expose the logic of the whole — Chapter 1 was written specifically for this book, a kind of longer introduction, as it were, of what I have called here virtually a method for doing theology by regular referral to the eucharistic rite. I share in this chapter my own experience of grappling with the development of this method together with theological colleagues and with students. Chapter 2, "Deepening the Theological Dimensions of Liturgical Studies," was originally delivered as a conference, and it has something of a polemical edge. If, in the majority of the chapters I recommend that the attention of dogmatic theology should be directed more regularly to the foundational role of the liturgy, here I do the opposite by suggesting that specialists in the liturgy sometimes fail to engage their own discipline at sufficient dogmatic depth.

Chapters 3 and 4 are historical studies of liturgical fonts from the patristic period. I try to do here what I am urging in the previous chapter; namely, engage liturgical questions — in this case historical ones — at the theological depth they deserve.

Chapters 5, 6, and 7 all deal from various angles with the relationship between eucharist and fundamental theology. Through many years of teaching fundamental theology, I defined and developed the method I advocate and employ in these chapters. Since this discipline is foundational, what is accomplished in it will make its repercussions felt across the whole of dogmatic theology. In these chapters I try to show how fundamental theology, in order to perform its task adequately, must include a regular and methodical reference to the liturgical experience of the Church and listen to the disciplines which speak of this experience. I treat some of the specific themes of fundamental theology and try to indicate the fuller shape these receive by attention to the liturgy, above all to the eucharist.

Chapter 8 concentrates on what is the central content of Christian faith: the mystery of the Holy Trinity. Again, it is from what actually happens in the eucharist that any sort of trinitarian formulation or doctrine is derived, precisely because the eucharist is the sacramental form in which the whole work of salvation wrought by God — Father, Son, and Holy Spirit — is delivered to the community that celebrates it. Connecting trinitarian theology with the regular celebration of the eucharist prevents that theology from floating off into abstractions of interest only to theoretical types.

In Chapters 9 and 10 the energy shifts some. In these chapters I direct attention to two contexts in which the fruit of the academic study of theology can be shared in the Church's pastoral work. These are catechesis and preaching. Both chapters indicate how the eucharist can guide and shape these pastoral tasks.

Chapter 11, the final chapter, is directed to what might be called a eucharistic spirituality or eucharistic devotion. I focus here on the personal dimension of what private prayer before the Blessed Sacrament might mean. The center of eucharistic spirituality is found, of course, in the communal celebration itself; but private prayer and adoration of the blessed sacrament are an excellent means of personally digesting the immense riches of the actual celebration.

It gives me joy to be able to share the thoughts I have gathered together here in these pages. I hope that whoever reads them may be helped both to celebrate the eucharist with greater understanding and to pursue theology with the gladness which is lent that task by connecting it to the community's regular celebration of its greatest and most precious sacrament.

Chapter 1

EUCHARIST AND MASTER THEMES
IN THE THEOLOGICAL TRADITION

In 1988 the theological faculty at Mount Angel Seminary began a curriculum review in which my colleagues and I set ourselves the task, among other things, of finding concrete ways to achieve greater integration among the courses.[1] We asked how do the many, many courses — often overwhelming for students who have never been exposed to theology before — all hold together? We wondered if the shape of the curriculum could itself function as a pedagogical tool, showing a center to theology around which specific topics arranged themselves.

Facing these concerns as a faculty, we found that it led us to ask deeper theological questions than we had perhaps at first anticipated. This was exciting and fruitful for us. We had to ask ourselves where is theology's center, where is that center encountered, how is it reflected upon, how best is it unfolded and taught? Well aware that there is more than one way to answer all these questions, we were nonetheless able to arrive as a faculty at a unitive vision broad enough to accommodate the wide variety of approaches represented in theology today and in our own faculty but focused enough to provide our students definite bearings with which they could enter upon and continue the serious study of theology. This approach to theology and the definite shape it has stamped upon our curriculum (where, yes, much of the same material that has always been there is still to be found) are perhaps best summarized in the oft quoted statement of Irenaeus of Lyons: "Our way of thinking is attuned

---

[1] Mount Angel Seminary in Oregon is a Roman Catholic seminary which prepares students for priestly ministry in many of the dioceses of the western United States. In addition to seminary students, lay students and religious also pursue the study of theology there.

to the Eucharist, and the Eucharist in turn confirms our way of thinking."[2]

In a very simple way we found that we could begin the study of theology by pointing to an experience already long familiar to our students: the celebration of the eucharist. This celebration makes the Church to be what it is. From it un-folds all the theology that will be studied. And this same theology in-folds back into the celebration. Said in technical terms, the unifying vision of our curriculum is a eucharistic ecclesiology. We are convinced that it can be a good way to do theology in any setting. We have found it to have particular relevance to students who are preparing to be priests.

This curriculum was a number of years in preparation. We used this work as a renewal for ourselves as a faculty and as an exercise in working more closely together across our various specializations. In the time since it has been implemented, in 1994, we have noted a greater capacity for synthesis in our students, more cross-referencing between courses on their part, and in general a greater sense of a common task among students and teachers at work on many different parts of the theological edifice. It is not the intention of this short reflection to articulate this whole vision and our experience.[3] Rather I wish to share here some of the fruits of my own part in it, how it has affected the way in which I think theologically.

I have the good fortune of teaching both at Mount Angel Seminary and the Pontificio Ateneo S. Anselmo in Rome, one semester every year in each place. My doctoral work was in patristics. Although I work a great deal in this field, through the years I have also taught fundamental theology, liturgy, sacraments, and spiritual theology. For this reason I have always felt a keen interest in the question of the relationship among the

---

[2] *Adv. haeres.* 4, 18. Cited in *The Catechism of the Catholic Church*, (hereafter CCC) 1327 in a section titled "The Eucharist - Source and Summit of Ecclesial Life."

[3] Some of my colleagues have written about this. See O. CUMMINGS, *Eucharistic Soundings*, Dublin 1999; E. SKUBLICS, "Communion Ecclesiology: A Vision of the Church Reshaping Theology and Seminary Formation" in *Pro Ecclesia* VII (1998) 288-306; "The Syllabus: Rethinking the Method" in *Seminary Journal* 5 (1999) 47-50.

theological specializations. I love it when one theological discipline listens deeply to another and lets itself be led in directions it would not have found within its own habits of discourse. But I do not wish simply to say that one discipline can usefully listen more carefully to others. Of course that is the case. Yet I want also to claim that there is for all theological reflection a foundational role which is to be assigned to the *celebration* of the liturgy and especially to the *celebration* of the eucharist.

I want to share here in outline form how I treat these ideas with my students at Mount Angel in lectures that I call "The Elements of the Eucharist and the Master Themes of the Theological Tradition." As I have already said, from the celebration of the eucharist all the theological effort of the Church can be seen to un-fold. And this same theology in-folds back into the celebration. Theology truly shows itself here as an *intellectus fidei*, a rational effort to understand the faith that is professed and celebrated in the liturgy, an effort undertaken so that, returning to the liturgy according to its rhythms, faith may be professed and celebrated ever more deeply and with ever greater understanding. The master themes that the Catholic theological tradition has developed through two millennia can all be shown to have their ultimate origin and their ever renewed impetus in the very shape of the eucharistic celebration itself. I distinguish eight such themes.[4] The presentation of these roughly follows the very order of the rite.

The first master theme is ecclesiology. The Mass begins when an assembly forms, and this is already significant. The coming together of many people into one place to pray under the headship of their bishop or a priest is already manifestation of the mystery of the Church. The various orders gather, each in its place, for the action of the eucharist. This action causes the Church to be; to *do* eucharist is to *be* Church. When theological

---

[4] Obviously this could be done differently, identifying more or less themes in more or less general or specific terms. I intend here a flexible pattern, one possible way of organizing and coordinating eucharist and the Catholic theological heritage. I treat the eight themes that follow in relatively uneven lengths, developing here in slightly greater measure themes not pursued elsewhere in this book.

reflection treats the theme of Church, as it does from any number of perspectives, the reality it treats is ultimately formed here and reaches its highest expression here.

Ecclesiology as an academic discipline can profit from directing some of its attention to the concrete nature of all that is involved in a community assembling for this celebration. Behind every one of the baptized who has come to celebrate eucharist stands a magnificent personal story of grace, of struggle and labor and rejoicing, and of all these united around that person's faith. All have received their faith through others who have believed before them and passed it on. This is *being* Church, and the passing on of faith has this celebration as its ultimate point of arrival. From hundreds of directions involving thousands of persons, faith brings many believers together into one place. This gathering of many into one place has a specific scope. This people disposes itself for undergoing a divine action. The many will be made one, not through some means of their own devising but by receiving from Christ himself that life which he receives from another, from his eternal Father. It is by receiving from the Lord what they themselves do not have and could never generate that these many who are gathered are brought into a unity which has divine origins. Again, the name for this unity is Church.[5]

In the eucharistic celebration itself many elements express the divine nature of the ecclesial reality which is occurring; indeed, these elements are the very means of embodying and ensuring the particular and precise nature of what is happening; namely, that Christ is acting and that the community is entirely defined and comes into being only through what he does and accomplishes. Thus, for example, in the person of the bishop or priest Christ is represented as the head of this assembly. It is he who gathers it; it is under his authority that it stands; it is his word which is gratefully heard and pondered; it is together with him that the community will dare to speak a word back to the Father and make its thanksgiving offering to him.

---

[5] See, for example, *Lumen Gentium* 4: "Hence the universal Church is seen to be 'a people brought into unity from the unity of the Father, the Son and the Holy Spirit,'" citing St. Cyprian, *De Orat. Dom.* 23.

And all this happens in a particular time and place. That time and place are also significant for ecclesiology, for in the eucharist the one time and place of a particular gathering — concretely existing in a specific culture and in a precise moment in history with all the life stories of those who have come together — are expanded and dilate and are made to contain in this particular form the mystery of the universal Church across the world and across the centuries and across the heavens extending to the community of saints in heaven. In any one gathering of a community to celebrate eucharist this whole reality of Church is expressed in the signs of the liturgy and caused to be. The Church is local and located in time, or it cannot come to be. But the local reality is always more than the sum of its parts. The local reality is an icon in which the reality of universal Church is rendered present. Thus, in the eucharistic prayer the local bishop is named, as is the bishop of Rome, with whom the local bishop and bishops across the world verify their communion and apostolic faith. The saints in heaven are named, and the dead are remembered. The year of the celebration is etched boldly on the Easter candle which dominates the sanctuary. And all this is contained in the language and cultural forms of the particular place. Virtually all of the major questions in ecclesiology are contained here in ritual form and in the people who enact the ritual. The balance and proportion with which the many elements of the rite are held together and sequenced can suggest the balance and proportion with which the academic discipline proceeds in its reflective work.

The second master theme is the Word of God and this as understood in dynamic relation to sacrament. Thus, Word and Sacrament together and the one never understood without reference to the other. The first major ritual action after the rites of assembling is the proclamation of the Word of God. Much of the theological enterprise is devoted to understanding the sacred scriptures, but it is in the liturgical assembly that the deepest encounter with the Word is achieved. Here the believer realizes that scripture is not so much a book as a living word from God, a word which, when announced in the assembly, defines the very event that is underway. It is God's intervention and offer of salvation in the here and now of a particular assembly.

It is the shape itself of the eucharistic rite which suggests that
Word and Sacrament be held tightly together in the same master
theme. Obviously scripture and sacraments are two rather
different fields within theology, but attention to the rite can point
a way of bringing the results of these fields closer together. In the
rite what is proclaimed in word is repeated at a different and
deeper level in the symbolic, sacramental action. The word is
brought to its fullness here, but it nonetheless remains the
indispensable foundation for the sacramental action.[6]

I identify as the third master theme the Paschal Mystery. If
word and sacraments can be considered as *forms*, the Paschal
Mystery is their *content*, the message they proclaim. In theology
this becomes christology, that is, all that can be asked and
wondered about and explored concerning Jesus of Nazareth, who
was crucified, who is proclaimed as raised from the dead by the
Father, who sends the Holy Spirit to gather all peoples into his
one body. Naturally reflection on the figure of Christ has occupied
the center of Christian theology from the beginning, but this can
never appropriately become sheer speculation shaped by the
ingenuity of a particular age or individual. It must always be
measured and ultimately judged by its conformity to the
Christ-experience of the believing community in its eucharistic
celebration. For it is there that the crucified and risen Lord
manifests himself in word and sacrament and joins to his risen
body all his faithful followers. It is this *faith* that christology is a
rational effort to understand.[7]

The fourth master theme is titled Anamnesis, Epiclesis, and
Eschatology. The rich, elaborate, and many layered dimensions of
the eucharistic rite call forth theological reflection in varied
directions. Anamnesis and epiclesis are technical terms which in
their strictest application name parts of the eucharistic anaphora.
Anamnesis is a celebrative narration and remembering of the
events of Christ's Paschal Mystery — his death, resurrection,
ascension, his coming again in glory — and an offering of these
to the Father. But a dimension of anamnesis pervades the whole
celebration: it is all remembering, and in the festive setting the

---

[6] This is developed below in chapter 6.

[7] This theme is also developed further in chapter 6.

remembered past is rendered present in mystery and becomes the event which the assembly enacts and participates in. This spurs theological reflection to a consideration of the past deeds of God and the culmination of these in Christ. Such reflection tries to understand and articulate how concrete, actual events from the past can, in the risen Christ, be present in a new time and place and form a new event, the liturgy, which derives from and was already contained in that past event. Ultimately Christian faith celebrated in the eucharist claims nothing less than that the very sacrifice of the risen Lord is rendered present. Theology seeks to penetrate this awesome mystery.

Within the liturgy epiclesis is the invocation of the Father that he send the Holy Spirit upon the gifts for their transformation and that the Spirit fill those who receive the gifts. None of what is believed to happen during the rite would be possible without the action of the Holy Spirit. This spurs theological reflection to develop a pneumatology, that is, a reflection on the role of the Holy Spirit in the salvation wrought by Christ. If in the anamnesis concrete events from the past are recalled in a festive narration, in the epiclesis the view moves beyond the limits of a strict chronology and understands the event of the liturgy also as a visit from the future. The risen Christ already stands in that definitive future in which he is established by his glorification, and through him the Spirit descends from that future in a new Pentecost upon the worshipping assembly and makes it to be one body, one spirit in him.

Rational reflection upon faith is not confined within narrow limits. It is meant to be as high, as deep, as broad as the contents of faith, which are divine in their proportions. And thus, reflection cannot help but seek some understanding of what is for human experience the baffling and intriguing encounter with time. Christian faith, above all as celebrated in the eucharist, achieves a new dimension within the struggle of the human experience of time and so places reflection on time at a new starting point. Thus, within the theological enterprise reflection ranges from a theology of history itself and its significance all the way to a consideration of the last things and the last times which are treated in eschatology. The eucharistic experience is the anchor and the guide for these reflections, and what escapes the firm and definitive grasp of the inquiring mind is nonetheless again and again encountered in the celebration. This encounter leads the mind ever forward in its quest.[8]

I delineate the fifth master theme as the manifestation of the trinitarian mystery through the eucharistic action. The mystery of the Holy Trinity is the central content of Christian Revelation. If, as I said above, Christian reflection has concentrated its attention on exploring the riches and treasures hidden in the figure of Christ, it is through this that it has come to an articulation of — this the language of reflection — the one God in the three divine persons of Father, Son, and Holy Spirit. What Christ himself revealed and what the Church announces to the world is that the triune God invites all people to share in the communion of the Father, Son and Holy Spirit, and by this sharing to live in a new communion with one another.

In many ways it can seem that Christian living and consciousness, as well as theological reflection itself, all tend to shy away from grappling with the mystery of the Trinity. Too difficult and elusive, too abstract and straining of the limits of logic, too complicated — these can be the complaints. All this can become the case if an understanding of the Trinity is sought in speculation unmoored from the foundation of its manifestation in the eucharistic celebration. The whole form of the eucharistic rite is thoroughly trinitarian in its structure. It is by moving within this structure in faith and with loving adoration that the mind learns to bear the blinding light of the divine revelation. For theological reflection to essay some grasp of what happens here it has found that it must name — in an attempt at adequacy — Father, Son, and Holy Spirit. But not only that. These are not spoken of in some sort of speculative abstraction or numbers game but always in conjunction with the community formed by those who share in this triune life; namely, the Church. Thus, it is the *form* of the rite that manifests this divine *form*. In one of the dimensions of this form, it can be said that in the eucharist the *Father* gives himself through his *Son* to the world in the *Church*, and the *Spirit* illumines and vivifies every dimension of this gift. In another dimension, the *Church* responds in thanksgiving by offering to the *Father* the very gift she has

---

[8] This is developed at greater length in chapter 7.

received: the *Son*. The *Spirit* effects the transformation of the *Church's* gifts into the Body and Blood of the *Son*. Here we see that this manifestation of the trinitarian mystery is at one and the same time participation in it. *Many* are *one*, through sharing in the death and resurrection of the Lord, in the *oneness* of Father, Son, and Spirit.

The trinitarian doctrine of the Church, achieved by theological reflection and expressing the central content of her faith, is rooted in the plunge into trinitarian life effected by the eucharist and the other sacraments. The doctrine protects and promotes a right understanding of this saving truth. But doctrine is not enough and does not comprise the whole of the theological effort. Speculation is natural to the human mind and comes the more naturally the greater the mystery. From infinite and divine treasures unending possibilities unfold. Yet this cannot mean speculation in any and all directions. It must always remain the Church's reflection on the Church's faith, which is not her own invention but is given her in revelation by God. This faith is professed and celebrated in the eucharistic assembly, and so communion in that assembly remains the measure and the judge of all theological speculation.[9]

The sixth master theme which I present is the moral life or, more precisely, the reflection on this which is contained in the whole enterprise of moral theology. The presentation of this theme at this point and not earlier is significant. Theological studies do not begin with this topic and for good reason, for Christian moral theology is not merely the presentation of a natural morality which all people of good will manage to value and pursue. It is, of course, at least this much and is based on it. But it is in its distinctive features that the real force and attraction of Christian moral theology is felt. Those distinctive features fall into clear relief when moral theology is treated in a precise context; namely, the context represented here by this placement in relation to the other themes. The place the theme holds in the order of my own presentation here or to my students echoes the placement of the same in *The Catechism of the Catholic Church*. The moral life is dealt with in Part 3 of *The Catechism*, and the

---

[9] This is developed at greater length in chapter 8.

logic of this placement is repeated at many points:[10] what the Church professes in its Creed (Trinity and Church)[11] and what it celebrates in the sacraments (Trinity and Church)[12] require and make possible a new way of living. What is under discussion is not merely a natural morality but a living according to the new dignity in which we are established by the sacramental life of the Church. The sacraments render people capable of loving with God's own love. Our love for God himself is brought to perfection not by our own efforts but by Christ in the Holy Spirit working within us. And we are called and equipped by Christ and the Spirit to love one another and all people not with whatever love we manage to muster but with the divine love which is communicated to us in the sacraments.

The consequences of all this, carefully thought through around every conceivable dimension of human living in every actual set of circumstances which characterize every epoch in which Christians have lived or are living — this is the magnificent heritage of Catholic moral theology. Its requirements are high and steep and, indeed, would be unreachable were it not for that from which the requirements derive. They derive from what God has done in the world through Christ. In Christ, God makes every man and woman new; he renews the whole creation and sets history itself on a new course. Where exactly does this take place? We can answer, in the celebration of the sacraments and above all in the eucharist. But the new divine life bequeathed to human beings in the sacramental celebrations is meant to extend outward from there into every corner of human existence. This does not happen automatically. To ensure that it does, solid thinking, rational reflection, an *intellectus fidei*, are employed so that we who are prone toward an old world and an old way of life may be ever challenged to live the consequences of the grace we receive. Because I celebrate the eucharist I *must* live differently.

The eucharist explains the very strong emphasis on justice and love of neighbor that distinguishes the Christian moral life.

---

[10] See, for example, CCC 13-17, 1692, 2558.

[11] These are the major questions dealt with in Part 1 of the CCC.

[12] These are the major questions dealt with in Part 2 of the CCC.

Some measure of these virtues are found in human nature itself and in other religions, but the force with which this is emphasized in Christian morality and the impressive history of the Christian community on this score are distinguishing dimensions of its life. The sustaining force of the eucharist has made possible in every epoch of Christian history both heroic charity and the spending of one's life for the sake of justice, even sometimes to the point of martyrdom.

The Catechism opens Part 3 quoting directly from a homily by St. Leo the Great, who is ever eloquent and ever quickly to the point. It is useful to quote him also here to summarize this discussion of the significance of the placement of moral theology inside the "sacramental logic." It is worth recalling the pedagogical purposes of this way of discussing theology: in a concrete way our faculty wanted to show how in various ways all that is considered in whatever theological discipline un-folds from within the eucharist celebration. Concerning the moral life, St. Leo speaks in this same way:

> Christian, recognize your dignity and, now that you share in God's own nature, do not return to your own former base condition by sinning. Remember who is your head and of whose body you are a member. Never forget that you have been rescued from the power of darkness and brought into the light of the Kingdom of God.[13]

The seventh master theme in this scheme is spiritual theology. Once again, the order of *The Catechism* in its four major parts explains the logic of this placement. Part 4 is called Christian Prayer. *The Catechism* describes Christian prayer as the personal and vital relationship with the living God professed and celebrated and lived in the Church.[14] This description of prayer, in fact, can be extended to all that the theological tradition considers under the name of spiritual theology or spirituality. *The Catechism's* definition of prayer is carefully formulated to relate this major theme of its fourth part with the three preceding parts. The relationship with God which is expressed through prayer is a relationship not with the God of one's own imagination but with

---

[13] Sermon 21, *In nat. Dom.* 3, cited at CCC 1691.
[14] CCC 2558.

the God *professed* and *celebrated* and *lived* in the Church. Each of those verbal forms in italics is meant to summarize a previous part of *The Catechism*. The triune God and the mystery of the Church are *professed* in the Creed (Part 1). The same are *celebrated* in the liturgy (Part 2). These realities are *lived* by adherence to moral requirements (Part 3). But all this has a "vital and personal" [15] dimension which is worked out uniquely in each individual's life (Part 4). *The Catechism* considers this dimension under the title of prayer. The theological tradition considers the same more broadly under the title of spirituality.

This is theology produced by the saints. But what occurs by the grace of God in individual holy men and women belongs to the whole Church as her treasure and as hers to share. This treasure is likewise the object of rational reflection within theology, not in the sense of subjecting the experience of the saints to some sort of cold dissection, but rather as an effort to understand its dynamics and the conditions which favor its flourishing. The experience of the saints likewise is a kind of guarantee, a testimony, and an exploration of all that is *"professed* and *celebrated* and *lived* in the Church."* Spiritual theology seeks to coordinate through careful thinking the experience of the saints with all of this: what is professed, celebrated, and lived in the Church.

There was a time when spirituality was not set apart out as a specific topic within the theological endeavor of the Christian community. This came about for historical reasons, not all of them happy, that it is now part of this discipline's task to understand as part of its own identity.[16] In the past the arena in which rational reflection on the content of faith was conducted was not the professional, academic setting, with its orderly and methodical ways of proceeding, which characterizes theology today. The personal, vital dimension suffused every dimension of reflection, be it about Christ and Trinity, the Church, or the moral life. Something is gained and something lost in separating out spirituality as a specific topic. In some ways it is odd to think that

---

[15] The expression is from CCC 2558.

[16] See H.U. VON BALTHASAR, "Theology and Sanctity" in *Explorations in Theology. I: The Word Made Flesh*, San Francisco 1989, 181-209.

personal holiness and experience of the divine realities are not necessarily requirements for conducting rational reflection on the faith today. In some circles these may even be considered an impediment to clearheaded thinking. Others may admit them as desirable, but even then they are not incorporated as a specific moment or dimension of theological method. There is surely something lost in this.

On the other hand, perhaps something is gained. Were this dimension not separated out as a separate theme, the sheer weight of the accumulation of genuinely valuable insights from theological reflection during the course of two millennia could cause us to lose sight of that which ultimately produces the best of insights and guarantees them; namely, the lives of the saints. I suggested above that in ecclesiology, in christology, in trinitarian reflection, in reflection on our experience with the mystery of time, there is a virtually infinite horizon toward which theological speculation can direct itself. Progress is made in all these disciplines today thanks to the rigorously applied scientific methods employed in the academy. But at some point the discourse developed in these contexts must regularly let itself be measured against and challenged by a criterion which will help the whole community to judge its worth. That criterion is the holiness of the saints as expressed in their lives, their prayer, their mystic experience, their own theological reflection.

Holiness, however, is an elusive something and has myriad faces. How can we know when and where and whose holiness can be applied as a criterion? I would not presume to offer a complete answer to such a pressing question; instead, I offer only an indication of at least two directions worth pursuing. First, sometimes in the life of the Church the witness of a saint is so strong that *de facto* it functions as a criterion. This can happen within the lifetime of the saint, and it can be extended for decades and centuries after the saint's death. There the witness is in all its force, and good theology would do well not to resist it; indeed, it should seek to understand it. Secondly, there is something which helps us even to measure the experience of the saints and the relevance at any given time of their holiness for theological reflection; namely, the Church's celebration of the eucharist and the theological themes that derive from it. If theological reflection wishes to pursue an understanding of these themes in as thorough a way as possible, then it can, as a specific moment in its method, comb for their riches the lives of the saints to advance its insights around any particular theme. The theme being pursued will find the saints that move the search forward.

The eighth master theme is mission, in technical theological language what is called missiology. The Church does not exist for herself but for the sake of the world. And yet the Church — a collection of many human beings of all stripes and colors — has nothing to offer the world if she herself is not first transformed and made into the one body of Christ in whom she partakes of trinitarian life. It is this that is meant to pass through the Church to the world. In fact, without this transformation there is no Church but only so many human beings of various stripes and colors.

Ultimately it is in the eucharistic celebration that the Church receives its mission to the world and is equipped for it. *Ite missa est* — from this the eucharist derives one of its names, "the Mass." It is as if to call the whole celebration by the name of its ultimate purpose: "the Sending." Rational reflection must also undergird and suffuse the Church's sending, the task of evangelization. As in all the previous master themes, the eucharist is a sure guide in the development of such reflection and a nourishment that lends energy to the task. From the eucharist the Church is sent into the world to share the riches of the divine life that have been received there. As I said above, discussing the moral life, a new way of loving is learned and imparted; and missiology is ultimately about strategies of love. Theological reflection is applied to various settings in which the Good News can be shared; first of all, strategies for helping and serving others in their needs (justice and charity); ultimately, strategies for inviting others to life in the Church and the divine communion that is offered at the eucharist.

Such reflection will keep the unique face of Christian charity in the world sharply in focus and will know how to distinguish it from mere social service programs. It will also articulate reasons why Christians feel compelled to evangelize, and it will be able to do so also when such evangelization is pointedly criticized or resisted. Looking inward toward believers, it will remind them that the Gospel is not fully lived without this sharing. Looking outward toward those who do not believe, it will undergird the invitation offered to all toward faith in Christ with an understanding that this invitation is offered with good reason and is a matter of ultimate concern for all: eternal salvation. Such understanding — theology! — helps the Church to hold its course, to be true to its mission, even when cultural forces and moods suggest that the world and the public life of its communities should not be disturbed by Christians peddling their faith.

In today's complex world where attitudes toward religious faith are extremely varied and the options are legion, there is a temptation which makes its force felt even within the Christian community: the temptation to consider Christian faith just one more among a variety of religious options. When this view is accepted by Christians, even only half consciously, the sense of what Christian faith is slides toward an assessment of it which is more sociologically than theologically conceived. The celebration of the eucharist is the strongest remedy against such tendencies. It is not possible to celebrate the eucharist as the Church understands it — an understanding which theology helps render precise — and come out from there assessing Christian faith as of relative value. One can only come out from the eucharist as sent, sent with what is of ultimate and decisive value for the whole world. The theological work represented by the eighth master theme grapples with all these questions, and it finds the strength to do so because its practitioners celebrate the eucharist as "the source and summit" of all that the Church does, of all that she is.

In conclusion, it should be observed that all these master themes are deeply intertwined; they are not merely separate theological specializations. It is the eucharistic celebration itself that reveals the way in which the themes are related. No ritual gesture or action, no prayer or its content can be understood without reference to the rest. And so it is in theology. If the eucharist is what gives impetus to the development of any of these themes, fundamental theology and its concerns are a glue which holds the discussions together. It should not be surprising that this specialization be used for this purpose. It is with good reason that it is called "fundamental." It is the foundation upon which the theological edifice is constructed. Its principle themes, clearly articulated, enable the edifice to rise.[17] If the eucharistic experience can make its force more felt in the construction of the foundation, then its repercussions will vibrate through the whole structure. This is my project and my hope.

---

[17] This is developed at greater length in chapter 5.

Chapter 2

DEEPENING THE THEOLOGICAL DIMENSIONS
OF LITURGICAL STUDIES

Introduction

In a conference at my monastery and at the seminary where I teach, a renowned biblical scholar spoke of the history of Catholic Biblical Scholarship in the twentieth century. In the course of this conference he made an interesting and important observation about the situation of biblical scholarship as we neared the end of the century. In the first half of the century those Catholic scholars who eventually devoted themselves to biblical studies were ordinarily priests, already trained in general in Catholic theology. In the revival of biblical studies launched in the last thirty years as a result of Vatican II, many Catholic scholars, both lay and clerical, have received higher degrees in various dimensions of the biblical sciences as practiced in the current academy; but it is now possible to do so without reference to, and professional training in, the whole sweep of Catholic theology. In short, a Catholic doctor in biblical studies can be highly respected in the field and yet practice its methods and apply its results while being largely innocent of the whole of Catholic theology.

Early in my own theological training I was grateful to encounter Bernard Lonergan's *Method in Theology*, and I learned from this work that the results of biblical studies, indeed of any specialization within theology, must be coordinated in a dynamic process with the other specializations, which only when taken together as a whole, can properly construct theology.[18] Specializations and specialists are tempted to take the results of their own fields and use them alone for facing questions and

---

[18] B. LONERGAN, *Method in Theology*, New York 1972. See especially 125-145. Longergan's discussion of method does not render explicit a normative conception of theology, nor is agreement on such necessary for specialists to be guided by his insights. Articulating a normative conception of theology is part of the task of Fundamental Theology.

making decisions that are appropriately faced and made only by all the specializations taken together in a dynamic process.[19]

What was observed about biblical scholars I have been able to observe first hand in the North American scene within my own field of specialization, patristics. Specialists across Christian denominations and of no denomination have rapidly multiplied in this field. The Catholic who wants to use the often very positive results of their studies must, it seems to me, take account at some point of the fact that these specialists also often face questions and suggest evaluations without sufficient reference to the whole dynamic sweep of Catholic theology. With my colleagues in this field I am often aware that, having specialized in patristics after my general training in Catholic theology, I work in patristics in a way that often differs from those whose professional training is only within patristics.

It seems to me that a situation not dissimilar to this exists in part today among people professionally trained in liturgical studies. It is possible today to have a degree in liturgy and to practice in the field and yet again face questions and make decisions without sufficient reference to, without sufficient knowledge of, other dimensions of Catholic theology. I want to be careful in my formulation of this observation. I make it wanting to be neither offensive nor inflammatory, and yet at the same time I wish to suggest it as a challenge, a challenge that may at least in part explain some of the very serious practical problems that we face in the North American Church today, a challenge which also, once identified, can be met if there is the will to do so.

It would not be difficult to point to any number of North American liturgists who are very well versed in theology. I gladly acknowledge the fact and profit from their scholarship. However, in my opinion it must likewise be admitted that much of what is advanced in liturgical circles today is being done in a way that is theologically naive when compared with the maturity of the Catholic doctrinal heritage. Let me try to describe the situation I am referring to by addressing some sample topics that can render my remarks more concrete. These are all areas where the theological dimensions of the matter, it seems to me, could be more deeply conceived.

---

[19] LONERGAN, *Method in Theology*, 137.

Vernacular

We may ask what *theological* principles are guiding the current search for an appropriate vernacular language that translates the riches of the Latin liturgy? Have such principles, whatever they might be, been sufficiently debated on the level of their consequences for doctrine? Has there been sufficient *theological* reflection on, say, the mystery of language itself, on the relationship of this to the inner life of God, within which life one of three is named Word? What bonds exist and can be expressed between a vernacular spoken in the twentieth century and the mystery of one of the Trinity becoming flesh and living a human life in first century Palestine and, more, his being proclaimed crucified and now risen, Lord of the universe? And this twentieth century vernacular — what bonds exist and can be expressed between it and the saints with whom we are in communion over time, who faced questions and gave answers in Creeds and Councils that are still considered normative for believing Catholics today? I am reaching toward profound questions, and how we answer them matters not a little. But questions of this nature cannot be adequately faced without the help of the best philosophically, historically, and theologically trained minds of the community. Has the question been faced on this level by ICEL or now by the various episcopal conferences of the English speaking world who must decide whether or not to ask the Holy See's approval of ICEL's work? A practical and blunt question can indicate the tendency of such bodies to foreshorten the theological task with which they are faced: Has a sufficient answer to theological questions raised about translations in a Lectionary really been given when a biblical specialist pronounces a text correctly translated (or interpreted)? But that is the view of a specialist. How does it coordinate with the perspective on that same text by the historian of exegesis or by specialists who know how that text bears on the perception of some doctrine? [20]

---

[20] This is an application of Lonergan's warning that theology requires a dynamic coordination among specialists in many fields to "curb one-sided totalitarian ambitions" to which specialists in a single field may be prone. See *Method in Theology*, 137.

Sacred Music and Art

The question of a language suitable to the liturgy places us very near the question of the meaning of sacred art. Virtually every liturgical concern and practice is expressive of a position — implicit or explicit — on sacred art. If we take just one example, music, we can perhaps develop some remarks to indicate directions in which a deeper and more carefully developed theological approach to the question of sacred art would be helpful. Individual composers of music for the liturgy in our time or in former times need not themselves be trained in depth theologically, though it is not likely that such training would be an impediment to the task of achieving good music. Nonetheless, a carefully developed theological understanding of liturgical music is necessary for the task of suitably judging it and for directing its future development.

Reliance on the three great transcendentals from classical philosophy enables us to frame the question in terms of Beauty, Goodness, and Truth. The relationship between art and the content of Christian faith can begin with the observation that a profound emotion accompanies the apperception of the form of Beauty, Goodness, and Truth becoming flesh. This emotion forms part of the very content of the Word uttered by God about Himself in flesh, such that it could be said that the Word is not fully apprehended without the emotion proper to it. But not just any emotion; rather the emotion proper to it. It is the office of sacred art — in our case here, music — to discover and express in form (the art form) the insight into emotion appropriate to the mystery of Eternal Goodness, Truth, and Beauty ("the form of God" to use an expression from Phil 2:5) having taken the form of a slave.

Admittedly, this is easier said than done, but we have at least been able to be clear on what must be done. Furthermore, theology can remind artists that they cannot possibly succeed in this office without the help of the Holy Spirit. This is more than pious exhortation. It lies in the very nature of the task, which theology alone is equipped to help us identify. No matter how great the genius of, say, the composer, now that the Word of the Father has come to dwell with us in very flesh, one could never discover the form of music appropriate to this action of God without the Holy Spirit whose work it is, from the moment of the Annunciation down to the present, to form from limited, finite materials a form of adequate expression for infinite Goodness, Beauty, and Truth in the world.

Obedience to the Holy Spirit in the creative act of shaping sacred art demands conversion of life (μετάνοια - a change of mind) and submission of the intellect and will to the *form and content* in which God utters his Word, to the *form and content* of Revelation. This is a prior given from which no Christian artist worthy of the name may be allowed to stray for the sake of what we might describe today as a more individually shaped form and content. The Christian artist exercises his task within this fundamental option, which history has shown is wide enough to allow for profound artistic achievement. This form and content of Christian faith is identifiable and clear. And again, though the artist need not be a theologian, theology is necessary to judge the suitability of a particular work of art for the liturgy.

Theology focuses for the artist the nature of the form which is to be created. Behind the form of a work of liturgical art lies a prior and indeed a divine form: the form of one who, though he was in the *form* of God, did not cling to that *form* but rather emptied himself and took the *form* of a slave. (Cf. Phil 2:5) Sacred music created by the breath of the Holy Spirit will be music that expresses by means of measured sound and silence the proportion (!) observed by God Himself in bridging what should have been an unbridgeable gap, the gap between eternal, infinite, divine life, and the passing, finite life of the creature. God bridges this gap with a delicacy and proportion which preserve intact the finite vessel into which divine life enters, a delicacy and proportion which from our human perspective can only be called a new kind of power and a new kind of wisdom, power and wisdom which puts to shame all worldly power and wisdom. It is the form of divine power and wisdom. Sacred music must be in the *form* of this same divine delicacy and proportion, and it must express for us the emotion proper to the realization of what an awesome thing God has done in becoming flesh, emotions of adoration, gratitude, love, devotion, and a cry for mercy at finding oneself in the presence of so great a God.

Thus, it is not enough for liturgists to have a merely general anthropological sense of the importance of music in the cultic rituals which human tribes shape. It will not do to leave unexamined or unchallenged presuppositions about music and art in general which are ours from a culture whose project is different from the search for that form for which the Christian artist searches. Philosophical precision and theological precision of a Christian order are necessary to keep us on task. Boethius can be of some help in illustrating what I am speaking about. Boethius speaks of *musica* in a threefold sense: (a) *musica instrumentalis* (instruments, made by human hands, using dead matter in the interests of "spirit," breath (b) *musica humana* (the human voice) (c) *musica mundana* (the music of the spheres). These three together are to form a sym-phony which involves the entire cosmos across all the levels of its being and discovers that song which lies at the foundation of all Being, the song that is Trinitarian love eternally exchanged and now that same love offered to the entire created order. It is a sym-phony which in fact penetrates the very heart of Providence's ordering of things, and this same symphony must be discovered and made to sound in Christian liturgical assemblies. As a commentator on Boethius puts it, "It is not a matter of cheerful entertainment or superficial consolation for sad moods, but a central clue to the interpretation of the hidden harmony of God and nature in which the only discordant element is evil in the heart of man." [21]

Music and Language Together

In Christian liturgy there is an especially close relationship between music and the language of the liturgy, be that the ancient Latin or a contemporary vernacular. Music must always be at the service of the word. This has been said often enough, but there are theological reasons for this which, when articulated, both can insure that composers do more than pay lip service to a dictum and, alternatively, can prevent music from being banal, excusing its low level by explaining that it is at the service of the word. One possible way of articulating this theology is to search to develop an understanding of the roots of words in the human body itself,

---

[21] H. CHADWICK, *Boethius. The Consolations of Music, Logic, Theology, and Philosophy*, Oxford 1981, 101.

in its pre-rational instincts and rhythms. Before there are words, there is the whole language of the body with its tremendous capacity to express the most beautiful, tender and nuanced intuitions of the interior life. Before there are words, there are shouts, exclamations, groans of pleasure, love, or pain. Words are a highly refined and precise version of such bodily expressions. If their refinement and precision sometimes allow us to forget their bodily roots, this much always remains to remind us: that no word is uttered without a mouth and a throat and air breathed in and out, and no word is heard without bodies in proximity. Their content reaches mind and heart by sounds entering an ear.

Theology sheds further light on what is up to this point a philosophical or anthropological discussion. Christian faith indicates something about the significance of a creature so finely and divinely crafted as to be capable of expression on so profound a level. It is in this capacity for refined expression that the human person exhibits evidence of being made "in the image and likeness of God." (Gen 1:26) Thus, the roots of words ultimately lie deeper than in the human body; they lie in the very nature of God Himself. Revelation carries this content: that God eternally utters a Word that is wholly one with Himself, that it is the very nature of God to be one by being more than one, that expression of Himself is in the very nature of God. It is this expression of God, his Word, which has become flesh and thereby bequeathed to human words, whose roots are in the flesh, the capacity to be swept up into this divine utterance, and this in a twofold direction, making out of human words God's eternal and wholly adequate expression of Himself and making likewise human words directed to God capable of sharing in the Eternal Word's direction of perfect return to his Origin. But if this is to be our language, it can only come about with some measure of theological competence and control that ensures it. There are other ways of speaking, and language, like all other human capacities, suffers the effects of the fall.

Language suitable to the liturgy and the music that is at its service have as their task allowing human words to resound (re-sound) in this the fullest dimension of the divine Mystery into which they have been caught up. Music surrounds the "emitted sound" which a word is with the resonances of its bodily rhythms,

rhythms whose connection with the very inner life of God in whose image they are formed must be discovered and likewise allowed to sound.

Lex Orandi, Lex Credendi

Many liturgists are justifiably fond of drawing attention to the important dictum attributed to Prosper of Aquitaine, "*... ut legem credendi lex statuat supplicandi.*" The phrase shows the dynamic relationship between liturgy and theology and sets in relief the more foundational role of liturgy. As is well known, liturgy exists in the Church before the answers given to pressing questions that come to be embodied in Creeds, Councils, or theological *summae*. Indeed, it is the shape of liturgy and what is believed to happen there which guides the process of the formulation of doctrine throughout, and it is the same which is used to measure the adequacy of such expressions.

Nonetheless, theology itself must understand this very dynamic, not only to protect the foundational role of liturgy within the theological enterprise but also to guard against the dictum's misuse. One example of misuse of the dictum on the practical level is a sort of implicit disregard of the *lex credendi*, as if it were somehow optional since it is not "as foundational" as the liturgy itself. A possible description of a "liturgist" formed by such an attitude would be of someone who knows all about the way Christians have prayed or might pray today but cares very little or knows very little about the relation of these ways of prayer to what the Church believes and articulates in theological discourse. But caring about how the Church articulates what is normative for belief cannot be optional for anyone who would be professionally identified as a Catholic liturgist. A little history shows that the relation between a *lex orandi* and a *lex credendi* quickly becomes reciprocal. There is something in the very nature of liturgy that gives rise to the need to articulate on a different level of discourse what happens in the liturgy, how it happens, and the significance of what happens. Indeed, without such articulation the shape of liturgy itself, which according to the dictum is also a *lex*, could be manipulated at will. And furthermore, without such articulation the believing community could not engage in dialogue, either among its members or with those outside the community, concerning "the reason for the hope" (1 Peter 3:15) which is grounded in what happens in the liturgy and that at the Apostle's urging a Christian should always be ready to give.

It seems to me that *lex orandi, lex credendi* can function as a sort of grid which, once laid over the contemporary liturgical scene, causes some things to fall into clearer relief. For example, generally no one would be so bold as to identify and justify explicitly such a procedure, but it sometimes appears that ways of worship are manipulated with a view toward causing a shift in some dimension of normative belief. This does not happen on any official level, so the dynamic is difficult to trace but nonetheless present for all that. It can come about when someone or some community for whatever reason feels justified in altering some liturgical practice of the tradition and has, as suggested, little care or knowledge of the effects of such an alteration for the theological heritage of the Church. Or it can come about more intentionally, in which case the original dynamic is actually reversed but not admitted to for strategic purposes. A new way of believing is controlling a new way of worship. I have in mind here theological positions at odds with the community's normative articulation being embodied and expressed in some liturgical practice. It is well known, even if a certain cynicism is necessary to know it, that if a liturgical practice which embodies a theological position at odds with normative teaching can be established, eventually that theological position can be established at least in the psyches of the theologically untrained (and unsuspecting) masses. It is not for me to impute motives, but it is useful to observe that theological agendas are operating, either consciously or not, either known or unknown, in anyone who discusses and makes decisions in any way about how liturgy should be celebrated. The current liturgical scene in North America could profit much from rendering these agendas more explicit, first for the sake of intellectual honesty and then for the sake of genuine and skilled theological debate on questions of huge concern to all involved.

Christian Faith's Unique Understanding of History and the
Celebration of the Paschal Mystery

One practical approach to deepening the theological
dimensions of liturgical questions can be to begin by attempting
a description of some problematic situation and then to follow
that with a theological analysis of the same. One possible
description of a problem would be that in liturgical circles there
is considerable talk about how some ritual or language should be
employed or proclaimed but far less talk that attempts to
understand what is believed to be happening in the liturgy. But
can the liturgical renewal that was launched by the Council really
advance without continuing efforts to understand as deeply as is
possible for the inquiring mind the Mystery that is celebrated in
the liturgy? Understanding what is happening will greatly help us
to speak appropriately about how ritual and language should be
employed. It is dangerous to confront these practical concerns
without sufficient theological understanding.

An anthropological understanding of some dimension of the
liturgy is not sufficient, even if it is necessary, to grasp what is
happening. For example, anthropological studies of the nature of
ritual and myth offer valuable insights into what is happening in
Christian ritual and into the narrative structure which shapes it
in so thoroughgoing a way, but only theology can fix the
distinctive dimensions of Christian ritual and "myth." Without
theology's contribution, ritual and myth, in so far as these
describe some of what is happening in Christian liturgy, fade into
a blend conceived as nothing other than another tribe's version of
its approach to the spirit world.

To render my concern more concrete, we may look at the
words of a song often sung during eucharistic celebrations today
which can serve as a representative example of the problem. The
refrain is "We come to share our story." From an artistic point of
view, the criticism could be advanced that this comes off as being
a bit didactic; but the problems with such a text from a
theological point of view are more serious, even if perhaps
elusive. Yet theology, among other things, ought to be prepared
even to track down the source of elusive problems. We may begin
with the observation that in some sense the statement "We come
to share our story" is true as a description of what is happening

in the eucharist, or at any rate it is at least aiming at an insight that we would not want to do without in an understanding of what is happening. The insight is that there is a narrative structure that pervades the eucharistic liturgy, and whatever is narrated there is somehow intimately related to the story of the lives that those in the believing assembly are living. Yet, expressing such an insight with no more precision or finesse than the blunt declaration "We come to tell our story" can in fact be very misleading. First of all, there are no words in this song that ever tell a story, leaving thus unanswered the justifiable question of what precisely is this story. The effect of this can be that there is no precise story. The singing community and even the individual is allowed to fill in the blanks as may seem best. Music is formation on a very deep level, but what guarantee can there be with lyrics like these that the minds and hearts of the worshippers are formed according to a *lex credendi?*

But we may also ask if there is not something misleading in referring to what is happening as "our story." In fact, the story that is proclaimed in liturgy is not immediately and directly the story of the gathered assembly. What is immediately and directly proclaimed is the death and resurrection of Jesus Christ and this in the context of the whole history of Israel and in the context of the apostolic Church. This must be the "our story" which any worshipping assembly gathers to proclaim, and as such it exercises control over and makes demands of any particular assembly that would call it its own. What that control is, what these demands are, theology can make explicit. In that sense the story is not ours until we make it ours by assent. And assent is a public act, publicly verifiable. If we were merely gathering to tell the story of a particular gathered community, not a community which identifies itself in communion with the Church across the world and across time, then the story would be entirely ours and ours to manipulate as we will.

We might further ask if "story" is the best word for describing all this. Is it precise enough? Once we get it straight that what is narrated in liturgy is ultimately the death and resurrection of Christ, does calling all that "story" not risk letting what is narrated there be regarded as no more than an edifying tale? At any rate, nothing in the word (or the song) implies the specific and unique Christian understanding of what in fact happens when the death and resurrection of Christ is remembered in a believing assembly. Scripture and Tradition have a word for this; namely, memorial or anamnesis. Do we not need these words to express adequately what in fact is happening? What has been believed and understood by the Church about the "storytelling" that goes on in the eucharistic assembly evokes a host of mysteries and questions that are wonderful to contemplate and to seek to understand. A past is narrated and believed to be entirely present. A future is revealed and likewise constitutive of the present. Is this believed with good reason? What makes it possible? On what grounds does the Church make such a claim? Who cares or should care about such a past being present, about such a future? What conditions are necessary for participating in such an event, for claiming it as "our story"?

Liturgical renewal as envisioned by the Council cannot advance at any depth without probing such questions as these. Not every believing Christian asks or answers these questions in the way that professional theologians do, but the Church knows that in some way or other these are every believer's questions before the mystery of the liturgy, and what is answered well and carefully by her best minds at work finds its way of sifting down to every level of conceiving and answering questions. Relatively few people, whether they be intellectually simple or sophisticated, are spiritually fed in the long run by approaches to the liturgy that would burke this level of questioning. For a time the novelty of some new practice or approach can claim some interest and seem to offer some promise; but if the liturgy is to feed people for a lifetime, in times as difficult as our own, then a theological effort at understanding it as deeply and precisely as possible is surely called for.

It is a fact that many worshippers are exceedingly bored in the presence of the reformed liturgy, a fact either denied or admitted with reluctance or with perplexity by those who are engineering liturgies precisely so that such could never happen. The problem probably does not lie, as is often explained, in the fact that those who are bored are simply unreformed curmudgeons who will never go along with what was, after all, a reform decreed by an ecumenical Council. By this time more than the curmudgeons are bored. Virtually everyone is or risks being so by much of what is served up for our spiritual nourishment.

The explanation may be that the whole community is lacking in theological depth, the kind of depth that is advanced by well trained professional theologians — not to mention the holiness and contemplation of believers [22] — but which always sifts down to the most simple of believers. Without the precision which theology can offer, the community risks simply celebrating itself, its story and not the story of Jesus. This is boring.

There seems to me to be little or no contest on the level of spiritual worth between the kind of liturgy represented by the "we come to tell our story" mood and the liturgy which understands itself, as the Scripture itself puts it, as "remembering the wonderful deeds of God." This latter is a catch phrase of the tradition around which a wealth of profound insight into what is happening at liturgy groups itself, not least of which is what Jesus intended by his command at the Last Supper, "Do this in memory of me." He commanded that we repeat his action of taking up bread and wine and that we repeat the words he said over them. This is distinguishable in meaning from the sacred meals of other tribes. His words and actions at the Last Supper refer concretely and precisely to his death on the cross, which he was to undergo on the morrow. This action and the command to remember it henceforth refer all memorial, all storytelling, to this central event of salvation history. But the crucifixion which is remembered is the crucifixion of one who is risen, and thus it is that, present to his Church as risen Lord, Jesus can associate with his sacrifice a community at a point far distant in time from the particular time in which he was crucified. This is what it means to be risen: that he is able to reveal and bestow what he accomplished in one particular time on every time and every place. The liturgy is and proclaims a magnificent and completely unexpected mystery: that the center and fulfillment of all time stands in the very midst of time. The past is completely recapitulated in the personal existence of the risen Lord, and so also the future of the human race, manifested progressively in the Church, is already present in him and revealed in the extension of the reality of his risen body to the Church.[23]

---

[22] Cf. *Dei Verbum*, 8 on how tradition makes progress in the Church.

[23] I have greatly condensed here thoughts that I developed under the influence of H.U. von Balthasar, G. Lafont, and others in chapter 5.

Conclusion

What might these concrete examples suggest for the title and project of this study, deepening the theological dimensions of liturgical studies? Without pretending to be exhaustive concerning a theological agenda for the future, I would like to group suggestions into three categories.

The first category has to do with collaboration among theological specialists. I think a much more thoroughgoing collaboration between theologians trained in Fundamental and Systematics needs to occur with those trained in history of the liturgy and its anthropology. What liturgists think about and say and suggest could be greatly deepened by such collaboration.[24]

A second category of suggestions might be described as developing a willingness and the will to engage issues at the deepest possible level. Too often in recent decades the word "pastoral" has been the excuse for shirking the full range of discipline that the whole community of believers and thinkers must undertake, each member in a particular way, if the faith is to survive in the richness in which it has been handed on to us and if it is to really nourish our contemporaries. Gnosticism in the patristic period, New Age theories in our own, and Pop Liturgy within the Church all three have something in common. First of all, they have a real capacity to attract because they very often successfully articulate what people's most genuine and indeed valid religious concerns are. But they likewise have in common that they cannot deliver the goods they promise, for to spotlight a need, an interest, a desire is only half the pastoral task. The other half is to receive the Gospel as the only possible fulfillment of these desires, to receive it with the complete metanoia, the completely new way of thinking, that it requires. Theology is systematic, comprehensive, and methodical exposure and subjection to this new way of thinking in all its consequences, attempting, as the writer of a summa might do, to face every conceivable question and to leave no question without an attempted answer.

---

[24] It is not the focus of my present remarks, but here it is at least worth noting that dogmatic theology for its part suffers from insufficient contact with liturgists, or perhaps better put, from insufficient attention to the liturgy itself. See chapter 5 on the theological project of S. Marsili.

In a third category of suggestions we might try to identify some specific theological questions that, if well developed, could be of great service in deepening the theological dimensions of our approach to liturgical questions. One such topic would be an ecclesiology more thoroughly derived from the shape of the eucharistic celebration itself. This is a call for a more vigorous application of the principle *lex orandi, lex credendi* to our understanding of the Church. It could counteract ecclesiologies, implicit or explicit, which are more sociologically or politically or "politically-correctly" derived. Included in a eucharistically derived ecclesiology would be a theology of Holy Orders which is "able to give a reason" (cf. 1 Peter 3:15) for the hierarchical structure of the Church and its liturgical manifestation, able to give a reason for different roles in the liturgy and the capacity of these distinctions to create unity.

Another topic deserving of greater theological attention is trinitarian theology. Whether concerning trinitarian theology as a topic of specialization or its general bearing on the liturgy, it is important to renew from the perspective both of history and of systematic thought how the Church's trinitarian faith derives from the Church's experience of the action of the Holy Trinity in the liturgy, again, above all in the eucharist. Yet that its roots lie in the liturgy does not restrict the advancement of insight into its mystery to liturgical categories. Such insight can and must be advanced also in the theoretical realm, not meaning by this shapeless speculation and production of some new doctrine but rather understanding something in the way that only disciplined and systematic thought allows. Such theoretical advance must find its way back to the liturgy, for there its coherence and adequacy are ultimately measured, but there also it makes its ultimate contribution; namely, a celebration of the mystery with the ever greater kind of understanding suitable to a mystery.

Finally, it seems to me that theology in general and liturgy in particular must both concern themselves more and more to dialogue in critical and challenging fashion with all that characterizes the contemporary *Zeitgeist*. The uniquely Christian understanding of history, which is manifested most fully in the eucharistic celebration, promises to solve what is one of the most anguishing dimensions of contemporary experience; namely, the meaning of time and history. To articulate correctly and well this uniquely Christian understanding of history, theology is needed. To understand at depth how it is manifested in the eucharist, and indeed by extension in all liturgy, liturgists will need this theology.

In a different direction, still dealing with our contemporaries, the Christian understanding of truth is something urgently needed in our times because for us truth is not an abstract set of correct principles, a gnosis however derived. For us truth is a person, a divine person, Jesus Christ; and, to connect this fact to the anguished experience of time, this Jesus Christ is met in history. This truth is life for us, and it is life delivered and received, full of transforming power, precisely in the community that is constituted by the eucharistic celebration. The best theology is needed to articulate this truth, and liturgists must understand the eucharist as offering no less than this.

Finally, Christian faith conceives itself as offering the only adequate understanding of that for which every human heart is made and the only possibility of attaining it; namely, the notion of what a human person is. A human person is that being so deeply loved as to be unique and irreplaceable.[25] At the ground of all being, both human being and divine being, is not an individual with his rights but a person, that is, one whose entire definition is derived by relation to another. The eucharist reveals this relation; the eucharist is this relation. It is the relation of Father, Son, and Spirit to one another and ourselves as summoned to communion within this communion.

---

[25] This formulation is by J. Zizioulas, whose theological project can in part be characterized by concern to develop understanding of the human person in light of the trinitarian mystery as revealed in the eucharistic assembly. See J. ZIZIOULAS, *Being as Communion, Studies in Personhood and the Church*, Crestwood NY 1993. For a study of the same and for this particular formulation of a human person, see P. McPARTLAN, *The Eucharist Makes the Church, Henri de Lubac and John Zizioulas in Dialogue*, Edinburgh 1993, 174.

Chapter 3

DISCERNING THE DYNAMIC
LEX ORANDI-LEX CREDENDI IN THE ANAPHORA
OF *THE APOSTOLIC TRADITION OF HIPPOLYTUS*

Introduction

The phrase *lex orandi-lex credendi*, expressing the dynamic relationship between liturgy and doctrinal expression, was not articulated as such before the first half of the fifth century.[26] Nonetheless, it has long been recognized as a succinct expression of a dynamic at work well before it was rendered explicit in this phrase. Indeed, it is considered a foundational description of the way things are and ought to be in the relationship. What the Church celebrates in liturgy is the foundation for whatever is articulated in doctrinal pronouncements. However, the dynamic is not so neat as all that, and historical study of the conditions in which the dictum emerged can be useful in requiring nuance of anyone who would wish to apply it and draw consequences from it today.

I propose here such a particular study: an examination of this dynamic, insofar as it can be uncovered, in the ancient anaphora found within the text known as *The Apostolic Tradition of Hippolytus*.[27] I want to focus the study further; namely, around

---

[26] Actually *lex orandi-lex credendi* should be considered a shorthand expression of the more precise assertion of Prosper of Aquitaine *ut legem credendi lex statuat supplicandi*. On this, see P. DE CLERCK, "'Lex orandi, lex credendi,' sens original et avatars historiques d'un adage équivoque," in *Questions Liturgiques* 59 (1978) 193-212. For the attribution of this to Prosper with a discussion of the extensive bibliography, see K. IRWIN, *Context and Text, Method in Liturgical Theology*, Collegeville 1994, 3-32. For a briefer summary of the question, see A. SCHILSON, "Lex orandi-lex credendi" in *LThK* 6 (1997) 871.

[27] This is how the text is generally named and cited, but fewer and fewer scholars any longer think it possible to assign with certainty the text to Hippolytus of Rome or to take it as representing Roman liturgical traditions, as once was the common wisdom about it. For a review of the literature with

questions of the Trinity.[28] It has long been observed that the dynamic *lex orandi-lex credendi* contributed to the articulation of the Church's trinitarian faith as this came to expression together with christological formulations. Nonetheless, in large part the attention of scholars has been on the liturgical influence of Baptism. Perhaps nothing was so influential and constant in exercising control over the shape of the Church's trinitarian faith as the risen Lord's command to "baptize in the name of the Father, and of the Son, and of the Holy Spirit." (Matt 28:19) And yet surely the trinitarian shape of eucharistic worship acted also as a guide, both consciously and unconsciously, in trinitarian doctrinal formulations. There would be any number of possible directions in which this reality could be explored in patristic theology.[29] The present study proposes to do so on a particular

---

strong arguments against its attribution to Hippolytus, see M. METZGER, "Nouvelles perspectives pour la prétendue *Tradition Apostolique*," *EO* 5 (1988) 241-259; "Enquêtes autour de la pretendue *Tradition Apostolique*," *EO* 9 (1992) 7-36. Nor does it seem possible to assign with certainty any other geographical location to the text instead of Rome. It seems best to recognize its value as "un bien de l'Église 'universelle' plutôt que de l'Église de Rome," as Metzger suggests in "Nouvelles perspectives" 255. It should be read in the genre of a church order, that is, compilations of traditional material adapted to new situations and presented as having apostolic authority. As such the material gathered there can come from different time periods and places. For this genre, see B. STUDER, "Liturgical Documents of the First Four Centuries" in *Handbook for Liturgical Studies, Volume 1, Introduction to the Liturgy,* ed. A. Chupungco, Collegeville 1997, 200-205. Despite all these complications, what interests me here is an ancient anaphora and its relation to theology. It is this understanding that I hope to advance in the present study, without pretending to solve the historical problems surrounding the text. For the date, see below, n. 33. The texts are taken from: B. BOTTE, *La Tradition apostolique de Saint Hippolyte. Essai de reconstitution,* (LQF 39) Aschendorff, Münster 1989[5]; *Prex Eucharistica. Textus e variis liturgiis antiquioribus selecti,* edd. A. Hänggi and I. Pahl (Spicilegium Friburgense 12) Fribourg 1968, 80-81.

[28] More often than not in an investigation for origins of trinitarian doctrine, especially at a primitive level, the weight will fall on evidence and questions of the relationship between Father and Son, with the question of the Holy Spirit lurking only implicitly in the background. In what follows I will consider binarian evidence as relevant to the search for trinitarian origins.

[29] This sort of study was suggested many years ago by J. LEBRETON, *Histoire du dogme de la Trinité II,* Paris 1928, 212. For a review of the *status*

genre of text, a eucharistic anaphora; in this case an anaphora which enables us to examine the *lex orandi-lex credendi* dynamic at a very early stage, before it was ever explicitly operating as a principle, as it was by the fifth century or as it is sometimes made to do, occasionally too woodenly, in our times.

I suggested above that the relationship between liturgy and doctrinal formulations is not so neat as the shorthand phrase *lex orandi-lex credendi* is sometimes made out to be. Not infrequently the picture that is drawn is something to the effect of there being a liturgy in place long before the community ever began to be reflective on what we would identify today as doctrinal questions. The liturgy's rituals, symbols, and euchological language — "discourse" of a different kind from doctrine — are more primordial and thus more foundational than doctrinal language. True enough. But the nuance that is lacking here, or perhaps better, the unasked question, is where have these rituals, symbols, and euchology come from? What meaning do they carry or intend to express? They are certainly in their own way expressing definite theological positions about God, about Jesus' relationship to God, about salvation, about sin, about eternal life, and so on. The euchology changes in order to express these theological positions, and there is no sense that such change is manipulative. It is, rather, a kind of progress in rendering more precise what the Church believes and is celebrating. In this sense there is a kind of lex that is already controlling the *lex orandi* and shaping it. Examining the anaphora of *The Apostolic Tradition* and its roots gives us an opportunity to discern in part this still more primitive dynamic that functions as a kind of *lex* in the shaping of the *lex orandi*. I will try to show here how that more primitive *lex* can be found in the biblical text itself, but the biblical text read in a particular way.[30] This is nothing other than the *regula fidei*,

---

questionis up until 1970, see A. HAMMAN, "Du symbole de la foi à l'anaphore eucharistique" in *Kyriakon, Festschrift Johannes Quasten II*, edd. P. Granfield and J. Jungmann, Münster 1970, 835-843. For a more recent discussion, see B. STUDER, "Liturgy, an Expression and Norm of Right Belief," in *Handbook for Liturgical Studies, Volume 1, Introduction to the Liturgy*, ed. A. Chupungco, Collegeville 1997, 60-63.

[30] So I am using *lex* here in a large sense. In some cases *lex* is applied with the strictness of a norm, as later with Augustine and Prosper; but in the larger

another useful catch phrase which identifies the dynamic by
which the early communities identified the faith that came to
them from the apostles. So apostolic faith — focused here in a
particular way of reading the Scriptures — is what shapes the
anaphora and explains whatever modifications and additions can
be traced from its textual ancestors. And this anaphora will exert
its influence on trinitarian expressions more precisely formulated
as a *lex credendi*. I hope that one of the values of such a study can
be to show more clearly how the eventually rather complicated
trinitarian doctrines do really have their roots not only in the
eucharistic experience of the Church but also in the biblical text
as this is read and established by apostolic faith. The Old
Testament is read by apostolic faith; the New Testament is
established by it. But, of course, the fullest context of such
reading is the liturgical assembly of the communities whose faith
comes from the Apostles.

1. *The Anaphora of* The Apostolic Tradition of Hippolytus

In what follows I want to examine the anaphora that is found
in *The Apostolic Tradition of Hippolytus*. The text is presented as
a model; that is, it cannot be taken as a fixed written text always
and everywhere pronounced as set down. It shows us rather the
way in which the presider at eucharist would have shaped such
a prayer. I will be building here on the analysis of this prayer by
E. Mazza.[31] On the basis of his studies I want to examine the

---

sense there is a sort of sliding scale that expresses the relationship of the
authoritative force in the dynamic between Bible, liturgy, and doctrinal
formulation.

[31] E. MAZZA, *The Origins of the Eucharistic Prayer*, Collegeville 1995,
98-176. P. Bradshaw expresses reservations about some of Mazza's
conclusion in P. BRADSHAW, "Introduction: The Evolution of Early
Anaphoras," in *Essays on Early Eastern Eucharistic Prayers*, ed. P. Bradshaw,
Collegeville 1997, 10-14. Bradshaw's reservations do not affect the arguments
that I will develop from Mazza. Mazza's analysis is perhaps too much
concentrated on the relation between the anaphora and the Easter homilies
of Melito and Pseudo Hippolytus, which will be discussed shortly below.
Though I accept this relation as outlined by Mazza and use it as a spur for
my own reflections, I will try to fill it out by reference to other patristic
literature of roughly the same period, not to mention many biblical
influences, which it is always important to detect. I will be arguing for a

dynamic at work when this prayer is considered as a kind of *lex orandi* that influences the shape of trinitarian theology. In doing this I wish to watch as well for clues about what shaped the *lex orandi*. As I have already suggested in general terms, we will see that this is a particular way of reading the Bible and preaching it. Mazza observes that the anaphora of the *Apostolic Tradition* "... has directly or indirectly inspired all the other anaphoras up until today."[32] This fact alone, I think, suggests the value of uncovering the theological dynamic at work in the shaping of the prayer. In addition to seeing a very early stage of a process and the intrinsic interest this holds, on the basis of this, one will have a fuller context for judging subsequent developments. Do they hold to the initial shape of the dynamic? Do they change it? In either case, why?[33] Now the text of the anaphora.

---

widespread common tradition that explains the themes that appear both in liturgical prayer and in theological texts. G. Dix in *The Shape of the Liturgy*, London 1945, 159 adduces a number of verbal parallels between the writings of Justin Martyr and the anaphora.

[32] Mazza, *Origins*, 176. Perhaps the statement is exaggerated, and yet even cut in half it expresses well the importance of the prayer.

[33] I focus the study on this anaphora because it is what has survived and is thus available to us for examination, but it should be kept in mind that in the actual course of things this anaphora is the surviving evidence of a naturally much more complex situation in which a common tradition about ways of prayer stands behind it. I agree with the consensus that the document can be dated to the first half of the third century. For me Metzger's description of the "Identification des utilisateurs du document" in "Enquêtes" pp. 22-26 is the strongest argument for such a date. Though the nature of Church Orders allows for new use of old material, the compiler of *The Apostolic Tradition* presents all the material as traditional, and it is likely that the material represented there is in some cases even older than the third century. The affinities that we will see between the anaphora and other sources of second century theology strengthen this likelihood. As regards the anaphora, the same common tradition is witnessed also in the anaphora-like prayer in *The Martyrdom of Polycarp*, XIV, 2, which will be discussed below. The Easter Homilies of Melito and Pseudo Hippolytus also testify to this common tradition. This connection is what is examined with Mazza below. P. Bradshaw would date the whole much later, even to the beginning of the fourth century. P. Bradshaw, "Redating the Apostolic Tradition: Some Preliminary Steps," in *Rule of Prayer, Rule of Faith: Essays in Honor of Aidan Kavanagh, OSB*, eds. J. Baldovin and N. Mitchell, Collegeville 1996, 3-17. It is necessary to distinguish, as does Bradshaw here, between the date of the final redaction and the dates for various materials within it. Concerning the

1.1. *Structure*

> Gratias tibi referimus, Deus, per dilectum puerum tuum Iesum Christum, quem in ultimis temporibus misisti nobis salvatorem et redemptorem et angelum voluntatis tuae, qui est Verbum tuum inseparabile, per quem omnia fecisti, et ⟨cum⟩ beneplacitum tibi fuit, misisti de caelo in matricem virginis; quique, in utero habitus, incarnatus est et Filius tibi ostensus est, ex Spiritu sancto et virgine natus.

> Qui voluntatem tuam complens et populum sanctum tibi adquirens, extendit manus, cum pateretur, ut a passione liberaret eos qui in te crediderunt.

> Qui cumque traderetur voluntariae passioni, ut mortem solvat et vincula diaboli dirumpat, et infernum calcet et iustos illuminet, et terminum figat et resurrectionem manifestet, accipiens panem, gratias tibi agens dixit: Accipite, manducate, hoc est corpus meum quod pro vobis confringetur.

> Similiter et calicem dicens: Hic est sanguis meus, qui pro vobis effunditur. Quando hoc facitis, meam commemorationem facitis.

> Memores igitur mortis et resurrectionis eius, offerimus tibi panem et calicem, gratias tibi agentes, quia nos dignos habuisti adstare coram te et tibi ministrare. Et petimus, ut mittas Spiritum tuum sanctum in oblationem sanctae Ecclesiae; in unum congregans, des omnibus qui percipiunt ⟨de⟩ sanctis in repletionem Spiritus sancti, ad confirmationem fidei in veritate, ut te laudemus et glorificemus per puerum tuum Iesum Christum: per quem tibi gloria et honor Patri et Filio cum sancto Spiritu in sancta Ecclesia tua et nunc et in saecula saeculorum. Amen.[34]

Perhaps a few preliminary observations about the language encountered here are in order before proceeding to a more systematic analysis. It is clear that we are already dealing here with a stylized liturgical language, presented to the reader as a part of a church order, that is, a text whose material is presented as traditional and normative. This is kerygmatic language, not theological language in the strict sense, that is, language that is reflective and discursive. It is throughout closer to the biblical language than to the language of theological reflection that one

---

anaphora, Bradshaw would also date it late, though he admits (p. 10), on the basis of parallels between the anaphora and passages in Irenaeus and Justin Martyr, that it may have taken its form before the end of the second century. He seems not to take into account the study of Mazza on the parallels with the Easter homily which we will follow here, which further strengthen this likelihood. But my purpose here is not primarily to solve the problem of dating but to uncover the dynamic *lex orandi-lex credendi*.

[34] *Prex Eucharistica*, 80-81.

encounters in, say, Irenaeus' *Adversus Haereses* or in Origen's *De Principiis*. Some of the language is certainly archaic, such as the title *puer* for Jesus Christ. All these are clues to gather for gaining some sense of the nature of liturgical language and for distinguishing it from language destined in other contexts to articulate a *lex credendi*. But let us proceed now systematically.

Mazza sees a three-part structure to this text: (1) the first thanksgiving, giving thanks for Christ's work of salvation and extending to and including the account of the Last Supper; (2) the second thanksgiving, which gives thanks for this present moment, from *memores igitur* to ... *tibi ministrare;* (3) the epiclesis, from *et petimus*... and extending into the final doxology.[35] The roots of this material — both the structure and the content — lie in different kinds of antecedents. In the first part of the text there is a single coherent arc of development. Mazza thinks the inspiration for the language and theology of this first half is to be found in the atmosphere of something like the Easter homilies of Melito of Sardis and Pseudo Hippolytus.[36] The second and third parts of the text seem, according to Mazza, rather more to lie in the line of development from the Jewish thanksgiving prayer *Birkat ha-mazon* and what Mazza shows to be a Christian version of the same; namely, *The Didache*.[37] I will use the structure identified by

---

[35] MAZZA, *Origins*, 149-152. But see V. RAFFA, *Liturgia eucaristica, mistagogia della Messa: dalla storia e dalla teologia alla pastorale pratica*, Rome 1998, 512-523. Raffa divides the prayer into two sections, not three; a first part characterized by anamnesis, a second characterized by epiclesis. This is the kind of disagreement that I don't think it is necessary to solve in order to proceed with the present investigation. Such schemes of division are useful for distinguishing different elements in the prayer and so to guide our discussion, but they cannot be proffered as being most certainly the original understanding of whoever may have composed the prayer. See also C. GIRAUDO, *La struttura letteraria della preghiera eucaristica*, Rome 1989, 294-295. Giraudo also discusses the material using a two part division.

[36] MAZZA, *Origins*, 107-129. I use the clumsy expression "in the atmosphere of something like" to indicate that Mazza does not claim a direct textual dependence between these Easter homilies and the anaphora. He is connecting theological worlds of thought that emerge in two genres, the Easter homily and the anaphora.

[37] MAZZA, *Origins*, 149-176. For the structure of the *Didache* and its relation to the *Birkat ha-mazon*, see ibid., 12-41. This relationship is strongly contested by RAFFA, *Liturgia eucaristica*, 506-511. Raffa thinks that the

Mazza to give order to the present study. We can keep our
bearings in the text by being mindful of the three-part structure.
And insofar as the antecedants of any of these three parts can be
uncovered, they will provide a direction for interpreting whatever
contributes to that which we especially wish to examine here;
namely, the contribution of the anaphora to trinitarian theology.

2. *The Anaphora Shaped by Easter Homilies*

In this first part of the prayer Mazza finds a number of
expressions that are paralleled in the Easter homilies of Melito
and Pseudo Hippolytus, where the expressions and their theology
are developed at greater length. Some of these expressions are
important also for determining the trinitarian theology found in
the anaphora, and we will come to these shortly. But first we must
gauge the importance of this connection between homily and
anaphora. Mazza explains the connection to it in this way: "The
only explanation possible is that (1) the literary genre of the
Easter homilies possessed some words and expressions that were
bearers of precise theological themes, and (2) these passages were
obligatory. They had to be used because they derived from the
typological interpretation of specific biblical quotations that were
the necessary point of reference of the entire celebration." [38]

We should think hard about the dynamic suggested here.
This shows it at a very early and fluid stage, long before it was
explicitly identified in the catch phrase *lex orandi-lex credendi*. The
deepest roots of what is happening here is a theology achieved in
the biblical text as a whole, a theology uncovered when the text
is read with the eyes of Christian faith and in a typological key.
From this whole biblical world there emerge particularly striking
phrases, taken from the Bible, expanded and explained in
homiletic form in the course of the Easter celebration as
represented in these two homilies.

---

prayers in the *Didache* can be explained by direct dependence on Old
Testament precedents. For my argument the difference does not matter
much. The point is that there are many witnesses to a whole common
tradition of prayer which is working its influence on the anaphora.

[38] Mazza, *Origins*, 128.

For his analysis of the material in the homilies, Mazza bases himself on the studies of R. Cantalamessa, who has examined them in painstaking detail.[39] From his work it can be seen that the structure of these liturgical homilies is in two parts: (1) The Passover of the Old Testament, as in Exodus 12, is read in a typological key oriented toward Christ; (2) then the Christian mystery of the Passover, is developed at considerable length, developing "doctrinal" points.[40] In a certain sense we can claim that we are right at the point of passage between biblical text, biblical preaching, and biblical language used in an anaphora that wishes to accompany the meal in memory of the Lord's death. So close is the language, style, and genre of these homilies to Jewish Haggada on the Passover, and the influence of Haggada on at least certain sections of the Gospels' accounts of the Last Supper and the Lord's death, that Cantalamessa claims, "... dovremmo concludere che l'omelia pasquale del II secolo è l'erede più diretta, la prosecuzione — non più canonica, ma ugualmente autentica — del kergyma neotestamentario."[41] In all this we have a sifting of texts which eventually gives us the

---

[39] R. CANTALAMESSA, *L'omelia "In S. Pascha" dello Pseudo-Ippolito di Roma. Ricerche sulla teologia dell'Asia Minore nella seconda metà del II secolo*, Milano 1967; and ID., *I più antichi testi pasquali della chiesa. Le omelie di Melitone di Sardi e dell'Anonimo Quartodecimano e altri testi del II secolo* (Bibliotheca "Ephemerides Liturgicae" 33) Roma 1972.

[40] "Doctrinal" is my word, not Cantalamessa's. This is what I want to call doctrine at a primitive stage, where its language is very close to the Bible, very close to the liturgy. What I am calling doctrine in this qualified sense is what Cantalamessa describes as "... il piano divino in Gesù Cristo il quale, preesitendo come Dio, si incarna, soffre, muore, risorge e risale al cielo, procurando una redenzione definitiva che ora viene offerta a tutte le genti." CANTALAMESSA, *I più antichi testi*, 15. The intimate connection of this kind of preaching to the liturgy is likewise suggested by Cantalamessa in what follows immediately what I have just cited: "Redenzione che nella celebrazione liturgica della veglia pasquale viene come sventagliata nelle sue implicazioni sacramentali e mistiche davanti all'assemblea dei fedeli, ad opera di Cristo stesso che parla in prima persona, in una sorta di epifania cultuale."

[41] CANTALAMESSA, *I più antichi testi*, 14. One can gain a sense of how close is the connection in language, style, and genre by comparing the homilies with 1 Peter. Of it Cantalamessa says that it "... partecipa dell'uno e dell'altra: della canonicità del Nuovo Testamento e del genere dell'omelia pasquale." Ibid., 14.

language and the structure of a eucharistic anaphora. What I wish especially to draw attention to in this study is that this language and structure are thoroughgoingly trinitarian, making reference to what we would call both economic and immanent Trinity. We have caught, as if in a freeze shot of an action film, the biblical language in its point of coalescence around the mystery of the Trinity. It is no accident that such a shot is captured where the Church celebrates eucharist, especially the Easter eucharist. Here the biblical text of both testaments comes thoroughly alive in the words and actions of the bishop who recounts with thanksgiving the story of the redemption which culminates in the Lord's words and actions at the Last Supper.

We who have lost the sense of how intensely significant for the Fathers was the uncovering of biblical types perhaps fail to grasp how natural, and yet how profound, was the application of biblical typology to liturgical rites and words. This was happening in a number of different contexts simultaneously, not merely in these two Easter homilies. Studying the Latin tradition from a different point of view, Mazza observes, "The ontological relationship (of participation) between the event and the prior announcement of it suggested to the early Fathers that they should take over, en bloc, the entire special terminology of biblical interpretation and apply it to the liturgy." [42] We should think about how profound an intuition is operating here. It is not simply seeing that interpretive tools in one field will work in another. Rather, some deep relation is intuited between the biblical events attested to in scripture and the signs and actions of the liturgy. The center in every case is the historical Christ in his paschal mystery.

A certain tradition is in the making and coming to a more condensed expression in the [still fluid] text of the eucharistic anaphora. It was, we may say, especially the celebration of Easter — with its homily and Easter eucharist — that slowly achieved a

---

[42] E. MAZZA, *The Celebration of the Eucharist. The Origin of the Rite and the Development of Its Interpretation*, Collegeville 1999, 120. Mazza is speaking of the Latin tradition as represented in Tertullian. For the same as unfolding in the Alexandrian tradition, see B. STUDER, "Die doppelte Exegese bei Origenes" in *Mysterium Caritatis, Studien zur Exegese und zur Trinitätslehre in der Alten Kirche*, Rome 1999, 37-66.

sort of settling toward some terms and forms that progress toward an increasingly precise theological meaning, such that they become obligatory, i.e., a *lex credendi*. Insofar as this anaphora excercises influence on subsequent theology, we have the dynamic *lex orandi-lex credendi* as commonly conceived. But it is also important to realize that the biblical world of images and thoughts is functioning as a *"lex credendi"* causing to grow a sense that there is something obligatory in the way of prayer, *lex orandi*.[43] Observing this dynamic with as much detail as can be recovered, it can be seen that the precise trinitarian theology that will emerge later has its deepest roots in the biblical text used in this way, i.e., in the Easter feast so preached, in the Easter eucharist with this kind of anaphora. Examples would be the trinitarian beginning of the anaphora; the relationship between Father and Son displayed in creation *(per quem)*, in redemption *(quem misisti)*, but even before all time *(Verbum tuum insepa-rabile)*, as the one who does the Father's will; or christologically in the expanded section describing the redemption; or ecclesially in the expression *populum tuum;* in the third part, the petition of the Father for the Spirit to come upon the gifts; the final trinitarian doxology, etc. It is this that we wish to examine in detail now.

2.1. *Overview of the First Part of the Anaphora*

Always with an eye to what relates to Trinity in this prayer, it is useful to begin by observing an overall structure in the first part. The prayer of thanksgiving is addressed to *God* through his beloved *puer* Jesus Christ.[44] And then a condensed account of salvation follows, concentrating on Christ as the one who fulfills God's will. In the course of this, the Holy Spirit is related to the

---

[43] The launching of such a dynamic development is already testified to by the New Testament text; for example, a *lex* for reading the biblical text as in 1 Cor 10:1-11, or a *lex* for celebrating eucharist as in 1 Cor 11:23-34.

[44] I will try in what follows to keep close to the language of the anaphora in my own analysis, and so will generally say "God" for "Deus" and try not to use the word "Son" except where "Filius" is used, even though it would be legitimate according to the overall purpose of this study generally to say "Father" and "Son," aware that we are speaking of the first and second persons of the Trinity.

Son's incarnation. The account of salvation climaxes in the description of the Last Supper, which does not stand apart as something in its own right.

Of course, the most significant thing to observe for the present investigation is that we have a thanksgiving prayer and that it is addressed to God through Christ. This structure will hold through all the subsequent centuries and developments. On it is based an instinct that will be engaged again and again in the articulation of trinitarian faith; namely, the distinction between the Father and the Son. This shape of prayer is not an innovation in this anaphora. It is already there in the *Didache*, whose structure in turn is inspired by the Jewish *Birkat ha-mazon*. In other words we are very close to biblical language and to the biblical thought world, to the Bible functioning as a *lex*. The primitive level of this euchological language can be further observed in the fact that the prayer does not specify *Pater* but says only *Deus*. And this one is thanked not through the *Filius* but through the *puer* Jesus Christ. *Puer* is to be related to the title *pais* of the *Didache*. "*Pais* remains the characteristic Christological title of the eucharist of the *Didache*, and it appears at the end of every strophe of thanksgiving in which Jesus' revealing work is commemorated. [Didache 9.2, 3; 10.2, 3]... Thus, the title of servant *(pais)* has a particular connection with the prophetic activity of Jesus, which consists in this: God gives through the revelation made by Jesus."[45] So we have from the start this clear distinction between Father and Son, but we should not think this to be anything like what later generations would call a subordinationist picture. It is more a question of τάξις, that is, an order, just like the τάξις of the Lord's baptismal command to baptize in the name of the Father, the Son, and the Holy Spirit (Mt 28:19). In the theology of the *Didache*, "Jesus is the eschatological and definitive prophet, and the attitude that one assumes in encounters with him is assumed in encounters with

---

[45] MAZZA, *Origins*, 38. In addition to its use in the *Didache*, παῖς is used three times as a title for Jesus Christ in the liturgical prayer found in *The First Letter of Clement*, 59. That the same title for Christ should appear a century later in this anaphora is a good measure of how conservative the language of liturgy can be.

God."[46] Here we have a Jesus still very much framed round by the world of Judaism and its leading images. To this world we owe the shape of a thanksgiving prayer addressed to God for what he has done through his servant, the prophet, Jesus Christ. This world is the original *lex* that is giving shape to a *lex orandi*.

2.2. *Details in the First Part from the Easter Homilies*

After this "primitive" beginning with its roots in the Jewish-Christian prayer the *Didache*, the anaphora develops an extended account of Christ's work. This account, significantly, makes Christ's whole work depend on God who sent him and whose will he accomplishes. Thus, the origins of the economy lie entirely in God (the Father), and it is for this that he is being thanked.[47] Much of the language for this section derives from the world of the Easter homilies.[48] Thus, as we have said, it is a theology developed from a particular Christian way of reading the Old Testament and from the celebration of the Christian Passover. In terms of a contribution to trinitarian theology, we can examine the nuances that this special language brings to the understanding of God and of Christ's relationship to God.

One of the strongest ideas to emerge from this language is the clear image of God having sent his servant Jesus to accomplish his will. *Quem misisti* is the first phrase to qualify Jesus Christ,[49] who then is described among other things as the *angelus voluntatis tuae*. Then again we hear the verb *misisti* with Jesus as its object, and this time it is specified that he is sent *de caelo*. When the description of the economy comes to the Passion, God's will is once again mentioned: *qui voluntatem tuam complens*.[50]

---

[46] MAZZA, *Origins*, 39.

[47] In the New Testament and in the liturgy before Nicea, "God" always refers to the first person of the Trinity. This too is a conservative way of speaking.

[48] So observes Mazza, but we could add to this that there is already language like this in Eph 1:3-10. It is a common tradition that explains all such similarities and not just, too simplistically, the dependence of one text upon another.

[49] Compare Eph 1:3.

[50] Compare Eph 1:9.

A clear theology emerges here. The origins of our salvation lie in God (the Father), and it is his will that we be saved. But this will is accomplished by another. And that other is sent from heaven itself. These are no small gains in clarity and in condensed expression for what lies more diffusely throughout the entire Bible.

Further, with a very short phrase, *in ultimis temporibus*,[51] which again is biblical shorthand, this whole act of sending is placed within the entire context of God's work for the salvation of Israel. The biblical text in which this idea is found already condenses admirably the two testaments, showing the qualitative difference between the one and the other: "In times past God spoke in partial and various ways to our ancestors through the prophets; in these last days *(in ultimis temporibus)* he spoke to us through a Son." (Heb 1:1-2) When a phrase like this is taken into a euchological text, it is meant to invoke the entire context and theological content of the biblical text. That is its apostolic authority. We see it being brought to bear here in the Church at prayer.[52]

We should notice the titles for Jesus Christ who is sent: *salvator, redemptor,* and *angelus voluntatis tuae.* All these are titles which indicate his role in the economy. It is the third that may strike us as most unusual or primitive since it has subsequently fallen out of use.[53] Mazza's connecting it with Easter homilies shows, however, why this particular title could be considered, as he suggested, "obligatory."[54] The homily of Pseudo-Hippolytus

---

[51] Compare Eph 1:10.

[52] Cf. also Gal 4:4. The language and thought of JUSTIN MARTYR, *Apology I,* 63 can also be compared.

[53] Especially for associated risks of a subordinationist interpretation, see J. DANIÉLOU, *The Theology of Jewish Christianity,* London 1964, 117-146. See also D.D. HANNAH, *Michael Traditions and Angel Christology in Early Christianity,* Tübingen 1999. Hannah examines many instances of angel christology; for themes associated with Is 9:5, see pp. 209-211. The title *angel* for Christ is found frequently in Justin Martyr. See, *Apology I,* 36; *The Dialogue with Trypho* 34: 2; 56: 4, 10; 58: 3, 10; 61: 1 and others. The widespread usage of this title in the primitive texts and the fact that it is found also in the anaphora is yet another example of the conservative nature of liturgical texts.

[54] See above at n. 38.

shows us that a particular theological concern lies behind the expression; namely to show that Christ has a real humanity, that he did not suddenly appear as a phantasm, but that he is the fulfillment of Isaiah's prophecy, which says, "For a child is born to us; dominion rests on his shoulders and his name will be *angel of great counsel,* wonder-counselor, mighty God, prince of peace, father forever." (Is 9:5 LXX) Pseudo-Hippolytus reads this passage carefully, connecting "a child born" (and thus not a phantasm appearing as a full grown man) with the term "angel," but going on to notice also that the very same is also called "mighty God." The conclusion in the homily: "God and man together, this great Jesus has come among us, so that no one may refuse to believe in him and believe that the sovereign Spirit has been contained in the body of a man."[55]

Other language in the anaphora reenforces this theological concern about God and man together in Christ. Immediately after the three titles mentioned, all of which, as we have said, refer to Christ in the economy, Christ is described, as it were, in his divine condition. Three, if not not four, phrases underline this: (1) *qui Verbum tuum inseparabile,* (2) *per quem omnia fecisti,* (3) *et (cum) beneplacitum tibi,* (4) *misisti de caelo.*

It is not difficult to understand that a phrase like *Verbum tuum inseparabile* would become "obligatory" in the context of an Easter homily or an anaphora. Obviously a title like this, with its unmistakable biblical origins, shows much about the relationship between the Father and the Son. "Logos" is a title which appears more than ten times in the homily of Pseudo-Hippolytus, and it is frequent also in Melito's homily. In addition to the force of this title as it occurs in the prologue of John's Gospel and in the tradition of the Wisdom literature which underlies this, it is worth referring it more specifically to an observation of Mazza concerning its use in the homily by Pseudo-Hippolytus. He postulates a desire on the part of the homilist to echo a passage in the Jewish paschal *Haggadah* which stresses that it was the Lord himself, not an angel or seraphim or any envoy who brought

---

[55] MAZZA, *Origins*, 107-108, quoting CANTALAMESSA, *I più antichi,* nos. 86, 87, 88. For comment on the difficult phrase "sovereign Spirit in the body of a man," see CANTALAMESSA, *I più antichi,* 120, nn. 75, 76. In another context we will return to the term *angel* below.

Israel out of Egypt. Likewise, in the Easter homily Christ is presented here with a divine title to make the same point. Christian prayer cannot say any less of the one who effects our salvation than the Jewish prayer says.[56] The phrase is taken over by the anaphora for the same reason. *Tuum inseparabile* only emphasizes the divinity the more. So, though Jesus Christ is active in the economy as savior, redeemer, angel of another's will, he nonetheless appears truly as God, as another and yet as inseparably united with God. The implications of such a phrase are not entirely worked out yet, but they will be in time, and their presence in a *lex orandi* will clearly have its influence on the *lex credendi*. "Inseparable" is a very strong theological affirmation for expressing the relation between God and his Word. We may say, for example, with the language from the yet to come Arian controversy, that there never was a "once" when the Word was not or that there is no God who is ever without his Word.[57]

When next it is said of this Word *"per quem omnia fecisti,"* the Word is associated with God in his work as Creator. This, of course, summarizes the position expressed in John 1:3, as well as in texts like Col 1:16, Heb 1:2, Rev 3:14. The thought occurs in the Easter homilies, but it is widespread throughout any sort of patristic literature of the period.[58] The point for the present study is to observe once again that the biblical *lex* has condensed itself into this pithy liturgical phrase, becoming part of the *lex orandi*. As such, it will be in place when a *lex credendi* will need to be

---

[56] See MAZZA, *Origins*, 113-114. But it should be observed that the paschal *Haggadah* to which Mazza refers clearly finds its roots in Is 63:9, "not an ambassador or an angel but he himself saved them." This text is frequently used in testimonia by Irenaeus, Tertullian, and Cyprian, showing again that we should look for a common tradition to explain these connections rather than for direct textual dependence. For the testimonia, see *Biblia Patristica* I, Paris 1975, 159; and II, Paris 1977, 159.

[57] Such concerns are very primitive and conservative and do not simply emerge at the time of Nicea. They are already expressed in the Apologists of the second century, especially by Justin. So again: a common tradition testifying to common themes, with the anaphora among the witnesses. For second century Apologists and Logos christology, see STUDER, *Trinity and Incarnation, The Faith of the Early Church*, Collegeville 1993, 45-52.

[58] For references in the homilies, see MAZZA, *Origins*, 115. Of this phrase he observes, "It would be difficult to find a patristic work that does not have passages very similar to this phrase."

formulated more precisely around this question. The deep instincts developed in the eucharistic experience of the Church will enable it to say that in the creation God did not act alone but through his Word.[59]

It is difficult to know exactly how the phrase *ut (cum) beneplacitum tibi fuit* should be understood. This phrase has no parallels in the Easter homilies. If it means something to the effect of "because you were well pleased in him,"[60] then there is an interesting piece of theological condensation exhibited in the phrase. Its biblical roots would be clear: it derives from the revelation of the Son by the Father's voice in the Gospels' scenes of the Lord's Baptism and his Transfiguration. These are revelations that occur in the economy. However, the anaphora takes the phrase from that context and uses it to describe the Word in what we would call his immanent relation to God. This transposition becomes clear from the context of the phrase. It is sandwiched between three other phrases, all meant to emphasize the eternal condition and divine status of the Word. Indeed, there is a thought implicit here that is not necessarily present in the Gospel texts of Baptism or Transfiguration; namely, that precisely because the Word was pleasing to God, God therefore sent him from heaven. For all this the community is giving thanks to God. This is a movement in theological reasoning that will eventually be expressed in something like an actual rule of reasoning, moving backwards, as it were, from what is revealed in the economy to some understanding of God in himself. Again, this is a gain in the *lex orandi* that will exercise its influence on the *lex credendi*, but we want also to observe that it derives from a meditation on, a transformation of, the biblical *lex*.

These are interesting possibilities, but we cannot be certain that this is the sense of the phrase. It may mean more simply "in

---

[59] The *per omnia facta sunt* with which, among other phrases, the Council of Nicea formulates a *lex credendi* concerning the divinity of Christ, rests on the by then centuries old tradition of this phrase and this theological concern in a *lex orandi*.

[60] So is it understood by R.H. CONNOLLY, "The Eucharistic Prayer of Hippolytus" in *JTS* 39 (1938) 350-369, here 356-357; so also R.C.D. JASPER and G.J. CUMING in *Prayers of the Eucharist: Early and Reformed*, Collegeville 1990, 35.

your good pleasure." [61] In this case the theological meaning is less complex, but it still has clear biblical roots. It means then to echo all the rich theology expressed in the hymn that opens the Letter to the Ephesians in 1:3-10, and here specifically, verse 9: ... γνωρίσας ἡμῖν τὸ μυστήριον τοῦ θελήματος αὐτοῦ, κατὰ τὴν εὐδοκίαν αὐτοῦ ἥν προέθετο ἐν αὐτῷ...

The final phrase that expresses the divine origins of the Word is *quem misisti de caelo,* but the whole phrase reads *quem misisti de caelo in matricem virginis,* and as such bridges over to a number of phrases that will show the other half of the concern that was discerned in the Easter homilies and is now showing up in the anaphora; namely, that Christ has a real humanity. The language piles up to stress this: *in matricem virginis, in utero habitus, incarnatus est, ex virgine natus.* And yet the grammatical structure, as well as several other phrases joined to these, manages to maintain a unity between the one described in his divine condition and the one become incarnate. First of all, the subject of all these phrases is *Verbum tuum inseparabile.* With this subject and especially with the phrase *incarnatus est* the anaphora remains still within the logic of the johannine prologue (now John 1:14), but the biblical logic is now shaped into liturgical language and becomes reason for giving thanks. Other ideas are added to the johannine scheme, most notably a threefold mention of the virgin-mother. Again, the doctrinal consequences of this are not explicitly worked out, yet nonetheless the homilies and now the anaphora are expressing a theological concern and instinct in joining such insistent language about virgin-mother to the more simple johannine *et Verbo caro factum est.* [62] This kind of language will be in place in the Church's prayer when the *motherhood* of Mary will be used to show the real humanity of Christ, when her *virginity* is used to reveal the divine origins of the one truly born of her.

Tucked within these phrases concerned with the real humanity of Christ, two other phrases will remain insistent on the

---

[61] So is it understood by BOTTE, *La Tradition apostolique,* 13 with n. 6. So also by RAFFA, *Liturgia eucaristica,* 519.

[62] A similar theological concern shows itself in JUSTIN MARTYR, *Apology I,* 63 and IRENAEUS, *Adversus Haereses III,* 19, 1.

divine origin. One of these is *Filius tibi ostensus est.*[63] This phrase is intimately connected with what follows: *ex Spiritu sancto et virgine natus.* The whole might be translated something to the effect of, "He showed himself to be your Son born of the Holy Spirit and the virgin." That is, the eternal Word sent from God now shows himself in a new condition, in being Son born of these two origins, Spirit and virgin. The phrase *ex Spiritu sancto*, which has no parallels in the Easter homilies, is clearly a tightly condensed summary of the Matthean and Lucan birth accounts. Although the Holy Spirit is not woven into this development in any entirely balanced and "coequal" way, the biblical *lex* was definitely making its force felt here, and the euchological phrase *ex Spiritu sancto et virgine natus* is not far from, even if less precise than, the later creedal *et incarnatus est de Spiritu Sancto ex Maria Virgine, et homo factus est,* a phrase not found as such before the Creed of Constantinople in 381. For our purposes here of detecting the trinitarian *lex* in the anaphora, it is significant to find the title *Filius* so closely associated with *Spiritus* in a prayer addressed to *Deus.*

For all that we have seen so far we might borrow and apply to the whole an observation that Mazza makes in a more narrow context: "It is as if the anaphora were a terse statement of what is more diffusely expressed in the homily."[64] And I want to add,

---

[63] The theological sense is disputed. BOTTE, *La Tradition apostolique*, 15, n. 1 cites B. CAPELLE in "Le Logos, Fils de Dieu, dans la théologie d'Hippolyte" in *RTAM* 9 (1937) 109-124 for the understanding of this phrase. Capelle argued that on the basis of other texts found in the corpus of Hippolytus, now of disputed authorship, that for him the title *Son* is applied only to the incarnate Logos and is not suitably understood to refer to his eternal condition. CONNOLLY, "The Eucharistic Prayer," 357-358 is more nuanced as he cites passages from *Contra Noetum*, generally no longer considered to be authored by Hippolytus, which show the Λόγος "as subject and υἱός or παῖς as predicate, together with verbs of manifestation or demonstration. But it is no longer really possible to comment on the anaphora from writings once considered to be of Hippolytus, except insofar as we have done so in this study in general, taking a wide range of ancient texts all witnessing to a common tradition. It is unlikely that Botte's citation of Capelle for the understanding of this phrase is correct. Virtually from the beginning *Son* is a privileged title for indicating Christ in his divine condition, and in the language of prayer it can be considered to have this conservative sense.

[64] MAZZA, *Origins*, 110.

a terse statement of what is more diffusely expressed in the Bible. For the homilies are already condensing exactly that — large blocks of biblical theology — around particular theological concerns; and the anaphora, in a different genre but in a same dynamic, is more tightly condensing the same.

In what follows a new dimension of this first part of the anaphora is introduced, now focusing the redemptive work of Christ on his Passion. The language and thought world continue to parallel what is found in the Paschal homilies. This parallel is evidence that the whole common tradition is condensing itself around the Passion. As these theological concerns condense into the phrases of the anaphora, there are yet further implications for trinitarian understanding. The first phrase, of which Jesus Christ or the Word is still the subject is *Qui voluntatem tuam complens et populum sanctum tibi adquirens.* Attention has already been drawn to the idea of Christ fulfilling God's will,[65] but here it can be further specified that this idea is placed in virtual apposition with the idea of acquiring a people for God. Thus, in his Passion Christ accomplishes God's will; namely, acquiring a people. This concept is rooted in the Old Testament sense of Passover. It is there that God acquires a people. The Easter homilies do not fail to pick up on this point, transposing it in the general schema of typology and various prefigurations.[66] In the Christian Passover, Christ's Passion, a people is acquired. This is a primitive version in an early anaphora of a dimension I think it is important to be alert to in searching for Trinity in relation to eucharist; namely, the mention of our participation in trinitarian life, and this precisely by means of the Lord's Passion. Of course, the anaphora does not say it exactly that way, but this is an implication worked out in time, the theme of Church as sharing in trinitarian life. Surely here we are at the liturgical beginnings of such a conception. It is language from the Passover of the Old Testament that prepares this theme of a *populum sanctum,* and it is the Christian understanding of typology which carries it over now into this eucharistic context. In this regard the anaphora also

---

[65] For more biblical background, compare John 4:34; 6:38; 17:4.

[66] Mazza cites Melito's homily in this regard, nos. 35-45. The idea is also expressed in the relatively very early *Letter of Barnabas* 5:7 and 14:6. For the biblical background see Lk 1:17; 1 Pt 2:9.

distinguishes the roles here between God and Christ. By his Passion *Christ* acquires the people for *God* (the Father): *"tibi adquirens."*

The fuller phrase here is ... *tibi adquirens, extendit manus, cum pateretur...* Such a phrase once again shows biblical typology at work. The image of extended hands is a set phrase with Moses as a type, whose hands were extended in the battle against Amalek (Ex 17:8-13). It likewise is influenced by Isaiah 65:2, very early understood as a reference to Christ's passion: "I have stretched out my hands all the day to a rebellious people."[67] This latter application is a fine illustration of how this kind of exegesis forms the foundation for later theological conclusions. The Isaiah phrase is clearly, for Christian logic, an image of Christ in his passion, but it is God who is speaking in the Isaiah text. Theological conclusion: Christ must be understood in the divine dimension.

It is not easy to know how to interpret the phrase *ut a passione liberaret eos qui in te crediderunt.* Botte, basing himself on the Ethiopian and other recensions, thinks the sense could be "to trust" or "to hope" rather than "to believe."[68] The exact sense of the verb need not be settled for the purposes of the present study, for in any case there is an interesting articulation by this phrase of a three-way relationship between Christ, God, and those who trust in God. Christ is active in saving through his Passion, but those who are saved are putting their trust in the one to whom this prayer is addressed, whose will Christ fulfills. Perhaps not too much should be made of this, but it is interesting that it is not a question of putting one's trust or hope in Christ but in the one in whom Christ himself placed his hopes. This draws the eucharistic assembly into a particular pattern of relating to God; namely, Christ's own pattern of trust in God.[69]

---

[67] Examples of this interpretation are *Letter of Barnabas* 12:2; JUSTIN MARTYR, *Apology I*, 34; IRENAEUS, *Adversus Haereses V*, 17, 4; *Proof of the Apostolic Preaching* 46.

[68] BOTTE, *La Tradition apostolique*, 15.

[69] This remains a valid theological point even today for the development of a full trinitarian spirituality. The force and logic of the eucharistic prayer addressed to the Father should result in stressing in spirituality not so much a concentrating on Christ but more precisely on Christ's relationship with the Father.

In the phrase *Qui cumque traderetur voluntariae passioni*, one is struck by the occurrence once again of a word referring to will, *voluntariae passioni*. However, here it is not God's will directly that is referred to, as in the previous two instances, but Christ, who is described as being handed over to "voluntary suffering." This is, from a theological point of view, what might be called a very loaded phrase, and it has its consequences for trinitarian theology. Remembering the theory of Mazza that the language of the anaphora expressed a certain obligatory use of language become standard in the development of a preaching tradition, here we see a phrase that has a well developed tradition behind it. Taken together with the other two uses which precede this — *Angelus voluntatis tuae* and *qui voluntatem tuam complens* — Christ is intimately associated with the will of God. If in his Passion he is *traderetur voluntariae passioni*, it could be said that in his Passion Christ is, as it were, incarnating the will of God; for he willingly suffers. Pseudo-Hippolytus says as much at one point in the homily: "The Word is the will [of God]." [70]

Such a concept is already found before Pseudo-Hippolytus is on the scene. [71] The theme is developed by any number of Christian exegetes usually around Isaiah 9:5 in LXX, where among the titles of the future Messiah, there is μεγάλης βουλῆς ἄγγελος. This is the obvious antecedant to the anaphora's *Angelus voluntatis tuae*. [72] Christ, coming to earth from heaven *(quem... misisti de caelo)*, transmits and realizes the salvific will of the Father. Elsewhere Pseudo-Hippolytus exclaims, "Envoy in the world of the will of the Father, divine dawn of Christ on the earth!" [73] Cantalamessa comments, "La redenzione è l'invio della volontà salvifica del Padre impersonata da Cristo." [74] For trinitarian theology the significance of this tradition of exegesis around Isaiah 9:5 is that there is a clear distinction between

---

[70] Homily n. 59. See also the interesting phrase in JUSTIN MARTYR, *The Dialogue with Trypho* 41, "... becoming subject to suffering according to his own will..." a phrase uttered in the context of a discussion on the eucharist. PG 6, 564C.

[71] See CANTALAMESSA, *Omelia in S. Pascha*, 158-160.

[72] See above, n. 53.

[73] N. 10.

[74] CANTALAMESSA, *Omelia in S. Pascha*, 160.

Christ and the Father, even if Christ is intimately associated with the Father. He is his Angel, his Word, and now his will. The concern for expressing distinction is confirmed by a text which Cantalamessa cites from *Contra Noetum:* "If the divine word is sent through Jesus Christ, then Jesus Christ is himself the will of the Father."[75] Having cited yet other texts, Cantalamessa concludes, "Sono voci diverse e sicuramente indipendenti d'una stessa tradizione cristologica ricca di contenuto teologico. Essa infatti, completa la personalità del Salvatore, aggiungendo alla qualifica di *rivelatore* (logos) della verità divina, quella di *esecutore* della volontà divina."[76] This is a very clear instance, then, of the dynamic we have been uncovering: an exegetical tradition around Isaiah 9:5 develops an obligatory concept, the *lex* that comes from the Bible. This language enters the *lex orandi* in this anaphora. It will form part of the euchological repertoire upon which a *lex credendi* that distinguishes Father and Son will rely; and which further provokes the deep instinct in the *lex credendi* to identify the Father's distinguishing characteristic as his being the source of all, including the Son and the Spirit.[77]

The next phrase to deal with is a richly concentrated description of the purpose of Christ's Passion: ... *ut mortem solvat et vincula diaboli dirumpat, et infernum calcet et iustos inluminet, et terminum figat et resurrectionem manifestet...* Mazza cites Perler here, who pointed out that this part of the anaphora echoes the triumphal hymn of Melito's homily, which has Christ saying, "It is I who have destroyed death, and triumphed over the enemy, and trampled down hell, and bound up the brute, and led the human being toward the heights of heaven."[78] For our purposes it is enough to note several things.[79] First of all, the images all are

---

[75] HIPPOLYTUS, *C. Noetum*, 13, cited by CANTALAMESSA, *Omelia in S. Pascha*, 160. The Hippolytan authorship of *Contra Noetum* is disputed. In any case, we see again this theme testified to widely in the common tradition.

[76] CANTALAMESSA, *Omelia in S. Pascha*, 160.

[77] For example, see the profound meditation of Athanasius on this theme in his promotion of Nicean faith. ATHANASIUS, *Contra Arianos* I, 20-21.

[78] MAZZA, *Origins*, 126, citing Melito n. 102.

[79] The background of these individual images and their relation to various parts of the Easter homilies is discussed by MAZZA, *Origins*, 120-127. To the parallels with the Easter homilies cited by Mazza could be added two examples of similar phrases with a similar force: *Letter of Barnabas* V, 5-6;

vivid, poetic condensations deriving from Scripture. So once again, the biblical *lex* is operative.[80] Further, one should note the rhetorical force of the piling up of these images. There are six images coming one after another, pounding home the why of the Lord's voluntary suffering.

Yet there is more. These phrases are all joined grammatically in one long sentence, the main clause of which recounts the Lord's actions and words at the Last Supper. As such, then, it is the Last Supper account which completes the development of this first part of the anaphora, begun in the very first phrase. The Supper account is not a separate unit in the anaphora, with a sense of consecration, as will become standard in later anaphoras.[81] Prescinding from why and how the sense of consecration developed, effectively making the Supper account a separate liturgical unit, it is worth observing the theological effect of including it as the climax of the whole narrative of the Lord's coming into the world. What this does is associate the Supper very closely with the Passion. Of course, everything about the Supper already accomplishes this, as do the Gospel accounts of the same. But liturgically it is especially forceful to formulate a long and rhetorically effective sentence which in essence says, "To destroy death, break apart the bonds of the devil, etc., he took bread and said..." This tight connection between the Supper and what the Lord did on the cross is a little more tenuous when the Supper account has an independent liturgical existence.[82] In

---

IRENAEUS, *The Proof of the Apostolic Preaching* 38. Both of these passages include the phrase "manifest the resurrection."

[80] For a more detailed examination of each phrase with its biblical background and use by authors of the period, see CONNOLLY, "The Eucharistic Prayer" 361-362. I do not examine all that here because it goes too far afield from my trinitarian focus. However, the texts examined by Connolly are yet more evidence of the widespread common tradition.

[81] On this and on this history of this observation in recent scholarship, see MAZZA, *Origins*, 134-135.

[82] In a different place, though perhaps not so far removed theologically, Cyprian understands the Passion of the Lord as being especially found in his willingness to suffer, a willingness that he made clear precisely during the Supper. It is thus that Cyprian includes the Supper as an integral part of the Passion. This is brought out clearly by J.D. LAURANCE, *"Priest" as Type of Christ. The Leader of the Eucharist in Salvation History according to Cyprian of Carthage*, New York 1984.

terms of trinitarian theology, standing behind all this is that the Supper itself is God's will, that Christ the servant sent to enact the Father's will does so especially in the giving of his body, which will be broken, in the giving of his blood which will be poured out.[83] Again, for all this the community is giving thanks: *Gratias tibi referimus, Deus.*

For the most part we have been taking the clues for our analysis of the anaphora from possibile parallels with the Easter homilies. In the long rhetorical phrase to which we have drawn attention there are also some interesting parallels in the writings of Irenaeus.[84] This is an important point of contact for the dynamic we are trying to search out, for Irenaeus' concerns are about right doctrine. That toward this end he is found speaking the same language that is found in the *lex orandi* represented by the anaphora is yet another confirmation of how the several *leges* cross fertilize each other without an absolutely strict priority assigned to one or the other.[85]

---

[83] In the homily of Pseudo-Hippolytus, n. 92, the relation between the Lord's death and the Supper is explained. Note especially the phrase "He did not desire so much to eat [the Passover] as to suffer [it]; eating was involved in freeing us from suffering." Cited by MAZZA, *Origins*, 136. BRADSHAW, "Redating" 9, following E.C. RATCLIFF, "The Sanctus and the Pattern of the Early Anaphora," *JEH* 1 (1950) 32, thinks the institution narrative is awkwardly integrated with what precedes it and so argues that it was likely a later addition. Understood theologically as I have suggested here, I do not find it awkward, but appropriate to the recounting of the history of salvation in the context of the celebration of eucharist.

[84] MAZZA, *Origins*, 139-140, cites *Adversus Haereses* II, 20, 3: "By means of his suffering the Lord has destroyed death, has dissolved error, has annihilated corruptibility, has destroyed ignorance, has manifested life, has shown the truth, has bestowed incorruptibility." Also cited *The Proof of the Apostolic Preaching* 6 and 38.

[85] It is not necessary for our present purposes to pursue further the special questions surrounding the nature of the account of the Supper in this anaphora. As far as I can tell, nothing further is advanced concerning the focus of trinitarian theology. For a discussion, see MAZZA, *Origins*, 134-139.

3. *The Second Part of the Anaphora: Anamnesis, Offering and Giving Thanks for the Present Moment*

It is only in the first part of the anaphora, the part examined so far in this present study, that the influence of the Easter homilies on the language of the anaphora can be discerned. For the rest, influence and evidence of the common tradition must be sought elsewhere. The second part of the three-part structure which Mazza apprehends in the anaphora is that which extends from *memores igitur* to ... *tibi ministrare*. This is a much briefer section, and it will be examined now only for what it may contribute to the trinitarian question.[86]

The single sentence that constitutes this second part has three elements: anamnesis, offering, and another rendering of thanks. The anamnesis has a theology different from that of the first part of the anaphora and from the understanding of the Passion as contained in the Easter homilies. There salvation is concentrated on the Lord's death. And consistent with 1 Corinthians 11:26, faithfulness to the Lord's command to "do this in memory of me," the memorial is a memorial of the Lord's death. But now in this part of the anaphora we have *Memores igitur mortis et resurrectionis eius*. The idea of the memorial also of resurrection is new. This affects the perception of the preceding part to which it has been joined. Now death and resurrection are set on the same plane, and both are the objects of the memorial.[87] The joining of a complete anamnesis with a formula also of offering has the effect of transforming the preceding account of institution, for it causes the weight to fall now principally on the institution, picking up on the command to "do this in memory of me."[88]

In any case, taking the text as it now stands, there are elements relevant to our trinitarian investigation. First of all, the

---

[86] The antecedants for this part of the anaphora will not concern us except insofar as they shed light on what is under investigation here. For a detailed analysis see MAZZA, *Origins*, 141-174.

[87] Mazza associates this with the understanding of Easter breaking out of its strict association with 14 Nisan and being associated more generally with Sunday. See MAZZA, *Origins*, 167-168.

[88] These are the remote origins of the separate institution accounts that are found in fourth century anaphoras.

prayer continues to be addressed to God (the Father), but he is addressed remembering the Son. This idea is combined with the idea of the worshipping community offering bread and the cup to God. Thanks is given to him that this can be done, and the action is further qualified as a priestly service.[89] There are many theological implications tucked into this framework. I suggested above, in connection with the idea of *populum sanctum*, that in searching out trinitarian connections it is important to be alert to formulations which speak of our own sharing in trinitarian life. In the anamnesis and offering this idea is even more strongly present. The idea here is a simple version of what will be developed considerably in later, more elaborate anaphoras. The worshipping community is offering to the Father the bread and cup which recall the Lord's death and resurrection. Thinking this through theologically, we can say that the community is now offering what the Lord himself first offered.[90] This is a very concrete and particular shape given to the idea of being brought into trinitarian life. It is striking too that this is qualified as priestly service. Such an image is likely rooted in the Letter to the Hebrews' understanding of the Lord's own death as a priestly act, as this is expressed from 5:11 to 10:39.

In addition to the action of offering being connected with the anamnesis, there is also the idea of giving thanks, a thanksgiving

---

[89] In Botte's critical edition, he notes that the Latin version's *ministrare* is too weak, and here he follows the other versions, seeing behind it the *Apostolic Constitutions'* ἱερατεύειν, a reading confirmed by the Ethiopic version. He translates "... de nous tenir devant toi et de te servir comme prêtres." BOTTE, *La Tradition apostolique*, 17.

[90] See the interpretation of the meaning of bread and wine later in the text at chapter 21, following the Latin translation, which indicates interesting exchanges of sacramental terminology between Latin and the original Greek: "... gratias agat [episcopus] panem quidem in exemplum, quod dicit graecus antitypum corporis Christi; calicem vino mixtum propter antitypum, quod dicit graecus similitudinem, sanguinis quod est." But it is really not possible to say more precisely how the relation between the Lord's offering and the community is to be understood in this part of the anaphora. That the two are connected is clear; how that is understood is not. On this problem, see R. TAFT, "Understanding the Byzantine Anaphoral Oblation" in *Rule of Prayer, Rule of Faith*, 32-40. Further it is necessary to use caution in using one part of *The Apostolic Tradition* to interpret another since the material thus compared may have different origins.

to be distinguished from that which characterizes the first part of the prayer. Now the thanksgiving is for this present moment of prayer, for the possibility of being able to enact this priestly service. Mazza sees the remote origins of this second thanksgiving in the structure of the Jewish *Birkat ha-mazon*, which exerted its influence on other Christian texts that may be considered in the same family line.[91] Important for our purposes is the comparison Mazza makes between our anaphora and a prayer found on the martyr Polycarp's lips in *The Martyrdom of Polycarp*. Scholars are virtually unanimous in understanding this prayer as an adaptation to martyrdom of a eucharistic anaphora.[92] It has a tripartite structure in which it is not difficult to discern a relation to the tripartite structure of the anaphora we are studying. In the *Birkat ha-mazon*, in the *Didache*, in *The Martyrdom of Polycarp*, and in the anaphora of the *Apostolic Tradition* this second part is always a thanksgiving for the present moment. The prayer of Polycarp can be used to understand more precisely what is being expressed at this moment in the anaphora. Polycarp prays, "I bless you for having made me worthy of this day and this hour, of taking part in the number of your martyrs and of the cup of your Christ, for resurrection into eternal life both of the soul and the body in the incorruptibility of the Holy Spirit."[93]

The parallel between this and the anaphora can confirm my suggestion that there is some sense here that the community is now offering what the Lord himself first offered. The Lord offered himself; the community now gives thanks that it can offer itself together with the Lord. Martyrdom is the acting out in very flesh of what the eucharist accomplishes ritually, but in both cases the offering is in the pattern of what Christ accomplished. Christ's death, martyrdom, the eucharist are all three a "taking part in the cup of Christ for the resurrection into eternal life." All three can

---

[91] See MAZZA, *Origins*, 153-161.

[92] See P. CAMELOT, "Introduction," in *Ignace d'Antioche et Polycarpe de Smyrne, Lettres; Martyre de Polycarpe* (SCh 10), Paris 1969⁴, 207. For the most recent discussion, see G. BUSCHMANN, *Das Martyrium des Polykarp*, Göttingen 1998, 226-257.

[93] *Martyrdom*, XIV, 2; cited by MAZZA, *Origins*, 154. Greek in SCh 10, 229.

be called priestly service. All three give thanks to the Father for this. In terms of trinitarian theology, we may say that the community by its anamnesis and offering stands in the same relation to the Father in which Christ stood in his Passion, a relationship in which the martyr also stands.[94]

It may perhaps be objected that in stating the trinitarian theological implications in this way I am reading back our own more developed notions into a primitive prayer. Methodologically, of course, such a pitfall is to be avoided. However, I would suggest that there is something not altogether wrong in a judicious use of such a backward moving hermeneutic. It may be that in this way there can be detected the primitive roots of what is later developed more explicitly. I think that is the case here. In this anamnesis of the anaphora we have all the elements of what is one of the most profound dimensions of the Church's experience of eucharist; namely, the incomparable grace of offering to the Father what Christ himself offered.[95] It is offered while giving thanks for being able to offer this priestly service: *offerimus... gratias tibi agentes...* In this dimension of eucharist we are at the heart of what can be exploited in any age for the development of a truly trinitarian spirituality.

4. *The Third Part of the Anaphora: Epiclesis*

Textually the third part of the anaphora presents us with the most difficult problems of interpretation. These difficulties, outlined by Botte in 1947, are not in any way now solved, apart from some possible but not provable theories that can explain some of the difficulties. The difficulties may be summarized, first, by observing that the epiclesis has two parts, one a request for the

---

[94] It is is not difficult to recall here Ignatius of Antioch's understanding of his own martyrdom in similar terms. Letter to the Romans, IV, 1: "...ἵνα καθαρὸς ἄρτος εὑρεθῶ τοῦ Χριστοῦ... ἵνα διὰ τῶν ὀργάνων τούτων θεῷ θυσία εὑρεθῶ." SCh 10, 98.

[95] This idea of participation is "hidden," as it were, in the text of this anaphora, which speaks simply of offering the bread and the cup. The bread and the cup are a "sacrament" of this participation (sacraments hide as well as reveal), and the experience of the Church in offering these will slowly be the basis for a more clearly elaborated theology of participation.

descent of the Holy Spirit on the offerings of the Church and another — unrelated textually to it! — a request that those who share in the gifts be filled with the Holy Spirit. In addition there are further problems in just how particular phrases of these two parts are to be understood, difficulties attested to by the comparatively stronger divergence here of the redactions in the various languages.[96]

These difficulties make themselves felt on the present enterprise. An almost word by word analysis like the one conducted in examining the first part of this anaphora is not advisable here, being too risky. And yet there are a few broad strokes of not inconsiderable importance that can be sketched out here. First, there is what is almost too obvious: *God (the Father)* is petitioned to send his *Holy Spirit.* This is a new petition, a different part of the prayer; and in it the Holy Spirit comes into clear relief, not to mention a precise relationship with God. He is called *"Spiritum tuum sanctum."* The difficulty with this first petition, however, is that oddly it goes nowhere. One would expect some expression indicating the purpose of the Spirit's coming, i.e., to sanctify the gifts, to fill them, to transform them. But there is nothing of the sort. Instead, there is an abrupt shift to the second petition, which has in common with the first only the mention of the Holy Spirit.

All the textual difficulties notwithstanding, Botte was still willing at least to draw the conclusion that the epiclesis developed in this anaphora in order to give it a clear trinitarian shape.[97] The way in which the Holy Spirit is introduced in this prayer, with his relationship to God and his relationship to the Church, will

---

[96] B. BOTTE, "L'épiclèse de l'anaphore d'Hippolyte," *RTAM* 14 (1947) 241-251. ID., "L'Esprit-Saint et l'Église dans la « Tradition apostolique» de Saint Hippolyte," *Didaskalia* 2 (1972) 221-34. For the differences in the versions, see BOTTE, *La Tradition apostolique,* 17. Mazza concludes his analysis of the problems by suggesting, "... the two parts of the epiclesis of this anaphora belong to two different strata of the text. The connection between the two sections is not a very good one, both from a content and a literary point of view. This can all be explained by supposing that the first part was added at a later time." MAZZA, *Origins,* 173. For his whole discussion, see ibid., 170-174.

[97] See BOTTE, "L'Esprit-Saint et l'Église," 227-234.

hereafter continue to exert its influence not only on subsequent epicleses,[98] but consequently on the trinitarian doctrine that is rooted in this eucharistic experience of the Church.

This observation, however obvious, is no small gain in collecting evidence for the dynamic of *lex orandi-lex credendi* in the eucharistic context. For the rest, we may risk now attention to a few details, mindful of the aforementioned difficulties. I want to look at two things: (1) the relation between the Holy Spirit and the cup and (2) the petition for unity.

4.1. *The Spirit and the Cup*

Mazza assembles some interesting texts in order to help understand the sense of the petition that those who participate in the holy mysteries[99] may be filled with the Holy Spirit, *in repletionem Spiritus sancti*. In fact these texts closely associate the Holy Spirit and the blood of the cup. One of these is found in a homily, once thought to be of Chrysostom but now attributed to Apollinaire of Laodicea: "Through the blood [the Eucharistic cup] spilled for us we receive the Holy Spirit, since the blood and the Spirit are united in one single being *(eis hen elthe)*, so that through blood which is connatural to us we can receive the Holy Spirit who is not connatural to us."[100] This idea does not originate with Apollinaire. It is found already in the homily of Pseudo-Hippolytus, who speaks of "the entire cup full of blood and the divine Spirit," or again, "slaked with the cup of gladness — that is by the blood itself, vibrant and inflamed, branded by the heat of the Spirit."[101] The connection between blood and Spirit may seem strange to us, but it came rather naturally to mind in the ancient world. As Cantalamessa writes, "In the ancient conception, accepted by Philo and especially by the Stoic school,

---

[98] MAZZA, *Origins*, 174: "With the epiclesis of the anaphora of Hippolytus is born the model itself of the Antiochene epiclesis, which from the anaphora of Basil will develop into the form known to us and will be the model of almost all succeeding texts."

[99] So, according to Botte, must we understand the difficult language at this point. See BOTTE, *La Tradition apostolique*, 17.

[100] PSEUDO-CHRYSOSTOME, *Sur la Pâque*, II, 7; cited by MAZZA, *Origins*, 142.

[101] Homily n. 7 and n. 25; cited by MAZZA, *Origins*, 142.

blood and spirit are intimately connected realities: the first is vehicle of the second." [102]

These texts do not bring us forward with any definite certainty. After all, Apollinaire is far removed in time from the *Apostolic Tradition*. And yet something in the anaphora's petition is already moving in the direction of this much later text; namely, that those who participate in the holy gifts receive thereby the Holy Spirit. The several texts of Pseudo-Hippolytus place the same idea in roughly the same time period of the anaphora. Cantalamessa goes so far as to say, "The spirit is, therefore, the notion by which the homilist tries to explain 'the real presence' in the Eucharistic mystery." [103] All this could be described as a primitive, sketchy theology of consecration through the Holy Spirit. This is in no way consecration in the sense of the fourth century and as we know it today. It is consecration in the sense that the Holy Spirit fills the gifts and vivifies them with himself such that those who participate in the gifts receive the Holy Spirit. [104]

4.2. *The Petition for Unity*

The several texts brought together by Mazza to understand the relation between the Spirit and the gifts are not meant to argue for any textual dependency on the part of the anaphora on these texts. At best they give some indication of the theological thought world that can explain such a petition. The same petition can be understood from yet another angle. Again, there is no direct textual dependency, but we can make some attempt to understand the petition's theological thrust.

It is particularly difficult to know how to interpret the phrase *in unum congregans* because it is not clear what precisely is meant to be brought into one. It can refer either to the Church,

---

[102] CANTALAMESSA, *La pasqua della nostra salvezza*, 330, cited by MAZZA, *Origins*, 142.

[103] CANTALAMESSA, *La pasqua della nostra salvezza*, 131, cited by MAZZA, *Origins*, 143.

[104] Deep in the background lies the biblical lex in the mysterious texts of John 7:38; 19:34; 1 John 5:6-8.

in the phrase which precedes it, or to the faithful in the phrase which follows it. Botte concludes that the ambiguity must be let to stand, letting it refer to one or the other, or even, presumably, both. Whatever the case may be, it should be observed that the petition of the anaphora makes a decided shift from the texts which are its ancestors in terms of structure; namely, the *Birkat ha- mazon* and the *Didache*. We have seen the structure of these texts is the same as that of the anaphora: (1) a general first thanksgiving, (2) a second thanksgiving for the present moment, and (3) petitions. The petitions of the *Birkat ha- mazon* and the *Didache* are for the eschatological gathering of Israel or the Church into the kingdom. In both the gathering is assigned to God the Father to whom the prayer is addressed. In the anaphora two differences can be noted. First, the work of gathering is assigned to the Holy Spirit. Second, the gathering is no longer the eschatological gathering of the whole Church, but the weight of the petition falls on the particular worshipping assembly. This is a big piece of theology, full of trinitarian implications. We have here a primitive version of something that later will be exploited more explicitly in theology; namely, the special role of the Holy Spirit in establishing the unity of the Church here and now and the way in which this is accomplished in concrete, particular eucharistic assemblies.[105]

In this same line it is useful to examine the phrase *ad confirmationem fidei in veritate*. It is this that the faithful's being filled with the Holy Spirit is meant to accomplish. Thus, this is no vague prayer for unity but one that would show itself through the confirmation of faith in truth. This would be the Spirit's gift in the community that celebrates this eucharist. Where does such a precise petition come from, and what is its concern? Mazza connects it with the thought world represented in Irenaeus. In his concern to show the falseness of heretical teachings and to indicate the concrete way in which truth can be

---

[105] The biblical logic or *lex* is, of course, rooted in 1 Cor 10:17: "Because the loaf of bread is one, we, though many, are one body, for we all partake of the one loaf." As Connolly says in "The Eucharistic Prayer" 365: "The eucharistic bread then, by its composition, is a symbol of the union of the faithful in Christ, and further illustrates the working of the Holy Spirit, *in the faithful*, by which this union is effected."

verified, Ireneaus develops an ecclesiology one of whose principle claims is that only the one Church benefits from the presence of the Spirit, and the Spirit's gift to the Church is, precisely, truth. *"Spiritus autem veritas,"* he says, or again, the Spirit is *"arrha incorruptelae et confirmatio fidei nostrae et scala ascensionis in Deum."* [106] The activity of the Spirit in the Church guarantees the truth of faith.

The point here is not to claim that the petition of the anaphora has a direct textual dependence on Irenaeus. It is rather that Irenaeus has in place a theology that explains the precise concern of the liturgical petition. Mazza concludes his more detailed examination of these materials by saying, "We can say... that Irenaeus has all the material needed by the redactor [of the anaphora] for constructing his epiclesis... We have to admit that the material of which the epiclesis of the anaphora of the *Apostolic Tradition* is composed depends on Irenaeus, but we cannot say that the epiclesis itself, in its entirety, comes from him." [107] As suggested above, where we previously found the influence of Irenaeus on the anaphora, such a find sheds light on the dynamic we are seeking to uncover in this study. Roughly speaking, we can place Irenaeus in the category of a *lex credendi*. His ideas, which are meant to be guided always by the apostolic Rule of Faith, condense themselves, among other things, around the idea of the Spirit guaranteeing true faith in the one Church. In the *lex orandi* of the anaphora we find that the petition for the Holy Spirit is focused on this precise concern. In this context it makes no sense to assign some sort of absolute priority to a *lex orandi* over a *lex credendi*. Both express the same concern in a different way.

The importance of the confirmation of the faith in truth is seen in the way in which the petition for that very thing leads into the final doxology which concludes the anaphora. It is faith in truth, confirmed by the Holy Spirit in the eucharistic celebration, that makes possible the praise and glorification of the Father which the community wishes to offer: *ad confirmationem fidei in*

---

[106] These and other texts from Irenaeus are all brought together by MAZZA, *Origins*, 147-149.

[107] MAZZA, *Origins*, 149.

veritate, ut te laudemus et glorificemus... From here the *"te"* unfolds into a splendid trinitarian and ecclesial doxology. We may say that this ultimately is the truth that the Spirit confirms. Put in the terms which interest us in this study, we may say that true faith *(lex credendi)* makes possible true worship *(lex orandi)*, which is praise of the Father through Jesus Christ in the Holy Spirit and in the Church. True faith apprehends the reality of God as Father, Son, and Spirit. This reality is the ultimate reason for the *lex orandi* which prescribes that the Father be praised through the Son in the Holy Spirit.[108] With this finish to the prayer we have again what we have already observed at several other passes: the Trinity is spoken of *together with* those who will share trinitarian life; namely "in the holy Church." Here we have the eucharistic shape *(lex orandi)* of what later will be the shape of the *lex credendi* in the Creeds of the great councils of the fourth century: belief in the Trinity expressed in three successive articles followed by profession of belief in the holy Church, in the one Church, catholic and apostolic.[109] But in this kind of doxology the formulation is more primitive. The Church is not a separate object of belief here, but the place — the only possible place — in which the objects of belief — Father, Son, and Spirit — are

---

[108] It will not prove fruitful to linger overlong on the divergences of the linguistic versions of the final doxology. The doxology of the Latin text is odd in that it seems to unfold in two successive waves, the second not being entirely logical grammatically. In the first wave we have *ut te laudemus et glorificemus per puerum tuum Iesum Christum,* and this continues in what I call a second wave with *per quem tibi gloria et honor Patri et Filio cum sancto Spiritu...* It is not logical to speak of giving glory to the Son through Jesus Christ. This probably represents some redactional effort to have a clear and clean final trinitarian doxology. Botte observes that it is introduced "mécaniquement" here and in other doxologies of *The Apostolic Tradition,* i.e., chapters 3 and 7. See BOTTE, *La Tradition apostolique,* 19, n. 7. We would not be far from the sense in understanding the doxology in one complete wave rather than two: *ut te laudemus et glorificemus per puerum tuum Iesum Christum per quem tibi gloria et honor cum sancto Spiritu in sancta ecclesia.* For the difficulties in interpretation here, see CONNOLLY, "The Eucharistic Prayer" 367-369. The trinitarian doxology, or at least the trinitarian shape, of the eucharistic prayer is already attested to by JUSTIN MARTYR, *Apology I,* 65. For the phrase "in the holy Church" in a doxology, compare Eph 3:21.

[109] On the close relation between the Spirit and the Church, see J.P. MARTÍN, "Il rapporto tra Pneuma ed Ecclesia nella letteratura dei primi secoli cristiani," *Augustinianum* 20 (1980) 471-483, especially 483.

properly praised.[110] Again, this is the dynamic we are seeking to uncover: in this eucharistic celebration — which is the place where the holy church manifests itself — the Trinity is experienced and known.

Conclusion

I said at the outset that I wanted to undertake this particular study as one instance of any number of possible studies on the dynamic of *lex orandi-lex credendi* as this occurs in eucharist in relation to Trinity. Some definite results have emerged, which can be formulated now into the following conclusions.[111]

First of all, the parallels between the language and theology of the anaphora and the language and theology of the Easter homilies enabled us to catch the dynamic at a very early stage, where whole blocks of biblical theology were condensing themselves in a christological key into particular phrases which became obligatory both in the homilies and in the eucharistic anaphora. I called this process of condensation a *lex* which precedes the *lex orandi*. This more primitive *lex* represents apostolic tradition as it unfolds in the life of the Church, that is, a particular way of reading the Bible and celebrating it.

Secondly, we saw that this "obligatory" language and the theology it embodies was used in the anaphora to express a christology concerned to show Christ both as divine and human. Further, this christology witnesses to the instinct to distinguish

---

[110] P. NAUTIN, *Je crois à l'Esprit-Saint dans la sainte Église pour la résurrection de la chair*, Paris 1947 shows this clearly in his study of the profession of faith as contained in chapter 21 of *The Apostolic Tradition*. Thus, "in the Church" is to be understood as "un complément de lieu." Nautin understands the phrase to be attached strictly to what immediately precedes it: "in the Holy Spirit." But as BOTTE, *La Tradition apostolique*, 51, n. 1 points out, it would also be possible to understand "in the holy Church" as attaching to all three persons of the Trinity: "... il faut y voir la conclusion de l'acte de foi répété à l'égard de chacune des personnes et qui n'est possible que dans l'Église." What Botte posits in the context of the baptismal interrogation seems even more likely in the phrase as it occurs here in the anaphora.

[111] Here I will allow myself to speak in the standard terms of trinitarian theology, specifying "Father" rather than simply "God" of the anaphora so that the points established can be clear.

Christ from the Father, both from all eternity and in the economy. He is the inseparable Word of the Father sent into the world by him in these last days.

Thirdly, we saw an anaphora in which the Father's will is accomplished in the Passion of Christ which he also willingly accepted, thus enacting in his own will and in his flesh what the Father willed. This Passion is intimately connected with the Last Supper, which the community now does by imitation in memory of him.

Fourthly, we saw that by means of the anamnesis and through offering the bread and the cup to the Father the worshipping community stands in a relation to the Father similar to that in which Christ stood in his Passion. This liturgy is characterized as priestly service in the presence of the Father, a priestly service which parallels Christ's own death, conceived likewise in the Letter to the Hebrews as a priestly act. Christians feel the privilege of being called to this conformity to the Passion, this priestly service; and for this they give thanks to the Father, just as the martyr gives thanks for the privilege of such conformity in the giving of his life.

Fifthly, despite a number of difficulties surrounding the text and exact understanding of the epiclesis, significant material emerges at this point in the anaphora regarding the Holy Spirit. The Spirit is called the Father's Spirit, and the Father is petitioned to send the Spirit onto the Church's offering. Those who receive the gifts are thereby filled with the Holy Spirit, and this toward a precise end; namely, the confirmation of faith in truth. It is true faith which makes true worship possible, and this true worship is expressed in the climax of a doxology which is trinitarian and ecclesial in form: glory and praise to the Father through his Son with the Spirit in the Father's holy Church.

This anaphora offers a privileged look into the theological world of the Church's eucharistic experience at the beginning of the third century. In this study we have been able in part to see where such a world comes from, that is, from the Easter homilies and the dynamic which formed them. We have also been able to gain a sense of where it can go, that is, toward ever more precise formulations of trinitarian faith. I have used from time to time in these pages the expression "the Church's eucharistic experience." Hopefully it is clear by now why sensitivity to this is necessary to an eventual understanding of the Church's trinitarian doctrine. Here I have only studied the anaphora from a textual point of view. However, if we combine what has been learned from this with a realization of how much more forceful still is such a text when proclaimed in a believing assembly, when it is accompanied by ritual and gestures, when the bread is eaten and the cup drunk; when we remember that this is done Sunday after Sunday; when we remember that at Easter catechumens who have professed faith in the Father, Son, and Holy Spirit and were then baptized into that name were next taken to celebrate such a eucharist, then we have a sense of something that is marking the consciousness of the worshipping community little by little at a very profound level. This something is certainly a sense of God addressed through Jesus and in the Holy Spirit. Any articulation of trinitarian doctrine will ultimately have to rest on a consciousness so marked. In this sense then, despite all the theological forces that were already operating in advance of the anaphora, it is surely the *lex orandi* that establishes the *lex credendi*.

Chapter 4

UNCOVERING THE DYNAMIC
LEX ORANDI-LEX CREDENDI
IN THE TRINITARIAN THEOLOGY OF ORIGEN

The present study investigates several instances of the dynamic *lex orandi-lex credendi* in Origen.

Origen is not generally considered a major witness to things liturgical in the third century, even if, because of the extent of his writings, it is inevitable that questions touching on the liturgy emerge. Origen is an interesting case study, for he brings us to a different level of the dynamic between *lex orandi* and *lex credendi*. He is both appreciated and held suspect for what is called his spiritualizing tendency. For him the concrete celebration of the liturgy is a means to a more interior liturgy or feast, as he explains, for example, against Celsus: "I think that this is what Paul had in mind when he called the feast that is held on days set apart from others 'part of a feast' (Col 2:16); he hinted by this phrase that the life which is continually being lived according to the divine word is not in 'part of a feast' but is an entire and continual feast." [112] An entire and continual feast in the heart of one devoted to the word — particular celebrations are meant to nourish that.

Nonetheless, it would be too much to conclude from this and like comments that Origen underplays the ontological density of what is occurring in the liturgy itself. After all, he does well to

---

[112] Contra Celsum VIII, 23. English taken from *Origen: Contra Celsum, translated with an Introduction and Notes by H. Chadwick*, Cambridge 1953, 468. For a useful discussion of Origen's attitude toward liturgy in general and his spiritualizing tendencies, see C. MAZZUCCO, "Culto," in *Origene, Dizionario, la cultura, il pensiero, le opere*, ed. A.C. Castagno, Roma 2000, 107-110. The major study for this question as focused on the eucharist is L. LIES, *Wort und Eucharistie bei Origenes, Zur Spiritualisierungstendenz des Eucharistieverständnisses*, Innsbruck 1978. See also W. SCHÜTZ, *Der christliche Gottesdienst bei Origenes*, Stuttgart 1984.

recall that liturgy must reach an interior dimension for each one who celebrates it. Yet something of substance is already occurring in the liturgy. The dictum *lex orandi-lex credendi* was articulated explicitly in fifth century Western controversies over grace.[113] In this study I want to observe the dynamic at work in the formulation of a doctrine much more central; namely, the Trinity. With Origen we are in the pre-Constantinian church, that is to say, at a more primitive stage of the dynamic, at a more primitive stage of trinitarian theology. Examining how Origen moves within it sheds considerable light on the relation between liturgy and doctrine.

The Dialogue with Heraclides

A good measure of how seriously Origen takes the foundational role of the liturgy is found in the theological controversy reflected in *The Dialogue with Heraclides* and the way in which he refers to the eucharistic prayer to establish a doctrinal point. The *Sitz im Leben* for *The Dialogue* can only be reconstructed in general terms, but terms significant enough for the precise point under examination in the present investigation. A local council has brought together a number of bishops because of a doctrinal problem in the teaching of one of their number, Heraclides. Origen is invited to the council as a theological expert.[114] The doctrinal problem has to do with the distinction between the Father and the Son and probably arises from the use by Heraclides of a eucharistic prayer addressed to the Son.[115] In any case, Heraclides is unclear in how he understands the relation between Father and Son, and the text reports Origen's close cross-examination of the bishop and then his own exposition of

---

[113] See pp. 45-48.

[114] See J. SCHERER, SCh 67, 13-24; P. NAUTIN, *Origène, sa vie et son œuvre*, Paris 1977, 388-389; H. CHADWICK, *Alexandrian Christianity*, Philadelphia 1954, 430-436; R. Daly in *Origen, Treatise on the Passover* and *Dialogue of Origen With Heraclides and His Fellow Bishops on the Father, the Son, and the Soul*, translated and annotated by R.J. Daly, New York 1992, 19-26.

[115] On this, see J. SCHERER, *Entretien d'Origène avec Héraclide*, Paris 1960, SCh 67, 24; P. NAUTIN, *Origène*, 117 notes that the problem of eucharistic prayers addressed to the Son was still being dealt with by the Council of Carthage in 397.

how he thinks the question should be understood. It is in this latter part that Origen makes reference to the eucharistic prayer, but first it is worth seeing some of the discussion which precedes this reference.

The text gives a stenographic report of a council which helps the reader to witness firsthand the difficulty which the third century Church was still experiencing between the theological alternatives of Monarchianism or Adoptionism. Strongly marked by Justin Martyr and other apologists who considered the Logos as clearly distinct in relation to the Father,[116] Origen tries to steer a middle course between the two more radical alternatives. Heraclides is less skilled a theologian than Origen, but Origen is able to press his point in a way that appears to have persuaded the bishop. Chadwick summarizes Origen's position well: "Only the doctrine that the Logos is both separate from and one with the Father avoids heresy."[117] Origen is aware that the language that expresses this will be paradoxical and even scandalous for some. The cross-examination concludes with the following interchange: *Origen:* "The Father is God?" *Heraclides:* "Of course." *Origen:* "The Son is distinct from the Father?" *Heraclides:* "Of course, for how could He be son if He were also father?" *Origen:* "And while being distinct from the Father, the Son is Himself also God?" *Heraclides:* "He is Himself also God." *Origen:* "And the two Gods become a unity?" *Heraclides:* "Yes." *Origen:* "We profess two Gods?" *Heraclides:* "Yes. [but] the power is one."[118]

Origen has managed to achieve the point that is most important to him: the clear distinction between the Father and the Son, even while naming them both God and speaking of their unity. The cornered Heraclides agrees, but not without at least blurting out his principal concern: "The power is one." He is looking for some term to express the unity, and he is citing a traditional formula.[119] Origen grants his concern and begins his own extended discourse with the words, "But since our brothers are shocked at the statement that there are two Gods, we must

---

[116] On this see, D. PAZZINI, "Figlio," in *Origene, Dizionario*, 163-164.

[117] H. CHADWICK, *Alexandrian Christianity*, 433.

[118] Dialogue with Heraclides, 2, 15-27, SCh 67, 56-58. English, Daly, 58-59.

[119] It is based on 1 Cor 1:24 and Rom 1:4. See J. SCHERER, SCh 67, 59, n. 1 for other patristic references to this formula.

treat this matter carefully, and point out in what respect they are two, and in what respect these two are one God." [120] He proceeds by collecting scriptural examples of ways in which things that are two are also said to be one. The method here is meant to achieve a certain loosening of categories in minds that are too rigid to entertain paradox. And yet even with the examples that he employs one must distinguish the level of *earthly* examples of two and one from the *divine* reality of two and one in the Father and the Son. If Adam and Eve are two yet one *flesh* and Christ and the righteous man are two yet one *spirit,* the Son and the Father can be two yet one *God:* "... the appropriate word... when Christ is united to the Father is not 'flesh' or 'spirit' but the more prestigious word: 'God.'" [121] There is a tremendous intuition expressed here by Origen, in a phrase perhaps too tightly packed to reveal its force on first hearing. But it is worth thinking about carefully. He is suggesting that "God" is a term not just vaguely useful for expressing a common monotheistic notion of the deity but in fact more precisely suited for expressing a unique unity which is peculiar to God; namely, the unity of Father and Son. It is precisely at this point that Origen makes reference to the Church's eucharistic prayer, and it is his instinct to do so to which I wish to draw attention.

He is aware that his language is paradoxical and that it balances only precariously. (This is the nature of theological discourse when it approaches the heart of the mystery as in the present case.) And so he instinctively searches for firmer ground to help his listeners to follow the subtlety of his thought. (It should be recalled that he is trying to help those who may be scandalized.) This firmer ground he finds by reference to the whole Church's experience of Eucharist. He makes two points, the first of which overlaps the second. He appeals to the need for a universal common practice on prayer in this regard, perhaps alluding to the possible practice in the church of Heraclides of a eucharistic prayer addressed to Christ: "In some of our prayers we maintain the duality and in others we introduce the unity." [122] In fact those who do not pray in this way are already separated from

---

[120] Dialogue 2, 28-31, SCh 67, 58; English, Daly, 59.
[121] Dialogue 3, 23-28, SCh 67, 60; English, Daly, 60.
[122] Dialogue 4, 4-6, SCh 67, 62; English, Daly, 60.

the Church, and Origen names again as examples those separated either for Monarchian tendencies or Adoptionist ones. He wants to help the particular church of Heraclides avoid a similar separation from the greater Church. "Care must be exercised in the way one speaks of these things because this subject has been the cause of much agitation in this church." [123]

If the need for a common practice in the whole Church is the first of Origen's points, his second follows closely on its heels. He observes that the kind of eucharistic prayer that is normally found in churches — and thus normatively to be applied — is a prayer in which the proper relation between Father and Son is expressed: "Oblation is constantly made to God the all-powerful through Jesus Christ by reason of his communication in divinity with the Father. Nor is it made twice but (once) to God through God." [124] With this last phrase Origen is once again aware that he is pushing up against the limits of paradox, but it is the "constantly made oblation" of the Church which requires of him to go this far. An example of such a prayer roughly contemporaneous to Origen is the anaphora of the *Apostolic Tradition*, a prayer in which God is clearly addressed through Jesus Christ. [125] By appealing to the need for a universal common practice, Origen, of course, is not suggesting that there be one same text in all the churches. Even the text in the *Apostolic Tradition* is offered only as a model. But he is appealing to a structure of the prayer that must be found in all the churches and probably in most cases already is. This structure is prayer offered to the Father through Jesus Christ. A great deal of theological sifting had already gone into the production of an anaphora such as that found in the *Apostolic Tradition*. [126] To the fruit of such

---

[123] Dialogue 4, 20-23, SCh 67, 62; English, Daly, 60.

[124] Dialogue 4, 31-34, SCh 67, 62; English, Daly, 60-61. Nautin thinks that Origen is arguing here for a change in the practice of prayer, that rather than address "God through Christ your Son" it should be said "God through God." This seems unlikely, and Nautin has not been generally followed in this. See P. NAUTIN, *Lettres et écrivains chrétiens des IIe et IIIe siècles*, Paris 1961, 221-232.

[125] Nautin makes this connection in *Origène*, 117.

[126] For an example of the theological influences that went into this prayer, see E. MAZZA, *The Origins of the Eucharistic Prayer*, translated by Roland E. Lane, Collegeville 1995, 98-176.

sifting Origen makes appeal here. In language that helps him focus this aspect of the prayer on the problem for which the local council has been called, Origen says, "an offering to God through God." This means an offering to the Father through the Son. So, both Father and Son are God; in some sense, then, two Gods; but two can be one in a way that is unique to God, appropriate to God, just as Adam and Eve are one in a way that is appropriate to flesh.

We see here the language of theology searching for a precise rendering of a *lex credendi*, language rooted way down inside the reality of what is accomplished in the eucharistic prayer, the *lex orandi*. The eucharistic prayer is "an offering to God through God." That there are two who are one must find formulation then in the *lex credendi*. Origen finishes with this appeal: "Let these conventions be kept," meaning, most probably, let us hold to this *lex orandi*.[127]

The Treatise on Prayer

One would wish for a further discussion in *The Dialogue* of what in effect is delivered here in not much more than a few tightly packed sentences. Fortunately, however, elsewhere in Origen's writings this same theme is taken up at a little more length. These passages secure the interpretation offered above and reflect further on it theologically. They are chapters 14:1 to 16:1 in the treatise *On Prayer*. 15:2 is often cited in connection with the passage from *The Dialogue* that we have just examined: "And so when the saints give thanks to God in their prayers, they acknowledge through Christ Jesus the favors He has done."[128] Origen is referring to the eucharistic prayer here.[129] But once

---

[127] Dialogue 5, 10-11, SCh 67, 60; English, Daly, 61. The interpretation of this line is disputed, and the text is corrupt at this point. Daly and Chadwick think the reference is to the *lex orandi*; Scherer thinks it refers to the agreements that are meant to be the outcome of this debate.

[128] De Orat 15:2. GCS 3, 334. English taken from *Origen, Prayer, Translation and Introduction by R.A. Greer*, New York 1979, 113.

[129] Nautin draws attention to the phrase εὐχαριστοῦντες... θεῷ and διά Χριστοῦ Ιησοῦ and even connects it to the language of the anaphora in the *Apostolic Tradition*. P. NAUTIN, *Origène*, 117. The saints are not the saints in heaven but the baptized who offer the Eucharist through Christ.

again it is worth noting that he does so in order to secure an even broader theological point. Or put another way in order to emphasize the dynamic I am trying to uncover: from the eucharistic prayer *(lex orandi)* Origen was led to make a particular theological point about prayer in general, and once again it concerns the distinction and relation between the Father and the Son *(lex credendi)*.

The whole context is important for understanding why Origen makes the point just cited. His concern is clearly expressed at the beginning of a particular development where, typical of the way he would unfold almost any point, he calls his reader to the higher, more spiritual understanding of what is under discussion — in this case, prayer. Though one can pray for earthly, material needs, this is not the highest form of prayer. "You who wish to be spiritual, seek through your prayers heavenly and great things, so that in getting them as heavenly you may inherit the kingdom of heaven... And as for the earthly and little things you need for your bodily necessities, the Father will supply you with them in proportion as you need them." [130] This is the reason for all that he develops in what follows.

He first distinguishes four terms for prayer, following the Apostle as in 1 Tim 2:1: supplication (δεήσεις), prayer (προσευχή), intercession (ἔντευξις), and thanksgiving (εὐχαριστία). Of these four terms it is prayer (προσευχή) that he associates with his concern for the highest, most spiritual type, defining it as "something nobler [than supplication] offered by a person with praise and for greater objects." [131] Having defined his terms thus, he goes on to find biblical examples of each of the four types, and one of the examples he finds for προσευχή is striking for its trinitarian implications. The initial clue for Origen is discovered in his habitual very close reading of the text. Thus, the verse "A prayer (προσευχή) of Habakkuk the prophet" (Hab 3:1-2 LXX)

---

[130] De Orat 14:1. *GCS* 3, 330. English, Greer, 109. See the same expressed in *Contra Celsum* VII, 44: "His prayer is not concerned with any everyday matters; for he has learnt from Jesus to seek for nothing small, that is, sensible, but only for things that are great and truly divine which, as God's gifts, help in the journey to the blessedness with Him attained through the mediation of His Son who is the Logos of God." English, Chadwick, 432-433.

[131] De Orat 14:2. *GCS* 3, 330. English, Greer, 109.

will, of course, be of interest to him. He cites the prayer: "In the midst of the two living creatures (ἐν μέσῳ δύο ζώων) you will be known; as the years draw near you will be recognized." He sees in the reference to the two living creatures [132] an allusion to the Son and the Holy Spirit, [133] which inclines him to the interpretation then that prayer in the strict sense is properly addressed only to the Father, the "prayer of Habakkuk the prophet" functioning as the biblical warrant.

After considering other biblical examples of all four types, which does not offer an especially tidy or simple vision of prayer, Origen tries to come somehow closer to the heart of the matter. And to do this he focuses once again on the term prayer (προσευχή): "Now if we are to take prayer in its most exact sense perhaps we should not pray to anyone begotten, not even to Christ Himself, but only to the God and Father of all, to whom even our Savior Himself prayed... and to whom he taught us to pray." [134] For prayer in the strict sense of the term, Origen takes most seriously the fact that Christ himself prayed to another. In this fact the distinction between the Father and the Son is thrown into clear relief, and Origen underlines it. Granted the clear distinction, he considers three possibilities: (1) that prayer should be addressed to the Son and not the Father, (2) that it should be addressed to both, (3) that it should be addressed to the Father alone. The first possibility is ruled out as absurd. The second possibility is ruled out by the *lex orandi* as found both in the Bible and the liturgy. If we were to pray to both, then we would expect prayers addressed in the second person plural, but no such prayers can be found. Thus, the only conclusion is that "... we should pray only to the God and Father of all..." Yet he does not leave it at that, but feels compelled not only by the biblical

---

[132] This would perhaps better be translated "two living beings," according to the LXX. Nothing in the Greek text would make Origen think necessarily of "creatures" with the ontological implications of this for the Son and the Holy Spirit.

[133] See De princ. I, 3, 4 where Origen is explicit on this: "'In the midst of the two living creatures thou shalt be known' is spoken of Christ and the Holy Spirit. For all knowledge of the Father, when the Son reveals him, is made to us through the Holy Spirit." English taken from *Origen on First Principles*, *translation by G.W. Butterworth*, London 1936, 32.

[134] De Orat 15:1. *GCS* 3, 334. English, Greer, 112.

examples to which he has alluded (the trinitarian dimensions of the prayer in Habbakuk and the Lord's own example and teaching) but also by the *lex orandi* as expressed in the structure of the eucharistic prayer to add, "and yet not [pray] without the High Priest, who was appointed 'with an oath' according to the verse, 'He has sworn and will not change His mind, You are a priest forever after the order of Melchisedek.'"[135]

It is at this point in his argument that Origen introduces the detail that we began with; namely, his reference to the very structure of the eucharistic prayer: "And so when the saints give thanks to God in their prayers, they acknowledge through Christ Jesus the favors He has done."[136] In what follows we see once again something similar to what was noted in *The Dialogue;* namely, the need to balance one statement with another. So, Origen explains, if prayer in the strict sense must be addressed only to the Father, it must also now be said with equal force "that no prayer should be addressed to the Father without Him [i.e., Christ Jesus]." The liturgy teaches this, as he has just noted; but the point in fact is grounded directly in the teaching of Jesus, which Origen is able to read with typical very close attention. Jesus said, "Hitherto you have asked nothing in my name." (John 16:24) It is in the "hitherto" that Origen finds his key insight. "Until Jesus taught this, no one asked the Father in the name of the Son." It would not have occurred to anyone to do so. Indeed, Origen is keenly aware that here we touch the precise newness of the Christian revelation; namely, that the one God and Father, to whom prayer had *hitherto* already been addressed, *henceforth* is to be addressed in the name of Christ and "no prayer should be addressed to the Father without him." "[Jesus] did not simply say 'ask me' or simply 'ask the Father.'"[137] It is prayer *to* the Father *through* the Son that constitutes the Christian newness.

In what follows Origen seeks to drive the point home. He admits a qualified way in which prayer to the Son is possible (15:3), but then develops a line of reasoning that he imagines in the mouth of Christ, based on Christ's own words, "Why do

---

[135] De Orat 15:1. *GCS* 3, 334. English, Greer, 112-113.
[136] De Orat 15:2. *GCS* 3, 334. English, Greer, 113.
[137] De Orat 15:2. *GCS* 3, 334. English, Greer, 113.

you call me good? No one is good but God the Father alone."
(Mark 10:18 and parallels)[138] It is as if Christ were saying to us,
"You should pray only to the Father, to whom I pray myself... For
you must not pray to the High Priest appointed on your behalf by
the Father (cf. Heb 8:3)... Rather, you must pray *through* the High
Priest..."[139] The image here is liturgical and biblical, but it is made
to extend beyond that to more general theological conclusions
about the Trinity. In all this unfolding line of reasoning there has
been a very fluid movement back and forth between the general
theological point that Origen wishes to establish (about the
Father and the Son) and the Church's *lex orandi* to support his
argument. As his argument relies on this *lex orandi*, it can also be
used as a *lex credendi* which insists that the way of prayer should
conform to all that has been said: "Since we hear Jesus saying
this, let us pray to God through Him, all of us saying the same
things and not divided about the way we pray. Are we not divided
if some of us pray to the Father and some to the Son...?"[140] He
might just as well have said the same thing in the local council
in the church of Heraclides. Perhaps experiences like this council
were the reason why he felt it necessary to develop this point and
extend it beyond simply the liturgical setting to a general sense
of prayer.[141]

Homily 13 on Leviticus

There is another passage worth examining in this context.
I choose it not because it displays as directly as the previous
two passages the dynamic between liturgy and theological
formulation but rather because it somehow enables us to gain a

---

[138] For further indications of how Origen understands this text, see
De princ I, 2, 13 with comments by P. NAUTIN, *Origène*, 119.

[139] De Orat 15:4. *GCS* 3, 335. English, Greer, 114.

[140] De Orat 16:1. *GCS* 3, 336. English, Greer, 114.

[141] Origen would not have distinguished as sharply as we do between
liturgical prayer and individual or private prayer, drawing some theological
conclusions from the one and different conclusions from the other. They are
all prayer, and as such fall into the category of a *lex orandi*, a *lex* learned first
from Christ himself and embodied in the Church's liturgy. What is learned
from such prayer is the clear distinction between the Father and the Son but
also that the Father should never be addressed without the Son.

glimpse of a general way in which the liturgy would have influenced, even subliminally, Origen's theological reasoning. Of course, Origen's theology is always intentionally constructed on the basis of the biblical text; for him theology is exegesis. In a homily on a passage from Leviticus we see how the Church's Eucharist worked its effect on the exegesis or theology which Origen constructs. Knowing his mind on the importance in the eucharistic prayer of carefully distinguishing Father and Son even while holding them together, we can see that same concern emerge in a context where nothing is in dispute but where the goal in preaching is simply getting to the deeper meaning of the text.

The passage on which Origen is preaching is Leviticus 24:5-9 (LXX), and it is in pondering the loaves of bread mentioned in this passage that a connection with the Eucharist will be made and then developed on the trinitarian question. According to the text, twelve loaves are meant to be "a remembrance before the Lord" as an entreaty or supplication before him.[142] Origen first notes that on the literal level twelve loaves of bread do not amount to much of a supplication. But, of course, the text has to be referred to the "greatness of the mystery" and "... if you turn your attention to that 'remembrance' about which the Lords says, 'Do this in remembrance of me,' you will find that this is the only 'remembrance' which makes God gracious to men. Therefore, if you recall more intently the ecclesiastical mysteries, you will find the image of the future truth anticipated in these things which the Law writes."[143] So far such a way of proceeding is not surprising to anyone familiar with Origen's exegesis. He has interpreted the word *remembrance* in the Leviticus text with the same word in the New Testament and thus established that the Leviticus text is actually speaking about the "ecclesiastical mysteries," clearly in

---

[142] LXX has ἀνάμνεσις for remembrance. We have Origen's homily only in a Latin translation, where commemoratio is the term used.

[143] Homily on Leviticus 13:3, 3. SCh 287, 208. The English translation is taken from *Origen, Homilies on Leviticus 1-16, translated by G.W. Barkley*, Washington 1990, 237. Unfortunately, because we are limiting our discussion to trinitarian questions, we cannot take up the interesting eucharistic theology implied in the statement that the Eucharist "makes God gracious to men." For something similar see also Homily 9:10, 1 on Leviticus.

this context meaning the celebration of the Eucharist. This connection seems obvious enough to him, and he presumes his listeners are satisfied, saying, "There is not much more to discuss about these things because it is enough to be understood by a single recollection." [144]

Then, typically, Origen offers another possible explanation, suggesting straightaway that "Every word of God is a loaf..." And then this causes him to seize on other details of the text and wonder what is the significance of the requirement that these loaves be made with "fine wheat flour" and that they "must always be placed in the sight of the Lord and must be set forth upon a clean table." The answer is that there are different kinds of words of God — loaves — and those made of fine wheat flour "contain secrets and speak about the faith in God or the knowledge of things." Abraham served this kind of bread for his divine visitors (Gen 18:6), whereas Lot had only a more common kind of bread (Gen 19:3). What is striking about where this particular line of argument finishes is the trinitarian shape that is the hidden meaning of the finer loaves: "And you, therefore, if you have knowledge of the secrets, if you can discuss wisely and carefully about faith in God, about the mystery of Christ, the unity of the Holy Spirit, you offer loaves 'from fine wheat flour.'" Religion that restricts itself to moral exhortation is a loaf of another kind: "But if you use common exhortations for the people and only know how to treat a moral issue which pertains to all, you know you have offered a common loaf." [145]

The next detail which Origen takes up has an odd lack of clarity about it, which is the signal to him that there is a certain mystery after which he is meant to inquire. The text says, "Let each loaf be two tenths," but it does not say of what. It is for the reader to wonder. In what Origen discovers he will speak of the relation of Father and Son to each other in ways that recall what we have already seen in *The Dialogue* and *On Prayer*. The precise details that enable this are three numbers in the text: *"two," "tenths,"* of *"one"* loaf. God himself is shown under the perfect number ten. If one speaks in the Church of the Father alone, that

---

[144] Homily on Leviticus 13:3, 3. SCh 287, 208. English, Barkley, 237.
[145] Homily on Leviticus 13:3, 4. SCh 287, 210. English, Barkley, 237-238.

would be only one tenth of a loaf. Likewise, speaking of Christ alone would be only one tenth. Then Origen must surely have delighted his listeners with what follows: "But if I should say that the Father is always with the Son and 'he himself does his works' or also if I should say 'the Father is in the Son and the Son in the Father' and 'he who sees the Son sees the Father,' and that the Father and Son are one, I have offered one loaf from two tenths of pure 'fine wheat flour,' the true loaf 'who gives his life for this world.'" [146] This is effective exegesis and preaching. Origen has collected into one rhetorical string five passages from the Gospel of John, delivered one after another, each of which shows the distinction of Father and Son as well as their unity. There are *two* parts to each statement, but *one* loaf, the loaf which comes down from heaven.

He stays with the point, insisting on it, refining the theological nuance. It is still a question, as we saw in the passages from *The Dialogue* and *On Prayer*, of balancing one statement with another: "... confessing the Father and Son, we make 'one loaf from two tenths;' ... How do 'two tenths' become one mass? Because I do not separate the Son from the Father nor the Father from the Son. He says, 'For whoever sees me, sees the Father also.'" [147] Even the two different positions in which the loaves are to be set — another "two" in the text — are designed to protect this mystery: "For if there should be one position [only], the word about the Father and the Son would be confused and mixed... but there are two positions, ... for we call that one who is not the Son Father and this one who is not the Father Son... and in this way we profess 'two positions before the Lord.'" All this is about balance, or to use the language of the present images, about measure: "It is in fact, if I may say so, the art of a great and very creative baker to preserve diligently these measures and thus to temper the word about the Father and the Son; to join them where it is appropriate and, on the other hand, to separate them where it is fitting that 'the two measures' in some degree are never absent and the one loaf never fails to appear." [148]

---

[146] Homily on Leviticus 13:4, 1. SCh 287, 212. English, Barkley, 238-239.
[147] Homily on Leviticus 13:4, 3. SCh 287, 214. English, Barkley, 240.
[148] Homily on Leviticus 13:4, 4. SCh 287, 216. English, Barkley, 240.

All this might well have been said to Heraclides or in the context of *On Prayer* where Origen himself "preserved diligently the measure" of prayer addressed only to the Father together with insistence that it nonetheless never be addressed without Jesus Christ. We have already seen that it is the very structure of the eucharistic prayer (the *lex orandi*) that, among other things, makes Origen sensitive to this. It would have been hard for an exegete with Origen's sensitivities to see the word *bread* in the biblical text and not think of the Eucharist, especially if the same passage contains also a word used for the Eucharist; namely, *remembrance*, not to mention also the detail of the bread being placed on a clean table in a holy place. But then, noting the connection, Origen typically extends the sense of all this to a more interior, intellectual and spiritual level, seeing the bread or loaf as right thinking about the Father and the Son. The numbers *two* and *one* are a guide for him in this, and it is not a big step for him to see a same *two* and *one* in this text as the *two* and *one* of the eucharistic prayer, the Father and the Son. Origen develops at greater length the doctrinal truth of which the loaf of the Leviticus text is an image,[149] but he does not need to leave the image of the Church's liturgical celebration behind to make this connection. Indeed, as we saw, this celebration was the first connection made at the beginning of his comments on this passage; and it is also actually the last one, as he concludes his homily. Commenting on the "holy place" where the loaves are to be eaten, he explains that the holy place means a pure soul. Then he connects that once again with the word of God, that is, this right doctrine about the Father and Son, and says, "In that place [i.e., a pure soul] we are commanded to eat the food of the word of God." To such a thought, how could he have failed to add, as he does, "Whence in like manner this law is also set before you that, when you receive the mystical bread, you eat it in a clean place; that is, you do not receive the sacrament of the Lord's body with a soul contaminated and polluted by sins. For 'whoever eats the bread and drinks the cup of the Lord unworthily will be guilty of the body and blood of the Lord...'"?[150] So, the bread come

---

[149] The word is Origen's at Homily on Leviticus 13:3, 3 and cited above at n. 33, alluding to Heb 10:1.

[150] Homily on Leviticus 13:5, 5. SCh 287, 220-222. English, Barkley, 243.

down from heaven is right doctrine about the Father and the Son, and a right way of praying to the Father through the Son, and the bread and the cup of the Eucharist — not different breads but one bread seen in all these various dimensions.

Conclusion

It is difficult not to be admiring of Origen's theological genius: the force of his thought, its surprising turns, his pioneering efforts into so many questions, the underlying spiritual drive, the range of what he considers. The sheer weight of his figure as a theologian in the early stages of the whole history of Christian theology makes him particularly interesting as a test case of what I have wanted to examine in this study. As I noted, Origen is not considered a major witness to things liturgical in the third century. The liturgy is not a direction toward which his thoughts habitually turn. Thus, when he was found to turn there anyway, as in the texts examined here, the impression is that here we are at the heart of the matter; here is a question that cannot be avoided. And the question we found concerned Trinity and the consequences for prayer. Origen relied on the universal Church's *lex orandi* to render more clearly the *lex credendi* in a particular church which was experiencing trouble in one if not both of these *leges*. It is a solid way to proceed theologically, and even Origen, who might be expected not to show much interest in it, employs it.

Yet we tried also to take the question further. Listening to Origen preaching, we attempted to trace to some extent the contours of his mind — the mind of a great theologian — and to see what may have caused it to turn this way and that. Deep inside his mind there lay a pervading sense of the Church's eucharistic experience such that the word *bread* in a text on which he was to preach could not help but find its clarification by reference to those "ecclesiastical mysteries." But this was not a reference to some liturgical text. In the end it was a reference for him to something that somehow mysteriously contained a content central to the very mystery of God; namely, two (Father and Son) in one (bread). Here, to use the language in which the present investigation has been framed, the ultimate *lex* is not a liturgical text or rite but the very reality of what God is. This reality keeps reflecting itself across the many layers of being; it is spoken of in hidden ways in the Scriptures; it is revealed in its final clarity by the divine Logos become flesh, who leaves to the apostles a command to baptize and to celebrate the eucharist in his memory. This *lex* likewise reflects the reality of who God is; the one who searches and knocks against the mystery finds it. And whenever the Church must say with precision what is believed to be so about God, as was required in the local church of Heraclides, then another *lex* is formulated on the basis of these others. Here one would hope not only for intellectual talent in the practitioner of theology but also for a spiritual knowledge of the deepest roots of the mystery. "And you, therefore, if you have knowledge of the secrets, if you can discuss wisely and carefully about faith in God, about the mystery of Christ, the unity of the Holy Spirit, you offer loaves 'from fine wheat flour.'" [151]

---

[151] Homily on Leviticus 13:3, 4. SCh 287, 210. English, Barkley, 238.

Chapter 5

LITURGY AND FUNDAMENTAL THEOLOGY: FRAMEWORKS FOR A DIALOGUE

In chapter 32 of the book of Genesis Jacob is said to have wrestled with "some man" until dawn, but the match was a draw. When the man asked Jacob to let him go, Jacob said that he would not do so before the man blessed him. Then the man told him, "You shall no longer be called Jacob but Israel because you have wrestled with God and with men and have prevailed." Then Jacob asked the man his name. He responded, "Why should you know my name?" After that Jacob named the place Penuel, saying, "I have seen God face to face, and yet my life has been spared." (Gen 32:23-33). This biblical story can set the tone for the project I would like to undertake in this short study. The story reveals the mystery with which liturgical theologians and fundamental theologians must both wrestle. The story is an image of the liturgy itself. We wrestle with all its material elements and in the end somehow experience the mystery of having seen God face to face. Likewise, Fundamental Theology in dealing with the nature of Revelation itself wrestles with the extraordinary and scandalous shape of that Revelation in the particular history of Israel and in the figure of Jesus of Nazareth. Wrestling with the symbols of the liturgy, wrestling with the form and content of Revelation — these are not two different wrestling matches, but rather different rounds in a same match.

The recent publication of the *Dictionary of Fundamental Theology* is an important event not only in the evolving self-identity of that relatively new theological specialty but also for the whole theological community.[152] The dictionary is a comprehensive and competent summary of a very wide range of questions with which Fundamental Theology is concerned,

---

[152] Cf. R. LATOURELLE - R. FISICHELLA, *Dictionary of Fundamental Theology*, New York 1994.

developed by an international team of scholars. It makes available to those in other theological disciplines the rich fruits of Fundamental Theology's recent efforts to define itself as a specific discipline, while at the same time advancing many of the concerns of the discipline itself. The relative youth of Fundamental Theology among the other theological specialties has been compared to the boy Jesus in the temple, only twelve years old; but those who hear him exclaim, "Where did he get this wisdom?" (Lk 2:47) [153] Indeed, Fundamental Theology has much to offer to other fields in theology, as the name itself suggests. At the same time, its own evolving self-identity has much to gain from a deepened dialogue with other theological disciplines. In this present chapter I wish to suggest a way in which Fundamental Theology and Liturgical Theology can enter into a dialogue which can be fruitful for both disciplines. I would like to launch a discussion and here will suggest some of the lines along which a dialogue could be developed.

In many ways much of the work which can make a dialogue between the two disciplines fruitful has already been done. In part what I want to do here is draw the attention of liturgists to Fundamental Theology and of fundamental theologians to Liturgical Theology. I would like to develop suggestions for both disciplines from work that has already been done. The importance of the dialogue presents a challenge in two directions. Odo Casel refused the dogmatic theology of his time precisely because it was unable to understand the liturgy.[154] But what would we say of a Fundamental Theology that is unable to understand the liturgy? It is weakened to the extent that it cannot do so. And some measure of this weakness is found in the fact that the *Dictionary of Fundamental Theology,* otherwise so wide-ranging in its dialogue with other theological disciplines, is lacking in specific discussion of the liturgy. In the other direction, Liturgical Theology has in large part remained but lightly influenced by what Fundamental Theology has accomplished in recent decades. Certainly there was not a sufficiently developed Fundamental Theology available for a Beauduin, a Casel, a

---

[153] R. Fisichella, *La rivelazione: evento e credibilità,* Bologna 1989[4], 17.
[154] This is discussed by S. Marsili in *NDL,* 1517b.

Guardini, all of whom sought to develop a specific identity for a Liturgical Theology. But in the more recent work of Salvatore Marsili one is struck by the fact that his efforts to create a true Liturgical Theology are very closely connected to the questions with which Fundamental Theology is concerned.

I have suggested that a dialogue can be launched by drawing attention to "work that has already been done." In what follows I would like to draw attention to the work of four different scholars, showing how in each a dialogue between the two disciplines could take place. I will begin with the work of Salvatore Marsili and his efforts to create a clear and specific identity for Liturgical Theology. Next I will turn to Rino Fisichella, one of the two editors of the *Dictionary of Fundamental Theology* and a scholar whose studies have done much to clarify the specific identity of Fundamental Theology. Ghislain Lafont is, among his contributions in many other fields, a fundamental theologian whose project there is conducted with a wide opening to the liturgy. Finally, there are parts of the enormous project of Hans Urs von Balthasar which can also be helpful in sketching a framework within which the dialogue I am proposing can take place. Obviously I can do no more than briefly indicate here what the extensive work of these scholars can offer to the dialogue which I am hoping to promote. But it can be a start.

Salvatore Marsili

Among the many projects of Salvatore Marsili were his efforts to create a clear identity for Liturgical Theology.[155] A key to his thought is his stress on the *event* character of liturgy. Liturgy is always the Word of God known in the reality which it acquires in the symbolic rite. Fundamental Theology has as

---

[155] The project of Marsili in this regard is usefully summarized by Kevin Irwin in his *Short Primer on Liturgical Theology*, Collegeville 1990, 25-29. Among the works of Marsili himself, I am drawing here from the following: S. Marsili, "La Liturgia. Momento storico della salvezza," in *Anamnesis I. Momento nella storia della salvezza*, Casale Monferrato 1974, 33-156; "La Liturgia nella strutturazione della teologia," in *Rivista Liturgica* 57 (1971) 153-162; "Liturgia e Teologia. Proposta e teoretica," in *Rivista Liturgica* 58 (1972) 455-473; "Liturgia," in *NDL*, 725-742; "Teologia liturgica," in *NDL*, 1508-1525.

part of its task showing how the Word of God is at the source of all theology.[156] But it is from this fundamental role of the Word of God that Marsili argues that liturgy is *the* source of all theology precisely because it is an *event* in which the Word of God is actualized. Indeed, doctrinal and moral teaching arise from within the inexhaustible source of the Word of God; Fundamental Theology explains and justifies this dynamic.[157] What Marsili stresses and what is relevant here is that this Word is fundamentally a proclaimed word, not merely a content captured in writing in the Sacred Scriptures, but a living Word that is what it is precisely by being proclaimed in the assembly of believers. The Word of God by its very nature always delivers an experienced knowledge of God, never a knowledge that can be had merely intellectually at arm's length. Liturgy is the place of this experienced knowledge because it is the place of the Word of God actualized as event by means of the symbolic rite. In the liturgy the truth which is peculiar and proper to Christianity — the announcement that God communicates with us in Jesus Christ — becomes an actual communication of salvation.[158]

Liturgical Theology as conceived by Marsili, rightly I think, does not wish to see itself just as of equal status among the other theological specialities. It is theology in a unique mode, on a radically fundamental level, and not just an effort to enrich Fundamental Theology and dogmatics.[159] It must be considered in special relationship to the data of Revelation which it is Fundamental Theology's task to reflect upon. In the liturgy the *reality* of faith itself is presented and is perceived. For Fundamental Theology to be reflection on faith,[160] it must be

---

[156] *Dei Verbum*, II, 8. R. FISICHELLA, "Theology: II Epistemology," in *DFT*, 1061-1065; R. LATOURELLE, "Fundamental Theology," in *DFT*, 328-331.

[157] R. FISICHELLA, *Introduzione alla teologia fondamentale*, Casale Monferrato 1992, 81-83.

[158] Cf. MARSILI, *NDL*, 1513, 1516; "Liturgia e teologia," 458.

[159] Marsili developed this point in contradistinction to his colleague C. Vagaggini, who he thought was too weak in his claims for liturgy as fundamental for the rest of theology. Cf. *NDL*, 1518-1519.

[160] R. FISICHELLA, "Prospettive epistemologiche circa il fondamento della teologia," in *Ricerche Teologiche* 2 (1991) 5-20.

reflection on *this* reality, not merely conceived as the truth of faith (content), but this reality as it is the salvation event of faith made actual. This is a challenge to the task of the individual theologian, who is confronted with this reality in the liturgy — this is the faith of the Church — and must respond not only with his academic reflection but, in order to remain faithful to the nature of the liturgical reality itself, must conduct his reflection in such a way that it be conducive to contemplation and adoration, which alone are adequate as responses to the reality contained in the liturgy. These thoughts are ways in which Fundamental Theology needs Liturgical Theology.[161]

Marsili claims that liturgy must be considered a foundation, alongside scripture, of a true and proper theology.[162] Scripture is the *announcement* of the Word of God; liturgy is its *actualization*. This implies theology in two phases: a biblical theology and a liturgical theology. As the Word announced (biblical theology) becomes actualized, the law of sacramentality is discovered as a necessary dimension of the Word announced. We have a Liturgical Theology when the discourse on God — and the God of which theology speaks is only the God of revelation (Fundamental Theology should make this clear) — is founded on that which Marsili calls the "sacramentality of Revelation."[163] This sacramentality is discovered by reflecting on the shape and scope of Revelation, and sacramentality is a necessary dimension because God's Revelation is communication with human, embodied beings; it is participation; and this cannot be realized except but through a sacramental economy. To speak of this sacramental economy means that the liturgy continues in time all

---

[161] In this context and by way of contrast it can be noted here that Liturgical Theology needs Fundamental Theology more to help understand the very fact of revelation itself and the response of faith. To this point we will return below.

[162] *NDL*, 1520b.

[163] *NDL*, 1520b. It should be noted that what Marsili means by "sacramentality" is different, at least in emphasis, from what fundamental theologians mean by the same term. Cf. FISICHELLA, *Introduzione alla teologia fondamentale*, 80. Marsili and other liturgical theologians are referring specifically to the liturgy, whereas fundamental theologians use the term in a more global sense. Marsili would claim that the global sense of fundamental theologians implies his liturgical reference.

of that reality of which Christ is the sacrament, since he was and is this sacrament precisely in time. Liturgical theology, therefore, is achieved when one speaks that discourse about God starting from Revelation viewed in its nature as a sacramental phenomenon, where there converge that event of salvation and that liturgical rite which represents it.

I suggested at the outset of this study that in part I wish to promote dialogue by drawing attention to "work that has already been done." As a first step in this conversation I am drawing attention to the importance and usefulness for fundamental theologians of Marsili's way of speaking, for it can add a fuller dimension to the fundamental theologian's own necessary task of developing discourse on the nature of Revelation. These points of contact, however, ought not confuse the identity of the two theological specialities in question. From the standpoint of Fundamental Theology, Liturgical Theology is a particular angle from which the Revelation event can and should be considered, but it is not sufficient in itself to embrace the whole discourse about Revelation that Fundamental Theology continues to develop and clarify. From the standpoint of discourse about Revelation, Liturgical Theology is a focused instance. It is discourse about God according to liturgical categories. Such categories are enumerated by Marsili at the end of his article on "Teologia liturgica" in the *Nuovo Dizionario di Liturgia*. They are (a) the sacramentality of Revelation; (b) the totality of Revelation found in the sacrament that Christ is; (c) the economy of salvation and of the liturgy; (d) the presence of the mystery of Christ; (e) the Word of God actualized. In all these ways, even if Liturgical Theology is a focused discourse, it is in a theological sense even more fundamental to theology than Fundamental Theology is fundamental to it.

But let us turn now to the work of a fundamental theologian to show how that specialty can also be of service to the work of clarification of the discourse that liturgical theologians are attempting to elaborate.

Rino Fisichella

Among fundamental theologians Rino Fisichella has done much to promote the work of developing a clear self-identity for Fundamental Theology as a theological discipline in its own right with its own methods, particular aims, and contribution to the entire theological enterprise.[164] Very important among his accomplishments was his work as one of the two editors of the *Dictionary of Fundamental Theology*, in which he played a major role in developing the well articulated plan of the whole, in selecting the various entries about which articles would be written, and in writing a great many of the articles himself.[165]

One example, relevant to the present discussion, would be the article written on Sign.[166] In the course of that article he offers a useful definition of sign: "all that which, being historically based, allows knowledge of the mystery by creating the conditions for interpersonal communication." [167] The need for a sign is part of the very nature of our being in relation with God, since he lives in unapproachable light and we need signs of the relation with him. Thus, there was the rainbow given to Noah, the stars that Abraham saw, circumcision given to the Jewish people. Or in the history of Israel there were the signs of the exodus, the time in the desert, Sinai. The person of a prophet himself was a sign as well as whatever signs he performed. All these lead to *the* sign: Jesus

---

[164] R. FISICHELLA, "Cos'è la teologia?," in C. ROCCHETTA - R. FISICHELLA - G. POZZO, *La rivelazione tra teologia e storia*, Bologna 1989³, 165-252; ID., *La rivelazione: evento e credibilità*, Bologna 1989⁴; ID. (ed.), *Gesù Rivelatore*, Casale Monferrato 1989; ID., *Introduzione alla teologia fondamentale*, Casale Monferrato 1992; ID. (ed.), *Noi crediamo. Per una teologia dell'atto di fede*, Rome 1993.

[165] *Dictionary of Fundamental Theology*, eds. R. Latourelle and R. Fisichella. For the plan of the whole, see XVII-XIX; and the very important systematic Index XXV-XXXI. Among Fisichella's articles are the following: "Credibility," 193-209; "Fundamental Christology," 108-113; "Christological Titles," 117-126; "Inspiration," 515-518; "Theological Language," 600-603; "Martyr," 620-630; "Method II: Fundamental Theology," 684-690; "Prophecy," 788-798; "Semeiology," 987-990; "Signs of the Times," 995-1001; "The Meaning of Revelation," 644-647; "Theology and Philosophy," 1075-1080.

[166] See "Semeiology: I Sign," 987-990.

[167] *DFT*, 988.

of Nazareth, whose life itself is full of signs. Indeed, such signs are one of the major themes of John's gospel. But Jesus himself is sign beyond himself, a sign of the trinitarian mystery. Fundamental Theology makes use of this kind of talk primarily in fulfilling its role of a new kind of apologetics, drawing the attention of unbelievers to the signs that are good reason for what believers claim about Christ. Liturgical Theology could make good use of Fundamental Theology's talk about signs, no longer to speak for apologetic purposes but to speak of the significance of sign in the liturgy.[168]

We need the signs of the liturgy for reasons similar to Noah's need for the rainbow or Abraham's seeing of the countless stars; namely, to know that we are in relationship with the invisible God. Ultimately, of course, we need the liturgy's signs to know that we are in relationship with the risen Christ, who has passed beyond our sight, not to withdraw from us but to be present in a way much more profound: in the Spirit. In this way the risen Christ, invisible but recognized in signs,[169] becomes a sign and a presence of the trinitarian mystery. Raised by the Father, he is with us all days to the end of time, in the Holy Spirit. The liturgy represents in signs this profoundly spiritual reality, which is no less than the whole mystery of Revelation brought to its fulfillment in the Paschal Mystery of Jesus Christ.[170]

Taking direction from Vatican II's *Dei Verbum*, Fisichella frequently stresses that the mystery of Revelation is given in the *form* of a word from God addressed to the human race, a word

---

[168] *DFT*, 997.

[169] See especially Lk 24:35. 1 Cor 11:26.

[170] Elsewhere in his work Fisichella discusses at length three reasons for the importance of signs. The first is epistemological. The second is for Jesus to point beyond himself to the Father, to show the dialectic of revelation, which is at once hidden and revealed. The third reason is provocation. Signs are designed to provoke one to belief. For this see FISICHELLA, *La rivelazione, evento e credibilità*, 179-199. In the present chapter I am trying especially to indicate how the *DFT* can be used as a handbook for liturgical theologians wishing to undertake the dialogue with Fundamental Theology. In Fisichella's lengthier discussion there would be much for dialogue between the two disciplines as each considers the importance of signs on epistemological, christological, and provocation to faith levels.

which requires a response from individual persons.[171] In the midst of such a discussion, attention to the liturgy could especially throw into relief the dialogical dimension of this word, as opposed to a mere content. Liturgy is in the clear *form* of God speaking to us and us speaking to God. This dialogue (with all its requirements and implications) is a constitutive characteristic of Revelation, which Fundamental Theology must make clear and has a better chance of doing by giving attention to the *form* of liturgy.[172] At the same time Fundamental Theology's particular competence to spell out the requirements and implications of this dialogue with God can protect the liturgy from an ever present danger; namely, degeneration into observance of a mere ritual form, rendering the dialogical form no real dialogue at all.

An historical example of this danger is illustrated already in the Old Testament in levitical ritual strictness (let this represent liturgy) vs. the prophets' call (let this represent Fundamental Theology) to return to genuine dialogue with God. God wants not sacrifices but that the people hear his voice.[173] There comes a time, after the work of the prophets, when in the Old Testament cultic ritual will lose its importance and give way to a cult exclusively centered on the Word of God. It is in this light that we must hear, "The Word became flesh and pitched his tent among us," (John 1:14) tent recalling the "tent of meeting." (Ex 40:1 ff.) The tent of meeting is now where this Word is made flesh and truly received. This is the place of true theology. Fundamental Theology in partnership with Liturgical Theology can indicate the path to this place of true theology. Fundamental Theology insists

---

[171] *Dei Verbum* I, 2: "... ut eos ad societatem Secum invitet in eamque suscipiat." I, 5: "Deo revelanti praestanda est oboeditio fidei..." In Fisichella, see, among others, *Introduzione alla teologia fondamentale*, 90-101; "Fundamental Theology: Whom is it For?," in *DFT*, 332-336; *Rivelazione: evento e credibilità*, 55-104; *Noi crediamo. Per una teologia del'atto di fede*, 77-95; 177-193.

[172] Indeed, the relationship between the *form* of Revelation itself and the *form* of liturgy is, I think, one of the most promising topics for dialogue between Fundamental Theology and Liturgical Theology. There is much to explore in asking to what extent does the drama of the liturgy (the form of liturgy, its shape) derive from the drama of Salvation/Revelation (its form, its shape).

[173] Cf. Marsili, *NDL*, 1511.

on the absolute and radical demands of the Word of God and on
the signs of its credibility.[174] Liturgical Theology shows that the
liturgy itself is the tent of meeting where this Word is made flesh
and truly received.[175]

In another important study Fisichella develops a theme in
Fundamental Theology which can be deepened by reference to
the Liturgy: the ecclesial dimensions of the act of faith.[176] After
introductory remarks which specify the importance of the theme
to Fundamental Theology and the need to develop new
approaches to the question which would permit the believer's
dialogue with our contemporaries who find the act of faith so
difficult, he offers an example of such a dialogue in a discussion
of the ecclesial dimensions — i.e., the communitarian dimensions
— of the act of faith. Christian faith is not merely by coincidence
or by accident a communal act just because many people seem to
do it, but it is communal in its deepest nature because it is shaped
and receives its character by its object, that is, by the Holy Trinity
itself. Faith in God is faith in a God in whom divine Persons in
relation to each other are the very essence of the reality of God.
The *community* of the Divine Persons is the ground of all reality.
Faith in this God is necessarily then trinitarian, communitarian,
in form.[177] But how and where specifically is this trinitarian form
encountered and expressed?

Fisichella will answer that it is found in the community of the
Church, but he does not make this claim arbitrarily. He arrives at
it carefully, basing his line of reasoning on an understanding of
the *person* of the believer, derived from an understanding of the
meaning of *person* within the Trinity itself.[178] The revelation of the

---

[174] FISICHELLA, "Credibility," in *DFT*, 193-209; "The Meaning of Revelation,"
644-647; "Semeiology: I Sign," 987-990.

[175] Cf. MARSILI, *NDL*, 1512: "In realtà la liturgia cristiana, in quanto
celebrazione del mistero di Cristo, nel fondo non è altro che continuata
attuazione sacramentale di quel primo avvenimento per il quale la Parola-Dio
si fece carne."

[176] FISICHELLA, "Ecclesialità dell'atto di fede," in *Noi crediamo. Per una
teologia dell'atto di fede*, 59-97.

[177] FISICHELLA, "Ecclesialità dell'atto di fede," pp. 70-73.

[178] In what follows I am attempting to summarize in a few pages what
Fisichella develops at some length. I trust I have been faithful to his thought,
though I unfold it here in an order slightly different from his own and with

Trinity of Persons within the one God is not given to us in the abstract. It is given only by means of the history of Israel and that history culminating in the person of Jesus of Nazareth, who is believed to be one of the persons of the Trinity become incarnate and ultimately crucified. Only through these historical facts read with faith is the trinitarian nature of God known. But not only is this revelation given in very concrete historical form, this historical form is never given apart from a dimension which always includes an invitation to us to participate in the intertrinitarian relations of the Divine Persons, to participate precisely as a person created for this in the image of the Divine Persons. (Cf. Gen 1:26)

So what is the essence of this being a person who can participate in the community of the Divine Persons? Jesus Christ himself reveals it in his personal history. On the basis of Phil 2:6-8, Fisichella notes that the human person of Jesus is he who is the eternal Son, he who is "in the form of God," as the scriptural text has it. As such he is qualified to express in human terms what is the nature of God. This consists in the "giving all" on the part of the Father — thus is he Father — and the "receiving all" on the part of the Son — thus is he Son. By this are the Divine Persons persons and by this are they by nature a perfect unity: because they are characterized and differentiated and united precisely in each one's giving all and receiving all. This giving all and receiving all of the Divine Persons is what is expressed visibly in human language in the facts of the life of Jesus of Nazareth.

The invitation to believe which is addressed to me by the proclamation of this life of Jesus is an invitation to participate in this community of divine giving all and receiving all, an invitation to become a person after the image of the Divine Persons. I am equipped for this act whereby I become a person because I have a personal freedom (also in this am I in the image of God) in which I am genuinely free to give all of myself and to receive all of my being... or not. If I keep all that I am for myself, I stand alone; I am a part of no community, no communion. When I give myself away, I become able to receive the other and be received

---

some expressions, developments, and emphasis of my own helpful to the present discussion.

by an other. This is to be a person, and it coincides with an act that is fundamentally communal.

To call this communal act also *ecclesial* is to suggest that the Church is the community within which this act of giving myself away becomes actually possible for me. Fisichella develops this line of thinking in a number of useful directions which it is not possible to into in detail here.[179] For the purposes of the present discussion, it must suffice to note that the act of coming into the community of the Church is an act whereby I "empty myself" (cf. Phil 2:7) of what is purely mine to receive the Other, that is, all that the Church has to offer me.

The expression "what the Church has to offer" must be carefully understood. It cannot be likened to or viewed on the same level as what membership in some organization or club has to offer. What the Church offers me is participation in the community that she herself is, and she is the community brought into unity "from out of the unity of the Father, the Son, and the Holy Spirit."[180] She is such a community concretely in history, and concretely in history she proclaims the story of Jesus and its authentic meaning, which can never be a meaning individually determined but, by the very object of what is believed, must be communitarian in form. But a community which believes what the Church believes carries within itself and offers a more profound reality still to the individual who joins the Church in her belief. Trinitarian life is carried within the Church and communicated through her, for she is formed profoundly in the image of the Divine Persons in virtue of the fact that she is the community of persons who have emptied themselves to receive life totally from the Spirit of Jesus sent from the Father. This is the "person" of the Church, the ecclesial "I" who believes, an "I" which surpasses in its understanding and certitude of divine realities the sum total of the understanding and certitude of the members. I become a person when I exercise my liberty to join

---

[179] Cf. FISICHELLA, "Ecclesialità dell'atto di fede," 77-95. In these pages Fisichella usefully models his own desire to dialogue with our contemporaries on why there are good reasons for believing in the triune God within the community of the Church.

[180] Cf. Vatican II's *Lumen Gentium*, I, 4, not cited by Fisichella but a helpful reference to the ideas being developed.

myself to this ecclesial "I" and thereby participate as person in the intertrinitarian community of Divine Persons.

These ideas are secured and deepened by reference to the liturgy. Fisichella himself suggests this at the end of his study: "Parlare della *lex credendi* senza fare riferimento alla *lex orandi* sarebbe pericoloso."[181] He offers only "uno squardo" at the rite of baptism to make this point, and we cannot do much more than that here. But in a dialogue between Fundamental Theology and Liturgical Theology on the act of faith, Fisichella's discussion draws our attention to factors that are of major importance. For the discipline of Fundamental Theology, in considering the ecclesiality of the act of faith, Liturgical Theology would wish to stress that the communitarian and ultimately trinitarian shape of faith finds its most dense and potent expression in the communitarian and ultimately trinitarian shape of the liturgy, with the countless implications that flow from this. Fundamental Theology should look with greater attention to the forms of liturgy and its implications for Christian living in order to speak authoritatively (a *lex credendi*) about the act of faith. It is the *lex orandi* which establishes the *lex credendi*. Liturgical theologians, in the context of Fisichella's discussion, are offered a very important dimension to the study of the communitarian and trinitarian shape of liturgy; namely, that really conforming oneself interiorly to the meaning of the exterior liturgical forms is an act that makes one a person in the deepest sense of the word, a person rendered genuinely capable of participating in the life of the Divine Persons in whom Christians profess belief. This is an understanding of person which, if exposed and explained carefully to our contemporaries who find the Church herself a stumbling block to faith, could attract non-believers to what should somehow be the irresistible beauty of faith celebrated in the act of adoration and thanksgiving which the Sacred Liturgy means to be.

I would like to turn now to the work of another theologian whose work in Fundamental Theology has much to offer to liturgists who would want to clarify the Liturgical Theology out of which they operate; namely, Ghislain Lafont.

---

[181] FISICHELLA, "Ecclesialità dell'atto di fede," 95.

Ghislain Lafont

Here my remarks about drawing attention to work that has already been done can apply especially to Ghislain Lafont's *Dieu, le temps, et l'être*,[182] for the book is demanding and the result of long, careful development. I cannot do it justice in any kind of summary, but I would like at least to draw attention to some of the ways in which the questions of Fundamental Theology treated there can help in clarifying a Liturgical Theology.

In Part 2 Lafont introduces a theme that is basic to the line of thought he wishes to unfold in the book: a principle of narrativity. He himself summarizes his ideas in five points. (1) The identity of a human being, both from the personal point of view of his individual birth and from the universal point of view of his belonging to humanity, is *founded* on a *narrative* which the human being accepts to hear. (2) This narrative owes its existence to *witnesses*, more or less directly encountered, but in any case real and personal, to whom one accords one's faith. (3) This narrative has to do with the whole of man, and therefore in a very real way with his body, that is to say with a spatial-temporal insertion in history. (4) The ambiance of this narrative is very naturally *feast*, or *celebration*, not as an escape from time and space for ritual benefits which would pertain to an *in illo tempore*, but as a high point which invests time with a certain rhythm and confers on it its true figure. (5) Man has a tendency, however, to *keep clouding over the narrative*, to replace it with narratives which are *produced* rather than heard, or with *constructed* descriptions and speculations, or, under the guise of legitimate scientific research, he contents himself with the reconstruction of the evolutionary process which sets *the stage for* the arrival of man, but does not give him birth. But the real issue is precisely birth.[183]

This principle of narrativity with these five dimensions is useful to the fundamental theologian in weighing the significance

---

[182] G. LAFONT, *Dieu, le Temps, et l'Être*, Paris 1986. Cited here according to English translation, *God, Time, and Being* (Henceforth, *GTB*), translated by L. Maluf, Petersham 1992.

[183] *GTB*, 133. For the whole development, see 121-133.

of the form in which the Christian Revelation is embodied; namely, a narrative of the history of Israel and — more toward the center of that Revelation — a narrative of Jesus of Nazareth which culminates in the narrative of his death and resurrection. With these five points Lafont proceeds to an examination of the narrative of the death and resurrection of Jesus and to its dynamic as a founding narrative which called the Christian community into existence and by which that community continues to live. Ultimately there is for Christians but one narrative: that of the Resurrection of the Crucified, with all of its consequences. This narrative "founds a history and a world." [184]

The first thing we will want to know, Lafont continues, is *"who* can make this narrative, *where* can it be heard and responded to, what *community* can stand between those who witnessed and those who hear the story today. The decisive question is one of *testimony."* [185] In Fundamental Theology this is a way of stating questions which are basic to the task of that discipline. It concerns the nature of Scripture and the community within which it can be properly interpreted and, within that community, who are authoritative interpreters.[186] Within the series of questions which Lafont proposes here, there is one which relates directly to the liturgy; namely, *where* can that narrative be heard and responded to. It is significant to the present discussion that this question emerges *within* and *surrounded by* questions which are treated in Fundamental Theology. This alerts the practitioners of both disciplines under discussion here. Lafont will go on to point out that this "where" of the narrative's being heard and responded to is especially the Eucharistic celebration. Thus, the attention of the fundamental theologian is drawn to the fact that his discussion of the dynamic of the narrative which founds Christian faith is not adequate without reference to the liturgical celebration of that narrative. The attention of the liturgical theologian is drawn to the fact that the nature of liturgy is not adequately understood without

---

[184] *GTB,* 135.

[185] *GTB,* 135.

[186] *Dei Verbum,* II. See also J. Wicks, "Church VI: The Church as Interpreter of Scripture," in *DFT,* 175-177.

reference beyond itself to what the narrative celebrated there accomplishes, for it "founds a history and a world." [187]

In answering the question *"who* can make this narrative," Fundamental Theology specifies and justifies the position that it is the apostolic witnesses who can do so and that the narrative is heard today in the community that descends from these witnesses. But the apostolic witnesses and the present community which is linked to them is inextricably related to the liturgical experience of that community. Lafont says, "The reality of the Resurrection and its fruit as new creation can reach man only through the mediation of the believing community that guards and transmits the apostolic testimony which it repeats and celebrates in the Eucharistic feast. It is only in the Church of the apostles that one can hear this narrative. It is in the Church that one professes faith in this narrative and that one celebrates its joy." [188]

Professing faith and celebrating the joy of the narrative — these are most basically liturgical realities. At the founding level, the decisive question is one of *hearing* and *commitment,* and not one of *reading* and *commentary.* Fundamental Theology is thereby reminded both of the ecclesial and liturgical dimensions of the act of faith on which it is its duty to reflect. [189] If one stands only before the text of the narrative, one is immediately geared to reinterpretation, that is, to a *production* of meaning. But the narrative that "founds a history and a world" is a *received* meaning, a dynamic with profound anthropological roots. [190] The proper ambiance of this *received* narrative is the feast, i.e., the liturgy. [191] When one hears witnesses, as opposed to standing alone before a text, then one is bound to the narrative received, to a meaning which the individual could never have *produced.*

---

[187] *GTB,* 135. I want to speak about the relation of liturgy to history and to world from a different angle below in discussing the thought of von Balthasar.

[188] *GTB,* 136.

[189] There is a strong point of connection here with the thought of Fisichella on the ecclesiality of the act of faith as discussed above.

[190] See above in the points which summarize Lafont's principle of narrativity, no. 1 p. 112.

[191] This is point no. 3 in the summary of the principle of narrativity. See above p. 112.

This distinction between a *produced* meaning and a *received* meaning, clarified by reference to the liturgy, can help the fundamental theologian to throw into relief what is at stake in the act of faith and by what exactly our contemporaries are being challenged when today's community of witnesses engages them.[192] Christian faith is fundamentally about faith in the resurrection of Jesus from the dead. This is the new and absolutely unique word that Christianity introduces into the long history of human longing and the search for meaning. And as Lafont points out, "... if it is possible to be sensitive to the wisdom and to the ethical grandeur of the Sermon on the Mount, to the posthumous aura of a man named Jesus, and still remain detached from an ecclesial community, it is no longer possible to do so when it is a question of believing in the risen Christ. In the first case, one receives a new inspiration toward the *production* of what one considers authentic behavior; in the second, *one receives the revelation* of one's origins and end in an interpersonal and community exchange, and also in the insertion into the bosom of a narrating tradition where one accepts to be at home and to take one's place."[193]

As his discussion unfolds, Lafont deals with another common theme in Fundamental Theology; namely, the inspired nature of the apostolic witness. The apostles themselves claim to speak under the impulse of the Holy Spirit and in virtue of the mission they have received from the risen Lord. The narrative within which the apostles express their testimony to the resurrection includes a *factual* dimension, though it is not pure fact or merely factual; for they themselves were not eyewitnesses of the resurrection itself. They themselves *received* the testimony, an inspired interpretation of a fact which was announced to them. Without this dimension of the apostolic experience being placed in a clear light, the resurrection is reduced to nothing more than a meaning *produced* by the apostles. Again, these ideas can be clarified and advanced by reference to the liturgy, and Lafont himself makes the connection. He says, "If the realism of the

---

[192] On these dimensions of the task of Fundamental Theology, see G. LAFONT, "Language: I. Philosophical Language," in *DFT*, 595-599; FISICHELLA, "Language: II. Theological," in *DFT*, 600-603.
[193] *GTB*, 136-137.

Resurrection is linked to the reality of the Church which witnesses and of the Spirit who attests, it is easy to see that the *place* where the witness is borne in a vital and effective way is the Eucharistic celebration." [194]

The purpose of the Eucharistic celebration — and by implication, of all forms of the liturgical assembly — is to make be *heard* this founding language in a founding manner and in such a way that it be *immediately responded to*. This emphasis on the festive place of the founding narrative not only clarifies an essential liturgical dimension of Christian life and faith, but it also makes it possible to render more precise the location of Fundamental Theology's task of reflection on the nature of scripture and its appropriate reinterpretations; otherwise said, on scripture and tradition or on Revelation and theology. Lafont next develops his thoughts in this direction. If it is true, he notes, that the founding narrative is essentially something heard and celebrated, it is nonetheless of great significance that it also remains something that has been *written* and something that is constantly being *re-said*. [195]

The process of writing and reinterpretation has anthropological roots as profound as those of the festive place of the founding narrative. Furthermore — and this is significant to the present discussion — the dynamic of reinterpretation is inextricably related to the dynamic of the festive place of the founding narrative. There is a spontaneous dialectic between, on the one hand, moments of proclamation, faith, and hearing and, on the other hand, the response of writing and reinterpretation. Both are necessary so that the founding narrative can be heard in ever new places and times. [196] Within this dialectic   and only within it! — what we may call a *"produced meaning"* of Revelation is legitimate. For within the dialectic writing and reinterpretation become *intellectus fidei*, but the entire effort is governed by faith, that is, by what one has first received, by what one has first heard. And to repeat: the place of this receiving and hearing in such a

---

[194] *GTB*, 139.

[195] *GTB*, 141 ff.

[196] Cf. *Dei Verbum*, II, 7: "Quae Deus ad salutem cunctarum gentium revelaverat, eadem benignissime disposuit ut in aevum integra permanerent omnibusque generationibus transmitterentur."

way that it can be immediately responded to is the liturgy. The liturgy functions as a criterion for an effort that must continue in the Church today; namely, a production of meaning (rooted in the received meaning) made suitable to our contemporaries in such a way that our own faith is deepened and others may come to believe.[197]

At this point there is directly posed Fundamental Theology's concern with the question of Truth.[198] What criteria do we have to judge the truth of what is written and the truth of a reinterpretation? For Lafont, "The truth of a reinterpretation is determined from the way in which the *founding narrative* makes itself heard in and yields, through the engendered production of meaning, the same effects of conversion to God and of human liberation as did the narrative itself."[199] This truth, he explains, will depend on three factors which function as criteria for reinterpretation: truth and liturgy, truth and ethics, truth and critical judgment. Concerning truth and liturgy, the truth of a reinterpretation is judged by its correspondence to the festive anamnesis in which the community hears and receives its foundation. But truth and critical judgement have to do with Fundamental Theology's concern to justify and properly locate the relationship of reason and faith. No one of these three criteria can be applied without the others. They are meant to constantly overlap and intertwine, mutually correcting and reinforcing one another.[200] It is a focusing of Lafont's notion of this mutual correcting and reinforcing that I would hope to promote in the dialogue between Fundamental Theology and Liturgical Theology.

We can conclude our reflections on Lafont's discussion with one final and important observation. He points out that in a

---

[197] This concern for dialogue with our contemporaries strongly marks the projects in Fundamental Theology of both Lafont and Fisichella. For Lafont's expression, see "Breve saggio sui fondamenti della cristologia," in *Gesù Rivelatore*, 120. For Fisichella, see his *Introduzione alla teologia fondamentale*, 42-51; see also, "Fundamental Theology: Whom is it For?," in *DFT*, 332-336; "Language: II Theological," in *DFT*, 600-603.

[198] Cf. *DFT*, I. DE LA POTTERIE, "Truth," in *DFT*, 1132-1137; FISICHELLA, *Introduzione alla teologia fondamentale*, 97-99.

[199] *GTB*, 143.

[200] *GTB*, 143.

reinterpretation which is true it ought to be possible to discern the recurrence of the founding narrative. But it is necessary to specify how. It is not present in the texts of reinterpretation (i.e., theology) in the same way that it was present in the oral preaching of the apostles, for theology represents a produced meaning, albeit one always governed by faith. Nor is it always possible, as the work of critical exegesis shows, to even retrieve the initial literary form of the founding narrative. Yet it ought always to remain possible to discern the *figure* of the founding narrative, the *profile* of the Christ it proclaims.[201] It is this figure of Christ which emerges from the written text of scripture, such that theology claims that the risen Lord is truly present in his word. It is this same figure which emerges with particular force in the liturgical assembly, where the Word is proclaimed, celebrated, and immediately responded to. It is by coming to know this Christ — his figure, his profile — in the celebration of the liturgy that we can detect whether or not the same Christ is expressed in the texts of reinterpretation. This is liturgy functioning as a criterion for theology.

Hans Urs von Balthasar

Lafont has insisted on the power of the founding narrative, which we have examined emphasizing its liturgical dimensions, to "found a history and a world." He develops that in the next part of his book, but at this point I would like to pass over to the thought of Hans Urs von Balthasar in his *A Theology of History*, where the discussion of history immediately opens into its liturgical dimensions.[202] Chapter 3 of this book is titled "Christ the Norm of History," and in it the discussion is such that it can be ranked as both Fundamental Theology and Liturgical Theology.[203] Again, what follows is my effort to draw attention to work that has already been done.

---

[201] *GTB*, 145. The notion of the *profile* or *figure* of Christ is very important in the whole discussion of Lafont, an idea that he carefully develops in, "La pertinence théologique de l'histoire," in *RSPT* 63 (1979) 161-202.

[202] H.U. VON BALTHASAR, *A Theology of History*, translated from the German *Theologie der Geschichte*, New York 1963. I will cite it according to the English version.

[203] H.U. VON BALTHASAR, *A Theology of History*, 79-107.

The discussion of that chapter can be ranked as Fundamental Theology since in the previous chapter von Balthasar has demonstrated that Christ, by recapitulating history, has become its norm. Now in this chapter he faces the difficult problem of discussing how the norm is applied. In essence, we will see that the norm cannot be applied except through a sacramental mediation, what Marsili has called "the sacramentality of Revelation," a necessary dimension of Revelation.[204] Thus, in this way the chapter also treats Liturgical Theology. Von Balthasar unfolds his argument in three basic steps, each of which I would like briefly to examine. The goal of all three of these steps is to demonstrate "the point of departure from which the individual historical existence of Christ can be so universalized as to become the immediate norm of every individual existence."[205] We might express this same idea in terms which have already become familiar to us by saying that what must be demonstrated is how the narrative of the individual historical existence of Christ can be claimed as a founding narrative which "founds a history and a world." This universalizing of the individual historical existence of Christ is a work of the Holy Spirit, who so interprets the life of Jesus as to expose the full depth of what has been accomplished in his Paschal Mystery. In a first step the work of the Spirit is individually worked on the Son himself during the forty days after the resurrection. In a second step, the work of the Spirit relates Christ, transformed in the mystery of his resurrection, to the historical Church of every age, a work which is expressed typically in the sacraments and most fully in the eucharist. In a third step the Holy Spirit completes this work in history by creating the missions of the Church and the individual. Let us turn now to a fuller treatment of each of these steps.

The first step examines the significance of the forty days after the resurrection, that mystery which above I called the new and absolutely unique content of Christian faith, the point at which every single person who hears of it is challenged to believe or not. Von Balthasar's discussion deepens our understanding of what is claimed about this risen one. We shall see that in him there is

---

[204] See above, 103-104 and *NDL*, 1520b.
[205] H.U. VON BALTHASAR, *A Theology of History*, 79-80.

worked a fundamental transformation of the experience of time such that history and every individual existence is offered redemption in him. This comes about first by the Holy Spirit, who is henceforth always the Spirit of the risen Lord, working a transformation of the individual historical existence of Jesus. It is this transformation which is manifested in the forty days.

The significance of the forty days is that they belong both to earthly and eternal time.[206] Christ's relationship with his disciples is continued *after* (!) his death. The gulf between the here and the beyond is bridged, and his intimacy with his disciples is renewed. All of the resurrection appearances testify to the fact that the risen Christ and the apostolic witnesses exist contemporaneously in the same time. The time of the risen Christ is "not the immutable relationship of an eternal present,"[207] nor is it "some fictitious appearance of duration, but time in the most genuine and real sense possible."[208] His time is not estranged from our time; it is continuous with it. Yet it is a time filled with his sovereignty and the glory of his divinity, and it reveals that all the fullness of eternity is present now *in* time. Thus, the Lord's earthly life, as far as he himself is concerned, is not past. The whole of it is taken up into his resurrection, for the one who is risen is he who was crucified in earthly time.

As far as he himself is concerned, the mode of time belonging to the risen Christ has not altered with his Ascension. Thus, "the mode of time revealed during the forty days remains the foundation for every other mode of his presence in time, in the Church and in the world."[209] What is revealed in the forty days represents the ultimate form of his reality, a form in which he is with us "all days even unto the consummation of the world." (Matt 28:20) But the forty days have a specific purpose: they serve to create a bond between the Lord's earthly life and the time of the Church. The center and fulfillment of all time stands in the very midst of time! Just as the past is completely recapitulated in the personal existence of the risen Jesus, so the future of the

---

[206] What follows is a summary of von Balthasar's discussion from 81-90.
[207] H.U. von Balthasar, *A Theology of History*, 83.
[208] H.U. von Balthasar, *A Theology of History*, 82.
[209] H.U. von Balthasar, *A Theology of History*, 84.

human race, manifested progressively in the Church, is already present in him and revealed in the extension of the reality of his risen body to the Church. "... for as the end of history, the *eschaton*, he is present at its center, revealing in this one particular *kairos, this* historical moment, the meaning of every *kairos* that can ever be. He does not do this from some point outside and above history, he does it in an actual historical moment..." [210]

This kind of talk is the work of Fundamental Theology. It faces squarely the scandalous nature of the Revelation which God has given: that in a particular historical person is found the norm of every human existence, the norm of history, and the unveiling of the very nature of God. From here von Balthasar passes over to what he calls the second level of the universalizing work of the Holy Spirit, the sacramental level.[211] Here we see clearly the link between the tasks of Fundamental Theology and Liturgical Theology. He takes as the first principle for the discussion he wishes to undertake a point already established; namely, the fact "that Christ's existence, and hence his mode of duration, in the eucharist and the sacraments is, as far as concerns himself, no different from that which belongs to the forty days."[212] Here still he is the risen Lord present with his earthly time (and thus all time) transfigured into his eternal reality, present in sovereignty and majesty and accompanying his disciples in their real time. The element of difference is that now he appears concealed under sacramental forms. Yet the forty days were expressly intended as an introduction and initiation to this form of his appearance. The dimension of faith shows how. For in both the period of the forty days and in the form of the sacraments the dimension in which it is possible for the risen Lord to appear is precisely the

---

[210] H.U. VON BALTHASAR, *A Theology of History*, 86. Lafont speaks of this as "An illuminating paradox: the *founding narrative* offered by Christianity is situated neither at the beginning nor at the end of time, but at least part 'in the middle of time.' We are dealing with the narrative of a concrete person, Jesus of Nazareth... whom all his contemporaries saw living and dying" (the language of history)... This Jesus is proclaimed risen (the language of origin and of fulfillment). So the testimony is at once precisely *situated* and *founding. GTB*, 137.

[211] For what follows, see H.U. VON BALTHASAR, *A Theology of History*, 90-97.

[212] H.U. VON BALTHASAR, *A Theology of History*, 91.

dimension of faith. This is because his appearance always implies the revelation of his divinity in his humanity, more specifically, the revelation of his divinity in the historical moment of his death on the cross.

The discussion of Fundamental Theology here enables us to make a precise observation about the nature of the presence of Christ in the liturgy. If, as far as concerns the Lord himself, his presence in the sacramental form of his existence does not differ from that of the forty days, then we are able to clearly express what he is doing in the liturgy. He is present "as interpreting, revealing and bestowing his earthly life, and in that sense bringing it with him, representing it, making it present." [213] Christ's presence in the sacraments, as in the forty days, is rooted in his earthly life.

Von Balthasar does not develop an application to each of the sacraments, but he does provide a principle for how each could be understood from this perspective. It is a principle of Fundamental Theology to be applied to Liturgical Theology. The development in regard to individual sacraments would be to point out how in each the personal, temporal-historical reality of Jesus of Nazareth is "thrown open to the recipient, offered to him, made available for his participation, assigned to him personally." [214] Jesus of Nazareth, crucified under Pontius Pilate, becomes contemporaneous with the recipient in virtue of his resurrection and in virtue of the recipient's faith. The divine life communicated in the liturgical action is inseparable from the historicity of Jesus. Obviously Jesus is not made present as he was in the historical past, but in mystery, in sacrament. Yet this should not be understood as some residue, his person somehow surviving but his actions themselves having become past history. It is rather that entire particular history that he lived in his person being made at one and the same time universalized and historically concrete.

In the eucharist all that could be said about sacraments and liturgy in general is given a new intensity, for here it is not simply some one aspect of his historical existence that is being applied

---

[213] H.U. VON BALTHASAR, *A Theology of History*, 92.
[214] H.U. VON BALTHASAR, *A Theology of History*, 93.

to the contemporary believer; rather his entire bodily reality is turned upon the Church and the individual believer, that bodily reality which achieved its supreme fulfillment as the bodily sacrifice on the Cross. When the risen one, risen in that very body in which he was crucified, turns this bodily reality toward the Church, he associates her with his one sacrifice. The bodily contemporaneity granted through the eucharist is not just vaguely somehow still being with Jesus, but it is quite concretely a contemporaneity with him in his sacrifice. And von Balthasar adds to this the beautiful reflection that when this happens, something takes place not only from the Church's and the individual believer's point of view but from Christ's as well. These are real meetings for him too! They are meetings for him with me in my time. He brings the glory and majesty of his divinity, henceforth inseparably bound to his humanity and to the history he lived, into my time; and in my time he is met by my faith.

This suggestion of von Balthasar can be developed toward a spirituality of the liturgy, which receives its impetus from Fundamental Theology's careful review of the details of Revelation. Here again we are instructed in the sacraments by the forty days. For in those days we see that the scenes in which Jesus is recognized by his disciples were significant encounters for him too. How pleased he must have been by Mary's exclamation of recognition, "Rabbouni!" (John 20:16) How satisfying for him Thomas' profound prayer, "My Lord and My God!" (John 20:28) What delight at John's recognition "It is the Lord!" and Peter's jumping into the water! (John 21:7) For in all these encounters the Lord enjoys the fruit of his passion: that those he so loved were beginning to understand how much they had been loved by him and how much had been accomplished for them. In the celebration of the sacraments, as he turns his bodily presence toward us, the risen Lord waits to receive our faith and our recognition; and our worship means to please him and honor him, to express some beginning of understanding how much we have been loved in the mystery of his Incarnation, his Passion, his Resurrection.

Again, all that happens in the sacraments is the special work of the Holy Spirit; and the Spirit works here in a way that parallels his work in the forty days. Just as in the resurrection it is the Spirit who awakens the dead flesh of Christ, the Spirit also awakens the matter of the sacraments, charging the form with an infinite content. This hidden work of the Spirit is manifested liturgically especially in the epiclesis, but the Spirit is, of course, at work long before any actual liturgy begins. For the Spirit loves Christ and wishes to please him with a bride that he himself forms to present to Christ, whom Christ in turn associates with his sacrifice and presents to his Father. We might say that the Spirit is always at work preparing the "vessels" for the liturgy, not merely chalice, plates, font, and all the symbols, but ultimately the vessel of each believer and an assembly of believers which he makes to be Church, all of which he "forms" in such a way that they can be filled with all the uniqueness and historical reality of an encounter in a new time with Jesus of Nazareth, the risen Lord, "my Lord and my God."

We can turn now to the third point that von Balthasar develops in this chapter, which is described as the Holy Spirit completing his work in history by creating the missions of the Church and the individual. I wish only to treat the question briefly here in order to complete this presentation of what von Balthasar has developed, though this third area offers much for future work between Fundamental Theology and Liturgical Theology. He notes at the outset of this third section that "The Christian does not only meet Christ in the sacraments, he lives continuously by his commandment and his law." [215] The way in which this is concretely to be done is the mission received by the Holy Spirit, a mission that is formed by the Spirit for the whole Church in a particular time and in which each individual member of the Church is given a unique share which can be called a particular mission.

This touches Fundamental Theology's theme of Church in its relation to world, culture, and history. [216] Significant to this present discussion is that this is a mission which can be discerned only as in strict relationship with and as deriving from the Church and the individual Christian formed as such in the liturgy. The first lesson which both Church and individual who would discern

---

[215] H.U. VON BALTHASAR, *A Theology of History*, 97. For this third section, see 97-106.

[216] Cf. J. DUPUIS - H. CARRIER, "Evangelization," in *DFT*, 275-291; M.C. AZEVEDO - H. CARRIER, "Inculturation," in *DFT*, 500-514.

their mission must derive from the liturgy is that mission, no more than the liturgy itself, is not a human work or a matter of personal choice and taste. In both liturgy and mission human nature and human liberty are always respected and indeed greatly honored, but these create neither liturgy nor mission. Both are a divine work, the work of the Holy Spirit. For a divine power is needed to create what the Christian's mission in the world is, since mission is far more than some ethical response in my life to the teaching of Jesus.[217] It is the life and death that Christ underwent in history brought into profound accord with the life in history that I am living. His particular life from a moment in history far different from my own is meant to function as the only norm and the only meaning of my time in history. Only the Spirit could bridge this otherwise unbridgeable gap. Within one same dynamic, the Spirit who raised Jesus from the dead and who forms and fashions the vessels for the liturgy also forms and fashions from the infinite wealth hidden in the life of Christ the wonderful variety of history, giving to the Church of every age and to every believer a unique time in which to live, a time which derives from the unique time in which Jesus of Nazareth lived.

Without going into further detail at this point, I wish to suggest here that a rich dialogue between Fundamental Theology and Liturgical Theology can occur precisely in what we might call the dialogue between liturgy and mission. In the "Ite missa est" with which every liturgical assembly is sent forth a profound mystery is occurring, and without reference to it the liturgy is not ultimately understood. It is no less than the assembly of believers being caught up into the very dynamic of God's kenosis for the sake of the world. It is their having been associated with the sacrifice of Christ such that he can say to them, "As the Father has sent me into the world, so do I send you into the world." (John 17:18; 20:21) It is the assembly in the "form" of "he who was in the form of God" taking "the form of a slave." (Cf. Phil 2:5-6) This form is the work of the Spirit. In the same way that liturgy is not ultimately understood without reference to this mission, Fundamental Theology must be careful

---

[217] Recall above Lafont's point about the difference between being persuaded by Jesus' example and believing in his resurrection.

to give the mystery of what is accomplished in the liturgy its full force in any discussion of mission, of history, and of culture. For the role of Christians as active players in the human family and human history is not adequately Christian unless it claims for itself an understanding that ultimately expresses belief in the full fruits of the resurrection, which includes the fact that Christians in every age are sharers in a divine work that is being done in the world, a work for which they are readied by being formed into the very body of Christ in the sacred liturgy. It is there that Christians in every age become what the Lord said to his first disciples: "You are the salt of the earth. You are the light of the world." (Matt 5:13-14)

Conclusion

I hope that I may have indicated in this chapter some of the ways in which a dialogue between Fundamental Theology and Liturgical Theology could be conducted. This is no more than a beginning, some few directions taken among many possible. Perhaps it can be useful in conclusion to draw together in a single and final focus the principle thoughts of the four scholars whose thoughts we have used for this dialogue.

From Salvatore Marsili we were able to emphasize that the Word of God, which stands as the foundation for all theological reflections and the implications of which it is Fundamental Theology's task to draw out, is fundamentally an *event*, an event necessarily sacramental, forever made new and actual in the Church in the celebration of the liturgy. Fundamental Theology profits by staying near to this fact as it unfolds for theology the implications of how the Word of God actually manifests Himself and lets Himself be heard.

From Rino Fisichella we saw that the signs from God that invite and challenge the world to believe are given new depth, given "body," in the liturgy. Both disciplines are advanced by attention to the *why* of signs and their necessity for our dialogue with the invisible God. The discussion of the ecclesiality of the act of faith draws the attention of both disciplines to the profound theological reasons why the act of faith and the act of liturgy are necessarily communal, and not merely vaguely communal, but specifically ecclesial. They are this because the object of faith and the aim of liturgy are participation in the intertrinitarian relationships of the Divine Persons.

If Marsili helps us to understand the event character of every announcement of the Word of God and Fisichella shows the ecclesial context of the signs that lead toward faith, Ghislain Lafont draws out the implications of the fact that the Word which is actualized as event within the community of the believing Church is Word in the form of narrative about the life, death, and resurrection of Jesus of Nazareth. The place of this narrative is not fundamentally the text but rather the feast, the celebration of the liturgy, in which the figure of the risen Lord is encountered and in which encounter a history and a world are founded. The texts of this narrative and its reinterpretation — the whole effort of theology as *intellectus fidei* — derive from this liturgical celebration of the narrative and are judged against the figure of the risen Lord encountered therein.

With Hans Urs von Balthasar we dealt specifically with the implications of the resurrection for both Fundamental Theology and Liturgical Theology. In the resurrection the Spirit so transforms the individual historical existence of Jesus that it becomes the norm and meaning of every other individual historical existence before or since. This magnificent transformation is actually applied to new times and spaces and individuals by means of the liturgy, where by faith every individual encounters Jesus crucified and risen as the meaning of his own existence, a meaning which gives him communion with all the saints and with the persons of the Trinity. This is the event of which Marsili speaks and which is actualized in the liturgy. To this transformation all the signs of Revelation of which Fisichella speaks, point; and the form and shape of this transformation is necessarily trinitarian and so ecclesial, as Fisichella also strongly emphasizes. The place of this transformation is the narrative of Resurrection celebrated within the Church of the Apostles in the liturgical feast, as Lafont has so carefully explained. The narrative celebrated founds a history and a world, as Lafont would say, because, as von Balthasar would say, from within the mystery of the Resurrection, applied anew through the liturgy to every age and individual, the mission of the Church and of the individual is created by the Spirit whom the Father sent to raise Jesus from the dead.

To wrestle with this particular narrative of Jesus of Nazareth, to wrestle with it as celebrated in the signs of the liturgy and in the community of the Church in a particular time, is to wrestle with all the meaning of our existence in the world and within the whole vast expanse of the aeons of time, and it is to exclaim with Jacob about our own particular place and time, "How awesome is *this* place. This is none other than the house of God and the gate of heaven." (Gen 28:17)

Chapter 6

THE EUCHARIST AND FUNDAMENTAL THEOLOGY

In the book of Exodus the question "why" is foreseen as a response of coming generations to the celebration of the Passover, and the answer that is to be given is striking: "When your children ask you, 'What does this rite of yours mean?' you shall reply, 'This is the Passover sacrifice of the Lord, who passed over the houses of the Israelites in Egypt... This is because of what the Lord did for me when I came out of Egypt... With a strong hand the Lord brought us out of Egypt... That is why I sacrifice to the Lord...'" (Ex 12:26-27; 13:8,14-15) The reply to "what does this mean?" is not a discourse on the value of ritual or the law. Rather, a history is to be recounted. (Cf. Deut 6:20,20-25) These texts can set the stage nicely for the discussion I would like to undertake in this chapter; namely, the relationship between Fundamental Theology and the eucharist.[218] Rites are celebrated that in every generation will provoke the question "What does this rite of yours mean?" and likewise in every generation a proper response to such questioning must base itself on the wonderful deeds of God in the history of his people. The answer is not an explanation of ritual but a reference to history. Fundamental Theology is that discipline which responds to the apostle's command: "Should anyone ask you the reason for this hope of yours, be ever ready to reply." (1 Peter 3:15)[219] What is the reason for the hope which the celebration of eucharist inspires in every generation of Christians?

---

[218] In the previous chapter the discussion focused more on the liturgy in general. Here the focus is sharpened around the eucharistic rite.

[219] R. Fisichella has suggested that the Deuteronomy text together with that of 1 Peter nicely orient the study of Fundamental Theology around one of its principle tasks: responding to the question "why?" and giving a reason for our faith. See *La rivelazione: evento e credibilità* (Bologna 1985) 30-38. I wish to use his suggestion here, together with the texts from Exodus, for the link between two disciplines: Fundamental Theology and Liturgy.

After I had developed the thoughts in the previous chapter, a major study on the question of the relationship between Fundamental Theology and liturgy appeared: A. Grillo's *Teologia fondamentale e liturgia.*[220] After recounting some of the history of the question in the theology of this century, he enters at length into a discussion shaped by philosophical, anthropological, and theological studies of the nature of sign and symbol and the role of these in the expression of religious beliefs and hopes. It is a study of great merit which promises much for the future dialogue between the two disciplines. As I have continued my own reflections on the question, I find myself inclined to develop an approach different from but not opposed to that of Grillo. Indeed, I hope it may be complementary to what he has done.

The method I wish to propose here and immediately to employ is relatively simple. It is to look concretely at some dimensions of a particular liturgical celebration — in this case the eucharist — and see what is offered therein for advancing the work of Fundamental Theology. At the same time it will become clear that categories and themes from Fundamental Theology can help to deepen a theological grasp of the eucharistic mystery. Fundamental Theology will approach the eucharist with questions and concerns that liturgical scholars are perhaps not inclined to pose. The present chapter is by way of sample and in no way purports to be exhaustive. Yet what I will be doing here can be further developed by attention to other dimensions of the eucharistic celebration than those treated here, and indeed by attention to other sacramental and liturgical celebrations.

Parameters for the Present Discussion

Fundamental Theology has as one of its principle tasks the development of a theology of Revelation. This is an ongoing work, and it has been approached from many angles. Attention to the concrete form of the eucharistic celebration offers new opportunities for this ongoing task. Vatican II's *Dei Verbum*, the document that may be considered the Council's statement on

---

[220] A. GRILLO, *Teologia fondamentale e liturgia, il rapporto tra immediatezza e mediazione nella riflessione teologica,* Padua 1995.

Fundamental Theology, orients the discussion of Revelation in a strongly trinitarian direction with the following opening sentences in the chapter titled "Revelation Itself": "It pleased God, in his goodness and wisdom, to reveal himself and to make known the mystery of his will (cf. Eph 1:9). His will was that men should have access to the Father, through Christ, the Word made flesh, in the Holy Spirit, and thus become sharers in the divine nature (cf. Eph 2:18, 2 Pet 1:4)."[221] This text states that God reveals two things: himself and his will. And actually it is the revelation of his will that is the revelation of himself, for his will is that we should participate in his divine life, a divine life that is — this is the revelation! — triune. Our participation is specific and precise in its form: we are to have access to the Father (1) through the Son (2) in the Holy Spirit (3). Thus, what are two revelations — God himself and his will — are experienced existentially as one: participation in divine life is knowing God as Father, Son, and Spirit.

With this basic principle the Council unfolds its teaching on Revelation. It is a principle which can be greatly deepened by attention to the eucharistic liturgy, for precisely there we may say God's will is realized. Precisely there our participation in divine life is actualized and made manifest; precisely there do we know God by having access to the Father through the Son in the Holy Spirit. The very shape of the eucharistic liturgy unfolds in detail this revelation of God in himself and of his will.

One way of mining some of the riches in this unfolding detail is to take account of the dynamic relationship between Word and Sacrament which thoroughly marks the form of the eucharistic celebration.[222] I would like first, therefore, to establish some basic principles which illustrate the significance of the dynamic relationship between Word and Sacrament and then turn to some details of the celebration in which that dynamic is expressed.

---

[221] *Dei Verbum* 2. Trans. A. Flannery.

[222] The dynamic of Word and Sacrament, of course, marks the normative celebration of any sacrament. Here it will be a question of examining the particulars of these in the celebration of the eucharist. Something similar could be developed in regard to the particulars of the other sacraments.

Basic Principles of Word and Sacrament in Dynamic Relation

We can begin with a useful remark by H.U. von Balthasar who observes that as the life of Jesus progresses two things stand out: (1) The Word becomes more and more flesh and (2) the flesh becomes more and more Word.[223] By the first he means that to the abstract nature of the words of the law and prophets Jesus imparts a divine, factual presence. By the second he is noting that Jesus increasingly unifies the scriptural words in himself, making his earthly life the perfect expression of all the earlier revelations of God. This idea can be extended in terms less immediately scriptural, i.e., ontologically: (1) the eternal Word, entirely in all that he is, becomes more and more flesh. (2) And all that is flesh is transformed more and more into all that the Word is. I want to suggest that this dynamic is the very dynamic that liturgy reveals, the very dynamic in which the liturgy consists. If Word becoming flesh and flesh becoming Word is what may be called the form or shape of salvation in history, it may also be said that liturgy is in that same form or shape.

S. Marsili made a similar observation in terminology slightly different from this. One of the great concerns of his work was to construct a clear way toward what he called a Liturgical Theology, by which he meant not just a theology that had a sort of liturgical tone to it but something much more fundamental; namely, the effort to found all theology in the experience of the liturgy and to let it be shaped by the categories of the liturgy.[224] We have a Liturgical Theology when the discourse on God — and the God of which theology speaks is only the God of revelation (Fundamental Theology should make this clear) — is founded on that which Marsili calls the "sacramentality of Revelation." This sacramentality is discovered by reflecting on the shape and

---

[223] H. Urs von Balthasar, "The Word, Scripture, and Tradition," in *Explorations in Theology, I: The Word Made Flesh*, Trans. A.V. Littledate and Alexander Dru, San Francisco 1989, 13.

[224] "La liturgia è un modo di essere della rivelazione, e da questo modo di essere della rivelazione nella liturgia (attuazione della fede) la teologia deve lasciarsi illuminare nella sua riflessione sulla rivelazione stessa." S. Marsili, "Teologia liturgica," in *NDL*, 1508-1525, here 1523. For a lengthier summary of Marsili, see previous chapter, 101-104 and A. Grillo, *Teologia fondamentale e liturgia*, 35-44.

scope of Revelation, and sacramentality emerges as a necessary dimension because God's Revelation is communication with human, embodied beings; it is participation; and this cannot be realized except through a sacramental economy. Yet within this discussion the primary category for Marsili remains the Word of God: "Questa categoria riassume e porta tutte le altre, ed è la categoria liturgica per eccellenza..."[225] This claim can be made because liturgy is actualization of the Word in the very assembly where it is proclaimed, and yet this Word cannot be actualized unless it achieves its sacramental dimensions. The Word as word proclaims all that Christ was and did in his earthly existence. That Word is seen as a sacramental phenomenon when the event which the words proclaim converges with the sacramental rite that represents it, thus becoming event of salvation in the midst of the celebrating assembly.

I find it useful to connect what Marsili is saying here with *Dei Verbum's* by now classic statement concerning the relationship between the actual words of the scriptural text and the events of salvation history: "This economy of Revelation is realized by deeds and words, which are intrinsically bound up with each other. As a result, the works performed by God in the history of salvation show forth and bear out the doctrine and realities signified by the words; the words, for their part, proclaim the works, and bring to light the mystery they contain."[226] A similar dynamic, and one rooted in this, is at work in the liturgy. The words of the Scripture not only proclaim the *events* of salvation history and the *mystery* contained in these.[227] When these *words* are proclaimed in the liturgy, they also proclaim the *event* of the *sacramental* celebration, which is that same event of salvation

---

[225] S. Marsili, "Teologia liturgica," in *NDL,* 1524.

[226] *Dei Verbum* 2. Trans. A. Flannery.

[227] The Latin here uses *mysterium.* Doing so, the document makes use of the more ample understanding of *mysterium,* which in patristic usage referred first to the deepest sense of the Scriptures and thus by extension to the liturgical celebrations of Baptism and Eucharist. The sacramental dimensions of this word may not have been intentional in the mind of the Council Fathers of Vatican II, but the use of the word here is fortuitous, for it allows us to extend the thought to liturgical celebrations, as would have been natural in patristic thought.

history actualized here and now. Put more simply perhaps: whatever it is that Scripture proclaims becomes sacrament.

In fact, when we look at the shape of the eucharistic liturgy, it is this very form that can be discerned. We are accustomed to this. We speak of the Liturgy of the Word and the Liturgy of the Eucharist. But now it becomes clear that this is not an arbitrary arrangement. It is liturgy in the same detailed form of salvation itself: words becoming sacrament, words rooted in events. And the reason why liturgy is in this form is because it is nothing less than the same thing. It is salvation history, that is, it is word becoming sacrament.

I would like to look now with greater care at the Liturgy of Word and the Liturgy of the Eucharist. But rather than divide the discussion into simply two categories, I would prefer to divide it into four. The first will concern the Liturgy of the Word, the next three will speak of dimensions of the Liturgy of the Eucharist in such a way as to enable us to observe the dynamic relationship with the Liturgy of the Word.[228]

1. *The Event Character of the Proclamation of the Word*

We can begin with an observation about the structure of the Liturgy of the Word. The Scriptures are read in a certain order, an order that follows the order of salvation history; that is, the liturgy begins with a text from the Old Testament and moves toward the climax of the proclamation of the Gospel. This is the order of the Liturgy of the Word because the Gospel is the climax and center of the Scripture, or put more comprehensively: because Christ himself is the fulfillment of the history of Israel. Thus, for a Christian, only from the perspective of the Gospel is the Old Testament text understood in its fullness, or again: only

---

[228] In what follows I am much indebted to a number of studies which have influenced me in a general way and which, for this reason, it will not be possible to cite specifically, except occasionally. In addition to the four authors studied in the previous chapter, I rely here on the following: J. CORBON, *The Wellspring of Worship*, New York 1988. P. MCPARTLAN, *The Eucharist Makes the Church, Henri de Lubac and John Zizioulas in Dialogue*, Edinburgh 1993. *Sacrament of Salvation, An Introduction to Eucharistic Ecclesiology*, Edinburgh 1995. J. ZIZIOULAS, *Being as Communion*, Crestwood NY 1985.

in Christ is the history of Israel understood. Some reading from the writings of the apostles forms a link between Gospel and Old Testament, a contemplative insight, a theological insight that helps bind the event of the Gospel to the event of the Old Testament.[229]

Noting this shape or form of the liturgy and the accompanying gestures, postures, signs and songs that surround it, our "children" may ask, "What does this rite of yours mean?" And theology has to be prepared to explain and justify it.

We have said that the Gospel is the center of this part of the liturgy. Why? How can this claim be made? On a most basic level, exegesis itself leads us to make such a claim. When one has finished with all the exercises that divide the Scriptures up into various pericopes and redactions and if there still remains some energy to try to put them back together again, it is not difficult to see that the Scriptures as a whole lead to a center. There is a center already to the Old Testament, even though it represents a host of theological traditions developed during well over a thousand years. Everything is organized around the Exodus, the wandering in the desert, the coming into the Promised Land. All things either lead to that, recount that, or look back to that. The whole of revelation for Israel is focused in what God manifested himself to be in these events. Every subsequent generation remembered and celebrated them, defined its present dealings with God in reference to them.

The New Testament functions within this thought world. It continues the sort of reading of the Scriptures that was already well established there, and it discerns in them — in the Exodus, the desert, the promised land — the foreshadowing and indeed some hint of explanation for the wonderful events that unfolded in the life of Jesus of Nazareth. Jesus becomes a new center for

---

[229] I am not speaking here necessarily of specific sets of texts as found in the Lectionary for the celebration of a given day, where this connection is sometimes more, sometimes less clear, as the case may be. The point is a general one about this structure in the liturgy. However, once the theological significance of this structure is grasped, as well as the sacramental (hear *mystery*) economy to which it is referring, profound and unexpected connections can emerge between the texts that will not appear when the texts are simply read side by side as texts.

such readers, and the texts of the New Testament are the written evidence of their way of reading the Old.

Jesus may be said to be a new center of the history of Israel, but his own life itself has a center. The Gospels especially lead us toward this center. A German exegete earlier in this century uttered one of those lucky phrases that has the quality of summarizing and suggesting so much all at once. The gospels, he said, are passion narratives with long introductions.[230]

This is well said. If we look at the kerygma of the primitive church as represented in somebody like St. Paul, we can see a situation that did not yet feel the need of something like the gospel genre. Paul preached only the death and resurrection of Jesus, and he managed to preach the Gospel without reference to the many words, parables, miracles of Jesus, not to mention the details of his birth. But in other circumstances and as the years passed, communities felt the need for a more extended narrative of the life of Jesus.[231] In the case of Matthew and Luke this need reaches back to the very origins and birth of Jesus. But in every case whatever was narrated about Jesus — be it the marvellous details surrounding his birth, be it the words and deeds of his active ministry — had as its purpose placing the mystery of his passion in its fuller context, a center which a preacher like Paul could never let us lose sight of. The four Gospels all lead clearly to this center, to the passion. The other writings of the New Testament unfold the consequences of such a center, showing in various ways that the believer is summoned to share in the Lord's passion and so in his victory.

Fundamental Theology, relying on solid exegesis, will make clear this center of Revelation in all its details and consequences.[232] But the liturgical celebration of the Word reveals something more, something which exegetical exercises themselves are not equipped to offer. The event of Christ, in whom all the other

---

[230] I regret that I have been unable to locate the author of this statement. I read it early in my theological studies and have remained under its influence ever since.

[231] On this question, as discussed within the discipline of Fundamental Theology, see R. LATOURELLE, "Gospel as Literary Genre," in *DFT*, 368-371.

[232] Cf. M. GILBERT, "Integral Exegesis," in *DFT*, 291-298.

events of Israel and indeed of all the world find their center and fulfillment, is "an hour which does not pass away."[233] Thus, the Scripture which proclaims Christ is doing nothing less than announcing and manifesting this hour (more specifically, some detail, some particular scene in this hour) as being the very hour of the liturgy itself.[234]

A key to Marsili's thought is his stress on the *event* character of liturgy. Liturgy is an event in the same sense as all other events in the economy of salvation — the intervention of the living God in human history, which, precisely because it is God's doing, cannot slip into the past. In a given liturgy specific words from the Scripture are proclaimed: "... the words, for their part, proclaim the works, and bring to light the mystery they contain."[235] The expression "the mystery they contain" deserves close attention. This mystery includes the power of the Word of God in every moment to be received anew as an actual communication of salvation. Every proclamation of the Word in the liturgy is a moment irreducibly new: the event of Christ (all the events of Scripture are the event of Christ) becomes the event of the Church, i.e., a particular assembly that here and now hears this Word.[236] The Word proclaimed in liturgy is not some pale reflection or residue of the event proclaimed there. It is the whole reality to which the words bear testimony made present.

The most complete example of what is being claimed here is found in the Liturgy of the Word at the Easter Vigil. Seven long readings of the Old Testament climax in the Gospel which announces Christ risen. The liturgy is the actualization of these words for the particular assembly that hears them. This is to say that the event of that liturgy is everything that the Scriptures proclaim — creation, exodus, exile and restoration — culminating

---

[233] On this expression, see the precise and compact formulation in *The Catechism of the Catholic Church*, 1085.

[234] This was discussed in the previous chapter in the section on von Balthasar. It is a question of explaining how it is possible that what Christ accomplished in one particular time can be made universally present in all times. This is the work of the Spirit, precisely as Spirit of the risen Lord. See 118-126.

[235] *Dei Verbum* 2, as cited above.

[236] Cf. J. CORBON, *The Wellspring of Worship*, 78-80.

in Christ's resurrection... in that assembly.[237] The particular assembly is the place, the time, the people, the moment in history in which Christ is risen.

None of these claims about the power of the Word could be made were it not for the action of the Holy Spirit, whose gift and creation the Scriptures are and whose inspiration is needed to understand them aright.[238] Put another way, the risen Lord himself must open our minds in the Spirit to the understanding of those words. When he does, our minds grasp nothing less than the wonderful reality that this moment of listening becomes in the very hearing an event of salvation, the same event that the words proclaim. The exodus of Israel out of Egypt is the exodus of Jesus from this world to his Father, and every believer discovers in penetrating the meaning of the Scriptures that he too is living this one and only exodus. The many events of the Scriptures are parts of one event: Jesus Christ, and him crucified, him risen, him crucified and risen in his church, in each believer.[239] This is the one and only center of the Scriptures. It is an hour which does not pass. The reading of the Word in the liturgy manifests this reality in the midst of the believing assembly, in the depths of our hearts.

It is the Spirit who writes the Scriptures, and it is the same Spirit who brings those Scriptures forward now to become flesh, to become sacrament. We turn to that action now. What is it in

---

[237] Such a context, created by the proclamation of the Word, is the context for the celebration of baptism and the eucharist that follows, that is, in the expression of von Balthasar, the Word becoming more and more flesh. Baptism and eucharist as celebrated at the Easter Vigil offer a separate opportunity for the kind of discussion we are conducting here. I do not pursue it at this point so as not to lose the thread of this more general discussion of Word and eucharist.

[238] On the intimate relation between Christ the Word and the Scriptures as Word of the Spirit, see H. URS VON BALTHASAR, "The Word, Scripture, and Tradition," 15-16.

[239] Herein lies the pattern and the task for the homily, an indispensable dimension of the Liturgy of the Word. One of the ordained, who by his ordination functions in that moment as a sacrament of the apostolic Tradition apart from which the Scriptures cannot be understood, must make these connections explicit for the particular assembly in its concrete circumstances: exodus of Israel, exodus of Jesus, exodus of us all.

the structure of the eucharistic liturgy that happens next and what does this reveal about the dynamic of Word becoming flesh, becoming sacrament? [240]

2. *The Bringing of the Gifts to the Altar, The Fruits of Creation and History*

The Prayers of the Faithful, though technically a part of the Liturgy of the Word, can be seen as functioning as a bridge between the first part of the celebration and what follows. What the particular assembly has heard in the Word should give form to its way of praying such that the needs of the whole world, in the particular moment of history in which it stands, and of the whole Church, also in a particular moment, are prayed for consciously and brought before God in the action that follows.

Gifts of bread and wine are brought to the altar. "What does this rite mean?" It is an action worth examining as if under a microscope, for on the basis of it Fundamental Theology is able to speak with greater clarity about a number of its central themes. It is perhaps worth imagining the scene in a very fine liturgy. A joyful procession accompanied by song starts down the aisle of the church. Bread and wine and various vessels and water and perhaps other gifts as well, money, are carried by the order of the baptized and brought to the bishop and/or deacon who places them on the altar and prepares them. [241]

---

[240] All that I have said here about the Liturgy of the Word need not be understood as applying only to that which precedes the Liturgy of the eucharist but would be valid for any celebrations of a Liturgy of the Word. This is true in a particular way of the Liturgy of the Hours. However, in the present chapter I wish to turn now to the unique way in which Word becomes Sacrament in the eucharistic celebration.

[241] In what follows I will make reference always to the bishop as the president of the eucharistic assembly. The same applies, *mutatis mutandis*, for the presidency of a priest; but it is useful to remind ourselves that the priest's presidency at the eucharist is as one ordained for such by his particular bishop, communion with whom he represents. Cf. *Sacrosanctum Concilium*, 44; *The Catechism of the Catholic Church*, 1142, 1369, 1561. On the importantance of using the expression "order of the baptized" at this point, see J. ZIZIOULAS, *Being as Communion*, 153, 216. On the significance of the deacon for this part of the rite, see 222.

Yet to understand the significance of the bread and wine we must look further and leave the church building to discover where this bread and wine have come from. It is worth tracing them all the way back to their literal, earthly roots — back to wheat planted in a field, its sprouting during a different season, its being cared for by skilled farmers, its coming to maturity and being harvested. Then it is ground and brought to the baker who exerts his own skills and raises bread in his ovens. And something similar must occur for the wine. Vines are cared for, pruned and cultivated, and grapes are gathered. There is need for the vintner's skills and the years of the wine coming to maturity in the cellar. Already many people have been involved, and seasons and years have had to pass that we might have the bread and wine brought forward in today's liturgy. Others still bring these gifts from the baker and the winery, purchasing them with funds earned in some other work. Thus it is that we may call the bread and wine the fruits of creation and history, the fruits of nature combined with human ingenuity: "which earth has given and human hands have made... fruit of the vine and work of human hands." It is of great importance that we notice carefully that these fundamental symbols of the eucharistic liturgy are not purely natural symbols, as is, say, water in baptism. They are in fact the product of the cooperation between the Creator and human beings.[242]

As these gifts are collected from outside the church and brought into the church, finally brought down the aisle to the hands of the bishop, there is articulated in this ritual action not only the relation between the order of bishops and the order of the baptized. In seeing this we see articulated also the global relationship between Church and world, between Church and all

---

[242] Those more poetically or mystically inclined will not find it difficult to think of wheat and grapes on a cosmic level as somehow recapitulating the whole history of the cosmos, which in fact stands behind the birth and growth of every living thing. Something similar is true, poetically and mystically, on the level of history. The wheat, the grapes, the wine maturing in a cellar somehow absorb the history of the times in which they grow. It sounds a little silly to say it, but the point can perhaps be made by observing that we do not celebrate eucharist with bread and wine that are centuries old. They must be fresh and mature, products of our time; and much of their significance lies in this fact.

creation, between Church and all history.[243] Through the work of the baptized in the world, the Church brings to the hands of Christ the fruits of the creation and the work of human hands. They are an offering with which we would wish to give thanks to the Father for all that he has done for us, in creating us and still more wonderfully in redeeming us.[244] But what offering could be made that would be worthy thanks to the Father? In fact, there is nothing. We have brought all we have, and yet we know that it could never be enough to be a suitable, a worthy thanksgiving offered to the Father.

Nonetheless, it is precisely in this condition of poverty before God that Christ comes to meet us and reveal his solidarity with us in this poverty. He will take our gifts into his hands, and he will transform them into his very body and blood, transform them into his Paschal sacrifice which he is continually offering in heaven. Fundamental Theology can learn much from close attention to what is happening here. Our attention is directed to the very stuff, to the material out of which an event of Revelation is made to occur in our midst. God's Word to us, his Revelation, is Jesus Christ, and not just vaguely Jesus Christ but Jesus Christ above all in the action of his Paschal Mystery.[245] And this Word is articulated to us in the syllables and words and phrases of bread and wine transformed. They become a language. The name of this language is flesh. They become the Word made flesh. Thereby the whole cosmos and the whole of history are rendered capable of something which by definition would be impossible to them. They are rendered capable of being God's adequate expression of himself. More: they are rendered capable of being an offering to God the Father, of being the thanksgiving and adoration that Christ's very sacrifice on the cross was and is.

A detail of the liturgy at this point can perhaps be useful in understanding this further. The relation between the gifts that the people bring and their very bodies and lives is especially made clear in the liturgy when incense is used at this point. First, the gifts themselves are marked out as holy. It is as if we can feel the

---

[243] Cf. J. ZIZIOULAS, *Being as Communion*, 151.
[244] Cf. *The Catechism of the Catholic Church*, 1359.
[245] Cf. *Dei Verbum* 4.

immediate future already invading these gifts. Bread and wine that soon will become his body and blood are already somehow holy! Then the altar is marked out as holy. The table on which the gifts lie is designated as the holy place which is truly the center of the world: the place of his Paschal Sacrifice. Then the incensing action shifts to honor the bishop as head of the body, after which the whole body, the assembly, is incensed to indicate that they themselves are what lies on the altar. The whole church is becoming a sweet smelling offering rising up to the Father; the whole church becomes a mysterious and holy place precisely because of what is about to happen. I say "the whole church," meaning first of all a building; but the building and the assembly which fills it are now manifesting a mystery, such that we may say that the whole Church everywhere in the world is this sweet smelling offering, and that mystery is manifested now in this particular assembly.

All these thoughts can emerge even before the gifts have been transformed! There is manifested here the relation between Church, cosmos, and history as God himself has intended it and revealed it. Within the Church there is manifested the relation between the various orders of ordained and baptized, also as God himself has arranged.[246] And yet up to this point we have only

---

[246] The theological points made here, all of great concern to Fundamental Theology, can perhaps serve as a caution against pushing too hard a current tendency in some liturgical circles to downplay this part of the rite, explaining it as consisting in no more than a simple placing of gifts on the altar. The intercessions for Church and world, the procession, the exchange between the various orders, the offering of gifts which represent cosmos and history for transformation (thus the old name "Offertory"), the holiness of what is about to happen — all of this should find its proper and clear ritual expression. It certainly does in the Eastern liturgical tradition. This is not to say that the current shape of the rite in the reformed Roman liturgy should not be subject to critical discussion. For a study of how the rites came to be as they now are, together with theological evaluation, see P. DE CLERCK, "L'apport des dons, liturgie et théologie," in *Vincolo di carità, la celebrazione eucaristica rinnovata dal Vaticano II*, ed. G. Dotti, Magnano 1995, 159-176. E. FOLEY - K. HUGHES - G. OSTDIEK, "The Preparatory Rites: a Case Study in Liturgical Ecology," *Worship* 67 (1993) 17-38 see the present rite as deficient, claiming that it removes the gifts and the givers from the ensuing words or actions. Mine is a more positive reading of the rite in its present shape, even if as de Clerck's study shows, there is room for a critical evaluation. In the

conducted a meditation on the *materials* of the language of Revelation. In turning to the following parts of the liturgy, the transformation of the gifts and the communion, we turn to the *content* of what is expressed in that language of Revelation.

3. *The Transformation of the Gifts*

In the eucharistic liturgy the gifts of bread and wine are transformed into the body and blood of Christ. This comes about through the action of the Holy Spirit, invoked in the epiclesis, and through anamnesis, that is, the narration in word and gestures of what Jesus did at the supper the night before he died and the memorial prayer which follows.[247] What does this transformation tell us about Revelation?

In some sense the answers that could be given to such a question are inexhaustible, for they would touch on the very center of the inexhaustible mystery of the eucharist itself. In any case, some attempt at an answer can be made. The transformation is nothing less than the mystery of the Word becoming flesh — and that mystery occurring, manifesting itself in our very midst. That the mystery occurs there reveals something about the assembly and indeed about the whole cosmos, the whole of history, to which this assembly is intentionally and consciously related. (This conscious, intentional relation is what was expressed by the Prayers of the Faithful and bringing the gifts to the altar.) It reveals that the cosmos is divinized and that history is become the specific place of the perfect and eternal dialogue which has always occurred between Father and Son.[248] Further, it reveals that this divinized cosmos and divinized history are not an abstraction but are as concrete

---

meantime, a sound point for Fundamental Theology can be developed from the rite as it now stands.

[247] Attention to the epiclesis and the anamnesis as such offers much for Fundamental Theology's reflection. This is developed in the following chapter. For the present I wish only to establish the point that the gifts are transformed by means of these ritual moments.

[248] That this dialogue is placed in history above all in the moment of Jesus' death on the cross is a claim grounded in the Scriptures. See G. Lafont's reading of Luke's passion account in *God, Time, and Being*, 162-164.

as the celebrating assembly. The very bodies and the very stories of the actual people in the assembly are transformed into the body and blood of Christ.[249]

This transformation of the gifts reveals and actualizes God's intentions for the world, and we can understand this in the terms provided by *Dei Verbum;* namely, participation in the divine nature which gives access to the Father, through the Son, in the Spirit. In every celebration there is a radical twofold movement, of the Father toward the world, of the world toward the Father.[250] In the first direction, the Father gives himself through the Son in the Holy Spirit. It is necessary to pause and to try carefully to grasp the depth and mystery of what this means. Without attention to this dimension of the eucharist, such trinitarian formulations are perhaps just pious and habitually uttered phrases. Yet what we are dealing with here is the form, the dynamic, the very shape of Revelation; namely, that the Father gives himself by giving his Son. This is "the Father who so loved the world that he gave his only Son." (John 3:16) But there is more. The shape of the liturgy here — epiclesis and anamnesis — reveals that the Father gives his Son in and by the Spirit who is Spirit of the Father; and the Father gives his Spirit an assignment, as it were; namely, to effect and illumine and clarify and arrange everything in such a way that the Son be known and that all who believe in him might live their lives entirely from the Son's life.[251] It is this precise trinitarian form that the transformation of the gifts reveals, that is, not merely or vaguely that the Father gives himself to the world; but concretely and specifically that the Father gives himself to the world in the giving of his Son, a Son at every moment accompanied by the action and work of the Holy Spirit.

And yet it is possible to be more concrete still. There is another dimension that is constitutive of the shape of this Revelation. It is the Church, that is, concretely the actual gathered

---

[249] Cf. *Lumen Gentium* 26, citing St. Leo the Great: "The sharing in the body and blood of Christ has no other effect than to accomplish our transformation into that which we receive." LEO, *Sermon 63*, 7 (PL 54, 357C).

[250] On this see J. CORBON, *The Wellspring of Worship*, 94-97.

[251] On this particular formulation of the Spirit's role, see H. URS VON BALTHASAR, "The Word, Scripture, and Tradition," 11-12.

assembly to whom the Father's Son is actually given. The Father does not just merely or vaguely give his Son to the world but he does so precisely through the Church.

Again, it is above all in the transformation of the gifts that this essential ecclesial dimension of the Father's self donation is revealed. Here Fundamental Theology has an opportunity to understand more clearly one of its principle objects of study: "the fact of Christian Revelation and its transmission *in the Church.*" [252] The case can be stated in provocative terms to make the point: the Father gives himself in the Son only through the Church. How can such a claim be made, and what is its nature? First of all, the point is not directly concerned or focused on the Church as institution or organization, though all the dimensions of the Church are interrelated, and one eventually arrives at institution and organization from the point being made here. Nonetheless, the point of focus here is on the transformation of the gifts: the gifts *which the Church* has brought are what is made into the body and blood of Christ. And this body and blood are given then to the Church as her food. The Father gives his Son, his eternal Word, to the world in a process in which the Word assumes humanity, assumes flesh, becomes flesh. And this flesh, this humanity, he takes from the Church; for the Church lays its humanity, its flesh, on the altar and these gifts are transformed there. Otherwise said: the Father gives himself in the Son *only* through the Church.

But why "only"? Of course, it is possible to see the action, the grace, the face of Christ in many situations in the world that appear to have no connection at all or only a very distant connection with either the Church conceived as institution or the Church conceived as eucharistic assembly.[253] Yet the Church that celebrates eucharist knows that her mission is to bring everyone

---

[252] For this expression, see the Congregation for Catholic Education's discussion of Fundamental Theology in *On the Theological Formation of Future Priests*, 6, 1. Emphasis mine. See also 6, 3: "... rational reflection on the Church herself as an institution desired by Christ to further his work in the world." To some extent this reflection must be part of Fundamental Theology's apologetical task, giving good reason for the Church's indispensable role in the dynamic of God's revelation.

[253] *Lumen Gentium* 8; *Unitatis Redintegratio* 3.

and indeed everything to the eucharistic table as a gift to be presented for transformation. This is the mission of the Church because "this being brought to the altar" is what has been revealed as the will of the Father for all.[254] So even in situations far from the institutional Church and far from the eucharistic assembly, the community that celebrates eucharist knows precisely from the celebration itself that all matter and all history have received in Christ a future which is nothing less than a share in his victory over sin and death. Thus, there is a dynamic secretly at work in the world which we may call a dynamic toward eucharist. In the same way that one can feel that the gifts placed on the altar are somehow already holy even before their transformation, one can see something similar in looking at the whole world, far from the institution, far from the liturgical celebration of the eucharist. All this is destined by grace for eucharistic transformation. In this way then we must say that the Father gives his Son to the world only through the Church.

An opposite direction also forms part of the radical movement of every liturgy; namely, that of the world toward the Father. This too has a trinitarian and ecclesial shape within which it must be described. The eucharistic action at the time of the transformation of the gifts reveals this shape. And again, it is uncovered within the dynamic of Word becoming flesh and flesh becoming Word. When the Father places his Son into the hands of the Church, he does so in order that the Church may do something with this gift; namely, offer it as its own back to the Father. Or the same mystery can be described from a different angle. When the Word assumes our flesh, he does so in order that he may offer it to the Father as what he is and has always been. This is flesh becoming more and more Word, more and more what the Son is.

All this is accomplished in the Holy Spirit. The Spirit who molded a body for the Word in the womb of the virgin Mary, the Spirit who raised the body of Jesus from the dead — this same Spirit now fills the gifts which the Church has brought and makes them to be one same thing: the body formed from Mary's body,

---

[254] Cf. 1 Tim 2:5: "God wants all to be saved and to come to know the truth."

the body raised from the dead.[255] And this is not some static body. It is the body crucified and risen which, standing at the right hand of the Father, forever offers itself to him in an hour which does not pass away. In the Spirit death disappears, and the body of Christ, formed from the whole cosmos and the whole of history, rises alive from the tomb and passes over to the right hand of the Father.

This too can be expressed in the provocative terms which Fundamental Theology should be prepared to employ: the world's passing over to the Father in this way can take place *only* in the Church. The logic of this "only" is revealed once again by the eucharistic celebration. What the Spirit accomplishes is done in a wonderful cooperation with the Church. Indeed, this is part of the Father's gift: that he not only gives us his Son in the Spirit but that he also offers us a critical role in the process wherein we may exercise our freedom to receive the gift or not, to offer it back or not. "When the Spirit encounters in us the response of faith which he has aroused in us, he brings about genuine cooperation. Through it, the liturgy becomes the common work of the Holy Spirit and the Church." [256]

It is perhaps worth securing these notions by brief reference to some liturgical texts. After the gifts have been transformed by the first epiclesis and by the anamnetic action of the narration of the Last Supper, the Church has in her hands the one whom the Father has given her. And she says, "We offer you his body and blood, the acceptable sacrifice which brings salvation to the whole world." (Eucharistic Prayer IV) Christ has let himself be handed over, the Spirit effects his assumption of the flesh, and now the Church offers this body and blood. This is the marvelous cooperation, the common work. But the Church in freedom likewise offers herself to the action of the Spirit. "Grant that we, who are nourished by his body and blood, may be filled with his Holy Spirit, and become one body, one Spirit in Christ." (Eucharistic Prayer III) And why be one body, one Spirit in Christ? The Church is not this is some static way but so that "he

---

[255] Cf. Rom 8:11: "If the Spirit of him who raised Jesus from the dead dwells in you, then he who raised Christ from the dead will bring your mortal bodies to life also, through his Spirit dwelling in you."

[256] *The Catechism of the Catholic Church*, 1091.

may make us an everlasting gift" to the Father. Already being this gift thanks to this eucharistic action, already a first fruits of the victory that is to extend to the whole cosmos and the whole of history, we, the Church, reach out to embrace that whole: "May this sacrifice which has made our peace with you advance the peace and salvation of all the world." (Eucharistic Prayer III) In praying thus, the Church is at work, doing the same work that Christ and the Spirit are doing in the world, in a marvelous cooperation.

4. *The Communion*

The final part of the eucharistic rite, the communion, manifests yet another dimension of what we have been calling the content of Revelation, Revelation experienced as an actual communication of salvation. The offering of the world to the Father climaxes in the "Per ipsum," and the communion rite begins with the words "Our Father." What is revealed here? What is the content of that part of the celebration which extends from the Lord's Prayer to the dismissal? We can answer — we must answer — with an answer that seems too easy, that says too much and nothing. But we must say it and try to give it its concrete content. The answer is: Love. [257]

From this point in the eucharistic celebration it can be seen that theology's discourse on love cannot be defined in just any old way and certainly not in a worldly way and certainly not by taking human love between individual human beings as a starting point, a starting point from which one might make a comparison with God's love, saying something like, "God's love is like that." For the Christian, in this moment of Revelation, love is not like anything. Love is. And what love is, is revealed by God. If anything, human love is like God's love in that it is at least a faint reflection of it. In any case, if what love is is revealed by God, this revelation occurs especially in the eucharist. All love is defined, true and

---

[257] On the need for Fundamental Theology to develop a credible discourse on the meaning of love, see G. O'COLLINS, "Love," in *DFT*, 607-609 and R. FISICHELLA, *Hans Urs von Balthasar, Dinamica dell'amore e credibilità del cristianesimo*, Rome 1981.

divine love is revealed here at this point in the celebration. The Church is now completely indwelt by the divine love of the Holy Trinity, and stands within the one love of the Father, Son, and Holy Spirit. This divine trinitarian love likewise has its form, its shape, its dynamic; and it is all revealed in what is possible for the Church in this moment.

The form of trinitarian love, revealed here in human form and language, is an uttering from the depths of a Son's being the name "Father." Its dynamic is that the Son's uttering that name echoes off of the Father's own utterance: "Son! Beloved Son, in whom I am well pleased." Further, this total and infinite love exchanged in the dialogue between Father and Son is known, experienced, acknowledged, enjoyed and honored by another — the Spirit — who proceeds from the Father, from the Father who ever begets a Son, who ever utters a Word. This is love. And from this eternal and divine love all love on earth must take its definition and its measure.

Love is a Father who ever utters his Word. This Word has become flesh, and so now if he says "Father," it from his flesh that he does so. And the Spirit is present at this utterance, knowing it, acknowledging it, enjoying it, and honoring it. The Paschal sacrifice of Christ has purchased for us adoption into this love, the Paschal sacrifice of Christ effected and accomplished in the transformation of the gifts which the Church has offered. As the first manifestation of this adoption the Church cries out with the Son and with the Holy Spirit, "Our Father!" This "our" is first of all the "our" of the Son and Spirit, but in marvelous cooperation we are made capable, always by the transformation of the gifts, of saying "our" together with them, indeed on the same level with them.[258]

If eternal love has this very definite form, the form of a Father begetting a Son and a Spirit who proceeds from this same love, then when this eternal love is manifested in the flesh, it will be in this same form. That form is the eucharistic mystery. The words of Jesus himself make this connection between forms: "Just as I have life because of the Father, so the one who feeds on me will have life because of me." (John 6:57) "There is no greater love

---

[258] Cf. *The Catechism of the Catholic Church*, 2786-2793.

than this: to lay down one's life for one's friends. You are my friends... I call you friends since I have made known to you all that I heard from my Father." (John 15:13-15) We could perhaps comment by saying that there is no greater love than a Father begetting a Son, and that the form this love takes in manifesting itself to us is Jesus' laying down his life for his friends. This same form is expressed in the liturgical act of receiving communion. And there is a revelation contained therein: "I have made known to you all that I heard from my Father." This is Love. It is Love come among us in the flesh. It is Love being Love by handing over everything. "Though he was in the form of God... he took the form of a slave." (Phil 2:5-6) This exchange of forms is the form expressed also in this liturgical moment. And for the communicant it becomes an action whereby each one is constituted as a person whose very being and entire existence derive from another (this is the form of the eternal Son's being), and it is a being one with that other by being other (an other) than the other (also the form of the eternal Son's being).[259]

The Son eternally begotten of the Father and the Spirit who proceeds from this love may both be considered to have their being from a self emptying of the Father. If eternal love manifested in the flesh is to be in this same form (cf. Phil 2:5-6), it will mean that what we can expect to see in the incarnate Son is a self emptying that begets another like himself, another to whom he has given everything that is his. ("I have given them the glory you gave me." John 17:22) The name for this other is Church — and every individual believer in whom, precisely through receiving communion, the Church mysteriously and mystically subsists. But just as within the godhead at the self emptying of the Father the Spirit is likewise present in a proceeding that is a knowing of this emptying, a knowing that is constitutive of the Spirit in the one and same divine substance which has as an attribute of its nature to be self emptying, so the Spirit is present with his own act of self emptying at the self

---

[259] For a discussion of this theme in the context of Fundamental Theology, see R. FISICHELLA, "Ecclesialità dell'atto di fede," in *Noi crediamo. Per una teologia dell'atto di fede*, ed. R. Fisichella, Rome 1993, 59-97. See also the summary in the previous chapter, 108-111. For a discussion of the same in the context of liturgy, see J. ZIZIOULAS, *Being as Communion*, 49-65.

emptying of the incarnate Word. [260] This kenosis of Son and Spirit, which is in the same form as the kenosis of the Father that eternally defines his relation to Son and Spirit — this kenosis of Son and Spirit is what is manifested in the transformation of the gifts. The begetting of another in the image of the Son — the Son who is *the* image of the Father (cf. Col 1:15) — is what is manifested in the reception of communion.

This other begotten in the image of Christ is, as I have said, the Church. But I do not mean here somehow just vaguely the Church as some freefloating abstraction. I mean very concretely this particular assembly being constituted as Church precisely in this eucharistic action. Here we see the Church constituted by the eucharist. In some mysterious way the eucharist precedes the Church; the eucharist makes the Church to be. We must say this first and understand this priority before we may say what we must also say and what is in some ways more obvious; namely, that the Church makes the eucharist. [261] The eucharist has priority over the Church in the dynamic which constitutes it because only in the eucharist — the eucharist which culminates in the communion that we are now examining — do we have the sign, the efficacious sign, of that which causes the Church to be what she is; namely, the one begotten by the kenosis of Son and Spirit, "one body, one Spirit in Christ."

The notion of oneness is essential to understanding correctly what we are saying here. The reception of communion is not merely the coincidental juxtaposition of so many individual believers, each of whom is sacramentally united with the Lord in his body and blood. It is all those individuals being constituted as

---

[260] Cf. Rom 5:5: "The love of God has been poured out in our hearts through the Holy Spirit who has been given to us."

[261] On this theme in the whole history of theology, see the two works of P. McPartlan cited in n. 25, especially *Sacrament of Salvation*, 30-44. In a document recently published by The Congregation for the Eastern Churches titled *Instruction for Applying the Liturgical Prescriptions of the Code of Canons of the Eastern Churches* (January 6, 1996) it is stated in n. 32: "The Church, therefore, understands herself in depth precisely starting from her nature as a celebrating assembly. In this sense, it should not be forgotten that, if the Church makes the eucharist, the eucharist makes the Church to the point of becoming the criterion of conformity for the same right doctrine..." Cf. *The Catechism of the Catholic Church*, 1396.

one body and as one body — *only* as one body! — united with the body's head, Christ, and animated by the one Spirit who has raised this body, the Church, from the dead. In this oneness which is accomplished by the reception of communion by all and in the sign which is thus made, we can then see in the Church the sign, the image, of the Holy Trinity, that is, many who are one.[262] And within this trinitarian dynamic we occupy a specific place, the place of the Son. The name for this — we have come full circle from where we started — is love.[263]

The sign of peace, unique to the Roman rite at this point, is a strong and powerful ritual expression of the love that the members of Christ's body must share among themselves as the condition for being united with their head. It places a sign of reconciliation and peace *within* the communion rite as a whole. We embrace one another in the peace that comes from the sacrifice offered, and thereby do we make a sign of the same reality signified in the sacrament to be received. We have prayed in the Lord's Prayer "forgive us as we forgive," and we make a sign right there of that intention before receiving "our daily bread." The sign of peace in its present traditional place, if properly carried out, has the potential for refusing to let those who celebrate this rite receive the body and blood of the Lord without realizing that the Lord who is received unites the assembly in himself as one body.[264]

---

[262] For more see J. ZIZIOULAS, *Being as Communion*, 78-89, 145-149.

[263] Cf. 1 John 4:10: "Love then consists in this: not that we have loved God, but that he has loved us and has sent his Son as an offering for our sins."

[264] In Eastern rites and in the Ambrosian and Mozarabic rites, the sign is placed before the offering of the gifts, as an expression of obedience to the Lord's command in Matt 5:23-24. This too is a powerful liturgical sign, but its meaning is different from the Roman rite's, where the stress falls much more strongly on communion. In some circles within the Roman rite today there is a suggestion of changing the placement of this sign to before the offering of the gifts. The suggestion is probably motivated by at least two concerns: the strong value of the sign as an act of reconciliation and concern for the ritual chaos that often breaks out during the exchange of peace in its present place. Before a change of placement of this rite is undertaken, however, it would be important to measure carefully whether those who celebrate in the Roman rite would want to lose this powerful expression of communion. If it is performed in a disturbing way, that particular way of performing the sign should be adjusted. Otherwise, disturbance is simply

One final element of theological significance in this part of the rite is the dismissal. The dismissal ought not to be understood simply as the banal announcement that "it's over; you can go home," but again as something revelatory in its form and structure.[265] It should be grasped within the dynamic of "As the Father has sent me, so I send you." (John 20:21; 17:18) "Ite missa est" — from this the whole eucharistic celebration derives one of its names, "the Mass." It is as if to call the whole celebration by the name of its ultimate purpose, "The Sending." Yet if the Church is sent into the world in the same way that the Son is sent, then that sending implies likewise a kenosis. Obviously — though we must pause to observe it — the Church has nothing to offer the world if she herself is not first transformed and made into the one body of Christ in whom she partakes of trinitarian life. "Not many of you are wise, as the world accounts wisdom; not many are influential; and surely not many are well-born." (1 Cor 1:26) So it is not merely a message, a "word" that the Church offers to the world. The Word of God has within itself this dynamic to become sacrament, which is to say, to transform our very flesh, our entire being. Only such a transformation and communion in Christ can mediate trinitarian life to the world.[266] This is what it means to be a kingdom of priests. In this communion the whole Church and each member becomes for the world what Christ is for the world: "life-giving Spirit." (1 Cor 15:45) And the Church becomes this in the same pattern whereby Christ and the Spirit are this; namely, a complete self emptying. "There is no greater love than this," and only love is credible to the world that does not yet believe.

---

displaced to another part of the liturgy, while losing something that has been in the Roman liturgy since at least the time of Gregory the Great.

[265] For a very useful study of dismissal rites in ancient liturgies, see A. KAVANAGH, *Confirmation: Origins and Reform*, New York 1988, 3-32.

[266] This transformation and communion, accomplished in the eucharistic celebration, can stand as a regular reminder to Fundamental Theology that "the reason for our hope" which it must always be prepared to give, is not merely some convincing message or way of arguing. The reason is grounded in this transformation and communion.

Conclusion

I hope that in this chapter I may have demonstrated further the value of what I am urging in the fruitful possibilities for dialogue between Liturgy and Fundamental Theology. In the previous chapter I examined the thought of scholars from both fields, attempting to show how useful such a conversation can be. In this chapter I have employed the simple methodology I am suggesting for furthering this conversation; namely, the examination of particular dimensions of liturgical celebrations with a view toward nuancing and sharpening the themes considered in Fundamental Theology, while at the same time bringing to Liturgical Theology some of the concerns of Fundamental.

The Word of God is the foundation for all theological discourse, and Fundamental Theology will always rightly insist on this. But I think the present discussion will have shown that this Word of God cannot so function if it is merely dealt with as some sort of guiding text to which subsequent discourse must somehow or other always make reference. The Word of God has a dynamic toward sacrament; that is, its proclamation in an assembly of believers becomes a communication of salvation for those who hear it, an event of salvation. This event is not simply so many words pronounced and heard, but the words find expression in signs and gestures and actions, all of which reveal the deepest mystery which the words contain.

In the case of the eucharist, the Scriptures proclaimed there reveal their deepest mystery in bread and wine exchanged by people who play different roles in the assembly, such that it becomes manifest that the whole cosmos and the whole of history are destined for transformation in the Spirit of the risen Lord. This transformation, which makes present the risen Lord's paschal sacrifice, and the communion which offers the participants a share in it, are a very concrete, ecclesial locus of Revelation. Here do we have that of which *Dei Verbum* speaks: participation in the divine nature, access to the Father through the Son and the Holy Spirit. The Word of God which Fundamental Theology places as the foundation of all theological discourse must be the Word of God in this its fullest sense. Liturgical Theology, for its part, understands from this conversation that such an encounter with the Word must necessarily be elaborated, among other ways, in theological discourse; for theological discourse at its best is the effort of the human mind to engage issues at the deepest possible level, to preclude false or insufficient understanding, to point the way to an ever more profound grasp of the mystery of faith. Then when our children ask "What does this rite of yours mean?" a coherent, adequate, and appropriate answer can be given. This rite is the reason for our hope, and the entire cosmos is invited to share in it.

Chapter 7

ANAMNESIS, EPICLESIS
AND FUNDAMENTAL THEOLOGY

Introduction

Fundamental Theology as a discipline in theology must concern itself with many things but above all with a theology of Revelation and the nature of the act of faith which is the proper response to the act of God revealing. From this, many other topics are drawn into its orbit, topics which often enough are treated in their own right in separate specializations: christology, trinitarian theology, eschatology, history, world religions, and so forth. Yet Fundamental Theology has its own particular angle from which it must consider these, always showing the foundational shape of the question, ever ready to indicate the dynamic interplay between the contents of Revelation and the use of human reason, likewise always able to justify this interplay. In recent decades a growing sense of identity for Fundamental Theology as a specific discipline within the theological academy has enabled it to make valuable contributions in grounding theological discourse and describing the way in which it properly proceeds.

Meanwhile other theological disciplines have their own histories of recent development. Liturgy is one of these. Tremendous work was done in the twentieth century in studying the history of liturgical rites and the texts which bear witness to these. From a different direction within liturgical studies, the nature of rite and cult, of symbol and of the body as instrument for worship are all being studied with great profit. Still other specialists attempt to deal with the theological content found in liturgical celebrations.[267]

---

[267] This theological work is so widespread as not to seem to require the bibliographical references which would prove my point. Such bibliography is extensive. As indicative of this work in an environment with which I am familiar and am myself working, I would mention for the liturgy the

However, it is no secret that specialization in theology can result in blind spots within the disciplines. Discussion across specializations is greatly to be desired. Such discussion freshens perspectives and enlarges them. Of course, I am not the first to urge something of the sort; and I only present myself within the discussion as one who is interested in it, along with others. Currently much theoretical groundwork is being done by scholars at the Istituto di Liturgia Pastorale at S. Giustina in Padua. Their discussions are developing categories, frameworks, and language which can build many bridges between liturgy and Fundamental Theology. Among other things, they face at length and at considerable depth the question of why the encounter with Revelation and the response of faith to it necessarily have a cultic moment that is foundational.[268]

I enter the discussion at a level less immediately theoretical, even while feeling encouraged to do so by the very theories being developed. My approach has been, and will be again in the present chapter, to look concretely at some particular dimension of a liturgical celebration to see what is offered therein for advancing some specific discussion within Fundamental Theology. But liturgy and how it is understood should not remain untouched by the exchange. Indeed, as G. Bonaccorso happily put it, "... una riflessione, cioè, che a partire della celebrazione

---

Pontifical Institute of Liturgy at Sant' Anselmo in Rome and the Istituto di Liturgia Pastorale at the Benedictine Abbey of S. Giustina in Padua. Many publications have emerged and are emerging from these schools to indicate the nature of the research they are advancing. For Fundamental Theology I would mention especially the specialization in that field at the Pontifical Gregorian University in Rome, whose programmatic *Dictionary of Fundamental Theology* is just one of the publications that continues to emerge from this fruitful environment.

[268] For the most recent collection of studies issuing from this school, see A.N. TERRIN (ed.), *Liturgia e incarnazione*, Padua 1997. Within this collection the study of A. Grillo can function as a *status questionis* of Padua's contribution. See A. GRILLO, "L'esperienza rituale come 'dato' della teologia fondamentale: ermeneutica di una rimozione e prospettive teoriche di reintegrazione," 167-224. See also A. GRILLO, *Teologia fondamentale e liturgia, il rapporto tra immediatezza e mediazione nella riflessione teologica*, Padua 1995. For an accesible discussion of the theological dimensions of the liturgy in categories being developed by this school, see G. BONACCORSO, *Celebrare la salvezza, lineamenti di liturgia*, Padua 1996.

comprende sempre meglio la fede, e a partire dalla fede comprende sempre meglio la celebrazione." [269]

Anamnesis and epiclesis are two fundamental ritual actions or dimensions of the Christian cult. Liturgists and liturgical theologians must talk about them all the time, encountering them at every turn. They are most fruitfully understood together, as distinguishable and yet inextricably intertwined.[270] They are particular ritual shapes in which the believing community encounters the God who reveals himself. If Fundamental Theology ought to take its form, its subject matter, its proportions from the form of Revelation itself, then it cannot afford to be ignorant of the tremendous force contained in the performance of the very ritual acts which provide access to this Revelation. Here I would like to talk about anamnesis and epiclesis in such a way as to indicate how attention to them can enrich questions classically engaged by Fundamental Theology. Liturgically we are dealing here with the ritual recalling of a sacred history and with the invocation of the Holy Spirit. What actually happens in the liturgy in these moments should have a great deal of impact on how Fundamental Theology understands history, eschatology, the nature of the Church (for it is in some sense constituted in these rituals), the unique Christian understanding of time, and much more.

In what follows I will, first, in summary form speak of anamnesis and epiclesis and their dynamic interrelation. In a second step I will attempt to focus some of the theological insights that immediately emerge from these rituals in such a way as to indicate how they can be brought more directly into the discussions of Fundamental Theology.

---

[269] G. BONACCORSO, *Celebrare la salvezza*, 89.

[270] This point is not always granted. Surprisingly, in B. Neunheuser's otherwise very useful article "Memoriale," in *NDL*, 765-781, he makes no reference to epiclesis, and the *NDL* has no separate article on it. This is certainly something of an omission in a dictionary of liturgy. Whereas liturgical scholars themselves would be able to note this as a shortcoming, theology (in this case, Fundamental Theology) is in a position to point out the theological consequences of such an omission. I hope this will become clear in the course of this chapter.

1. *Anamnesis and Epiclesis*

When I talk with students about how important it is to understand anamnesis and epiclesis always in close and dynamic relationship with each other, I express to them the admittedly impossible desire to be able to have emerge from my mouth two discourses at once, in such a way that one would not think that there comes first, for example, anamnesis with all that it means and then, after this, epiclesis with all that it means. Or vice versa. But since my wish is an impossible one, it is necessary to proceed step by step. Still, what the mouth cannot do, the mind can. That is, after all has been said — or in the present case written — then the mind must conceive of all the dimensions as occuring at once, as simultaneously unfolding and reacting to each other, as variously overlapping, as tones and counter tones which make sense only in relation to what they sound against.

So it is with the ritual realities of anamnesis and epiclesis. They are dimensions of a single rite, but different dimensions. They manifest the mystery in a different way, but they do so together. In what follows, proceeding step by step, I would like to lay out four dimensions of anamnesis and then to follow these (since it cannot be done simultaneously) by four dimensions of epiclesis which will roughly correspond to the dimensions laid down for anamnesis. In this way, hopefully, they can be spoken of in their own right and at the same time be seen in their dynamic relation to each other. Before presenting the four dimensions, I will offer a working definition of each term.

1.1. *Anamnesis*

Anamnesis is a word which in a general way describes that dimension of liturgy which is the remembrance of the wonderful deeds of God. Viewed from an anthropological direction, it is the kind of narrative usually identified by the technical sense of the word *myth*. This word can be used prescinding from judgements about the truth of a myth or narrative or how or on what level it is true, and it lets us focus on what most cultures have in common in the celebration of cultic rituals; namely, a recounting of the origins of the world and the community in language which shows the relation of the community with its gods. Christian liturgy has a narrative structure which permeates it, and we use the word *anamnesis* to describe that dimension and its significance. This can be done in four points. They will treat (1) Old Testament, (2) New Testament, (3) eucharistic liturgy, and (4) other liturgical, sacramental rites.[271]

1. The Christian understanding of anamnesis is rooted in the Old Testament notion of a memorial, captured in the verse from the psalm (Ps 111:4), "The Lord has made a memorial for his wonders." The great events of Israel's history, when narrated in a feast, become contemporary to the hearers, to those celebrating the feast. If other cultures believed that by the festive narration of the primordial origins of the cosmos, they could thereby be brought again within the realm of cosmic purity and power, it was Israel's unique position that something similar could happen regarding actual events from history. This position is a logical consequence — though Israel did not reason in the way that we describe with the word "logic" — of the fact that Israel understood the very events of her history to be a word of God to her, and as such, that word could not grow old or stale or grow weaker or lose its effect. "The Word of the Lord remains forever." Thus, it was enough to repeat the words which narrated the events to bring each new generation of Israelites into participation with the originating events of the community.[272]

This is especially clear in the celebration of Passover. We see in the Passover that when we say "narrate events" we mean far more than a thin monotone of words pronounced aloud. We

---

[271] What follows is my attempt briefly to summarize a great deal of material on the theme which represents the recovery of its importance in liturgical studies during at least the last fifty years. For a longer presentation, but still in summary fashion, see B. NEUNHEUSER, "Memoriale," in *NDL*, 765-781. It is interesting to notice how much liturgical scholars have appropriately relied on biblical research in both testaments, on Old Testament studies of the concept of ZKR and New Testament studies of anamnesis. Fundamental Theologians have noticed this same biblical research and its importance for some dimensions of their own work. However, they have not tended to notice the way liturgical studies have used this material.

[272] This unique Old Testament understanding of the nature of a feast is classically described in G. VON RAD, *Theologie des alten Testaments*, Band II, Munich 1965, 108-133.

mean a narrative in which words are surrounded by gestures and signs and indeed an entire elaborate meal in a particular place and with particular people. And in the context of that narrative recounted in this precise way on this particular night, the question inevitably arises "Why is this night different from all other nights?" The answer can be given that by remembering Israel's Passover from Egypt those who remember thereby pass over from Egypt with her. Indeed, this defines an Israelite. One becomes such by celebrating the feast.[273]

This (and the other feasts commemorating other events) are the memorial of the Lord's wonders that he has given Israel. And it is significant that this is given by the Lord. It is he who has worked the wonderful deeds, and it is he who makes it possible to celebrate them in such a feast. This is not without importance for a concrete understanding of Revelation, such as Fundamental Theology must conceive it. The primordial events which found the community and in which each subsequent generation shares by participation are not events produced and generated by the community's ingenuity, any more than the memorial feast is such. Both are received realities, which the community gratefully accepts to receive from God. A word that says precisely this about our knowledge of God is "revelation."

2. Jesus, the Jew, draws on all these notions the night before he dies when, in the context of the Passover meal,[274] he consciously and intentionally summarizes or recapitulates all of Israel's history in himself. In the signs of the meal which he selects, he is conscious that he holds all of Israel and all her history in his hands as he takes up bread and wine, and he identifies that whole history with himself and with the death he will undergo on the morrow, saying over it, "This is my body, this

---

[273] Cfr. Ex 12:26-27; 13:8,14-15; Deut 6:20-25; and the contemporary ritual of the Jewish Passover.

[274] We can prescind from the debates among exegetes, arising from the difference between the Synoptics and John on this point, about whether or not the historical Last Supper was actually a Passover celebration. The tradition represented in the relevant New Testament texts and the tradition of reading those texts all closely associate Jesus' last supper with the theological meaning of Passover. This is the relevant point here.

is my blood." This moment, this action, is unfathomably profound. This is not some vague identification of Israel's history with the story of Jesus. It is a sign unmistakable in its significance: Israel's history finds its fulfillment in the body that will hang on the cross, in the blood that will be shed there. This blood opens a new covenant, "the new covenant in my blood." And it is precisely in the context of these signs and their transformation that we receive Jesus' command, "Do this in memory (ἀνάμνησις) of me." (Cf. Lk 22:19-20; 1 Cor 11:25)

3. With this command the psalm verse, "The Lord has made a memorial for his wonders," shifts into its definitive christological key. And indeed, the Church slowly came to realize that the riches contained for her by being obedient to this command would be boundless. For this meal, repeated as received (not as invented by the community!) throughout the lives of believers and in each subsequent generation would be the context for the fulfillment of the Lord's promise about the Holy Spirit: "He will lead you into all the truth." (John 16:13) And we learn something here about truth and how it is received that must never be forgotten in formulating a theology of Revelation. For Christians, truth is not a proposition, a gnosis. It is a somebody, a person: Jesus Christ. And it is not he in some static form but he in the action of his dying and rising. This is truth and this is life. (John 14:6) And how do we know so? The experience of eucharist, repeating what the Lord himself gave us to do, reveals it to us.

The eucharist is a memorial of the supper on the night before Jesus died, but this supper pointed to the meaning of the cross, whose meaning is finally revealed in the resurrection and the rest of the unfolding of the Paschal Mystery. Thus to remember the supper, which by *fore*-shadowing his death already was swept up in its hour (into the "ontology" of that hour), is our way of remembering his death; for the supper now "*re*-shadows" for us that hour and is thereby swept up in it. Henceforth, all memorial, all anamnesis refers to this central event of salvation history. All remembering is ultimately a remembering of this. The risen presence of the crucified one is the eternally present *fact* of the new creation, the new covenant. In his resurrection all death — and so all the past — is swallowed up. The "technique" of memorial splices us into this *fact*.[275] This fact is also a future, for the resurrection contains as part of its very logic not only the defeat of past death but likewise of all death and all time subsequent to the historically grounded death and resurrection of Jesus. Thus, doing the meal as a memorial is also a remembering of the future, but to understand all these dimensions well we need to turn to the relation of epiclesis to anamnesis, which we shall do shortly. But first let us secure still more firmly some further dimensions of anamnesis.[276]

4. Although the Lord's command at the Last Supper rivets the Church's attention on the eucharistic dimensions of anamnesis, it is not difficult to see in a general way the anamnetic dimensions of all liturgy. To call the liturgical proclamation of the word of God "anamnesis," as *The Catechism of the Catholic Church* does,[277] is to claim that this proclamation inserts us into those primordial and originating events. But since Word always

---

[275] J. ZIZIOULAS, *Eucaristia e Regno di Dio*, Magnano 1996, 15 helpfully reminds us that the eucharistic meal not only has its historical roots in the Last Supper but also in those resurrection appearances during the forty days when the Lord ate and drank with his disciples. This is especially clear in Luke 24:30-31, but also John 21:13. That is, the risen Lord is showing himself in the signs that he made to refer to his death in the Last Supper. The risen Lord shows himself with other signs of reference to his death, most notably, in his wounds. Cf. John 20:20,27; Lk 24:40. That this memory of the death of the Lord is not merely backward looking but in itself has an eschatological thrust is shown by Paul: "For as often as you eat this bread and drink the cup, you proclaim the death of the Lord *until he comes*." (1 Cor 11:26)

[276] All thats have said so far is well summarized in a particularly dense paragraph of *The Catechism of the Catholic Church*, 1085. It is too long to cite in full here, but "In the liturgy of the Church, it is principally his own Paschal mystery that Christ signifies and makes present... His Paschal mystery is a real event that occurred in our history, but it is unique: all other historical events happen once, and then they pass away, swallowed up in the past. The Paschal mystery of Christ, by contrast, cannot remain only in the past, because by his death he destroyed death... The event of the Cross and Resurrection *abides* and draws everything toward life." Shortly after this, commenting specifically on the word "anamnesis," the Catechism cites *Dei Verbum* in a way that directly shows the relevance of anamnesis to Fundamental Theology. See n. 1103. For a discussion of similar material in the anthropological terms developed by the Padua school, see G. BONACCORSO, *Celebrare la salvezza*, 129-134.

[277] As in the previous note, CCC 1103.

has its dynamic drive toward Sacrament, the sacramental action itself also is expressive — and more densely so — of this same anamnetic element.[278] The most exquisite anamnesis which the Church performs is the eucharistic narrative, and in its most narrow technical and liturgical sense the word "anamnesis" refers to that prayer which immediately follows the words of institution wherein all the dimensions of the Paschal Mystery are remembered. But the whole anaphora is permeated with a narrative structure, and it grounds the "hour" of the liturgical celebration in the "hour" of Jesus' Paschal Mystery, which does not pass away.

Around the eucharist cluster the other sacraments and indeed all the liturgy of the Church. In addition to the other sacraments we should highlight in a special way the Liturgy of the Hours and the calendar of the liturgical year. All this is memorial. All this is the "Hodie" of the feast.[279] Only in this "Hodie" is the content of Revelation fully revealed, a content which we are easily inclined to identify too thinly simply with the Bible taken as a book. But no. The book is a means to an end: the presence of the living Word in the midst of the believing assembly, accomplishing and extending to that assembly what has been accomplished in concrete historical events. When we celebrate a memorial of those events, those events become the event of that liturgical hour.

1.2. *Epiclesis*

None of these magnificent claims of the worshipping Church would be possible without the action of the Holy Spirit, who accompanies the Son in every stage of his own work in the economy. Epiclesis is the liturgical manifestation of this indispensable role of the Holy Spirit in the economy of salvation.

By way of basic definition, this can be done simply: epiclesis is an invocation of the Father that he send the Holy Spirit to transform the gifts which the Church brings before him. This

---

[278] This relationship of Word and Sacrament and its relevance for Fundamental Theology was developed in the previous chapter.

[279] Cf. B. DE Soos, *Le mystère liturgique d'après Saint Léon le Grand*, Münster 1958, 22-27.

liturgical practice is also best understood by searching for its roots in the whole history of salvation. I remind the reader that the four points which follow are meant to parallel the four points developed on anamnesis. We proceed in this way precisely to indicate the intimate and inextricable relation between the mission of the Son and the mission of the Holy Spirit, expressed liturgically in an inextricable relation between anamnesis and epiclesis.[280]

1. Just as Christian anamnesis is rooted in the Old Testament notion of memorial, Christian epiclesis is rooted in the Holy Spirit's role in the shaping of the scriptural word of the Old Testament and, more foundationally, the shaping of the events to which that word testifies. It is all this that Christians profess, in what seems at first glance a somewhat laconic expression, in the line from the Creed which concerns the Spirit: "he spoke through the prophets." The Holy Spirit shapes all the events of Israel's history — and before that the very creation itself — in such a way that they are all "types" of Christ. The events themselves and the words that bear testimony to those events in the inspired scriptures are all mysteriously shaped so that they find fulfillment in the Son's Incarnation, in his death and resurrection. They have already foreshadowed it. They have accustomed a nation to its patterns. The history of Israel illumines and clarifies these;

---

[280] The relation between the mission of the Son and the mission of the Holy Spirit, or perhaps better, their joint mission, is, of course, a concern of dogmatic theology; and contemporary theology has concerned itself anew with an articulation of this traditional theme. In the West the work of Walter Kasper could be cited; in these East, John Zizioulas. Each argues in his own way the need for a simultaneity in christology and pneumatology, which simultaneity the liturgy illustrates. A useful analysis of the work of Kasper and Zizioulas precisely in this regard is E. PAVLIDOU, *Cristologia e pneumatologia, tra occidente cattolico e oriente ortodosso neo-greco, per una lettura integrata di W. Kasper e J. Zizioulas in prospettiva ecumenica*, Rome 1997. Of course, Fundamental Theology must be aware of this as well as of other doctrinal discussions; and awareness of the significance of the liturgical shape of this mystery could only be a boon. I take articles in the *Dictionary of Fundamental Theology* as indicative of current trends in the discipline. The articles on christology and the Holy Spirit are for the most part weak on the simultaneity question, something which would not happen were there greater sensitivity to the liturgical interconnection between anamnesis and epiclesis.

the history of Israel is the con-text (in the fullest sense of that word) in which the eternal Word (the eternal "text") is uttered in the flesh.

2. As the salvation history comes to the "fullness of time," it is the "work" of the Holy Spirit to form out of one particular human life a vessel capable of expressing the total being of God through the person of the Son. Thus, the Spirit overshadows Mary and forms the Father's Son in her womb (Lk 1:35). And the Spirit accompanies the earthly life of Jesus through each of its phases, appearing in visible form at his Baptism (Mt 3:16; Mk 1:10; Lk 3:22; John 1:32), driving him into the desert to be tempted (Mt 4:1; Mk 1:12; Lk 4:1), anointing him as he inaugurates his ministry in Nazareth (Lk 4:18), enveloping him in the cloud of the transfiguration (Mt 17:5; Mk 9:7; Lk 9:34),[281] being breathed forth from Jesus in his death on the cross (John 19:30), raising him from the dead (Rom 8:11), and being breathed on the apostles from his risen body (John 20:22).

When Jesus took bread and wine into his hands the night before he died, as we described it above, the moment and its possibilities had been long in preparation by the work of the Holy Spirit. "He spoke through the prophets," that is, the whole of Israel's history had been formed in such a way that it could all converge in this moment and its meaning. The Exodus, around which the entire history centers both before and after, was accomplished fact. Words of the Spirit-formed scriptures bore testimony to it. A memorial feast given by the Lord brought each new generation of Israelites under its force. Jesus himself had celebrated the feast many times during the course of his life, as had his disciples. A history, a language, a vocabulary, a set of rituals were all in place for Jesus' use in that moment. He takes into his hands what the Spirit, as it were, had prepared for him;

---

[281] The interpretation of the cloud of the Transfiguration as the Holy Spirit was very common in the patristic tradition, both East and West. It is supported by the noticing of the close rapport between the Baptism accounts and accounts of the Transfiguration in all the Synoptics, taking each as epiphanies of the Holy Trinity in relation to the Passion. The Baptism foreshadows the Passion, indeed launches Jesus on the road that leads to that Baptism ("I have a baptism to receive...") The Transfiguration follows Jesus' first explicit prediction of his passion.

and over it all he pronounces the words which the Spirit with whom he is anointed moves him to utter, "This is my body, this is my blood." Thus, together with the Spirit, does he express his own understanding of his mission, which brings the history of Israel to fulfillment. Thus, together with the Spirit, does he express his own willingness to pour out his life for the sake of the many. What the meal shows so magnificently and in so many layered ways, echoing with words and gestures and food thousands of years of history and the very creation of the cosmos — the same will be shown in the events that begin to unfold at the end of this very meal: Jesus' arrest, his death, his resurrection, his ascension, the Pentecost of the Spirit. All this the Spirit shapes into the events that are the perfectly articulated Word of the Father to sinful humanity, the life-giving Word of the Father.

3. The form and dynamic movements of the rites in liturgy echo the form and dynamic movement of salvation history itself, which in its own turn ultimately echoes the very form and dynamic movement of divine trinitarian love. We have seen that in its eucharistic liturgy the Church has been faithful in the celebration of a rite given by Jesus himself in the course of his earthly existence. To be sure, such a rite did not contain an epiclesis, even if the Holy Spirit was very much involved, as was noted in the previous point. But very soon in the course of the practice of eucharist in the various churches, some ritual expression of the Holy Spirit's indispensable action inevitably came to the fore.[282]

We have said that the epiclesis is an invocation that the Father send the Holy Spirit to transform the gifts of the Church, in the case of the eucharist, gifts of bread and wine. In the meal that Jesus gave to be celebrated in his memory he identified the bread

---

[282] We need not enter here into the complex historical question of the way various rites have had an epiclesis which is more or less explicit. Probably the clearest case of a not particularly explicit epiclesis is in the Roman Canon, and this is in part the reason for a clearer epiclesis in the new canons used in the Roman Rite after the reforms of Vatican II. But in all the rites an understanding of the Spirit's role is present, as J. Zizioulas, who is untiring in his insistence of its importance, himself notes when he observes that an explicit epiclesis is absent even in some eastern rites. See J. ZIZIOULAS, *Eucaristia e Regno di Dio*, 72. The concern is *theological*, not historical.

and wine with himself, more specifically with the death that he would undergo on the morrow. The bread broken is his body broken on the cross. The wine poured out is his blood poured out. These signs are meant to show that his death becomes a kind of nourishment for us. But in and of itself death cannot be a nourishment. It must be transformed, and such transformation is the work of the Holy Spirit. A prayer before communion in the Latin liturgy puts this very well: "Lord Jesus Christ, by the will of the Father and the work of the Holy Spirit your death brought life to the world." This transformation of death into life-giving nourishment for the Church is nothing less than the resurrection itself. It is the Spirit who raises Jesus from the dead (cf. Rom 8:11). The eternal Spirit is henceforth and forever Spirit of the risen Lord poured out on all mankind, and it is as Spirit that the risen Lord is present everywhere. The "technique" of epiclesis is a ritual means of splicing into the realm of this Spirit, not some vague Spirit but the Spirit who accomplishes for the Church in the eucharist what was worked in the resurrection itself. "If the Spirit of him who raised Jesus from the dead dwells in you, then he who raised Christ from the dead will bring your mortal bodies to life also, through his Spirit dwelling in you." (Rom 8:11)

The Spirit who molded a body for the Word in the womb of the Virgin Mary, the Spirit who raised the body of Jesus from the dead — this same Spirit now fills the gifts which the church has brought and makes them to be one same thing: the body formed from Mary's body, the body raised from the dead. It is precisely here in the eucharist that the Church is constituted as the body of Christ. The body taken from Mary, the body raised from the dead, the Church as body of Christ — these are not different or separate bodies. They are one and the same. And it is not a static body. It is the body crucified and risen, which, standing at the right hand of the Father, forever offers itself to him in an hour which does not pass away. In the Spirit death disappears, and the body of Christ, formed from the whole cosmos and the whole of history, rises alive from the tomb and passes over to the right hand of the Father.[283]

---

[283] I used the formulation in this paragraph in the previous chapter, 146-147, to speak from a different angle about the mystery of the transformation of the gifts.

If talk about anamnesis inevitably has about it a certain pull to the past, to a memory of the deeds of Jesus in history, then talk about epiclesis and the work of the Spirit — would that we could say it all at the same time! — clearly shows that "remembering Jesus" includes the paradox of remembering a future. Indeed, the Spirit pulls the weight of memory as much, if not more so, to the future as to the past. For there is only one way to remember Jesus crucified and to encounter him or, as the Latin tradition has long loved to consider the eucharist, only one way to have the sacrifice of Calvary present on the altar: Jesus crucified is none other than the now risen Lord, present to us in the Spirit.[284] And the risen Lord, freed from the bondage of time and space, even while being present in all time and space, is already living the future which is the recapitulation of all things in himself. (Cf. Eph 1:10) It is this Lord — "And the Lord is the Spirit!" (2 Cor 3:17) — who is present to the Church which celebrates his memorial. If the sacrifice of Calvary can be present anywhere beyond the historical Calvary, it is because where the risen Lord is present, — "And the Lord is the Spirit!" — he is present as the one once crucified there.

Much can be mined for theology from liturgical realties such as these, and we shall attempt to draw up something in the next

---

[284] I find Zizioulas too excessively critical or too little sympathetic to the Latin tradition on this point. For example, in *Eucaristia e Regno di Dio*, 12, he says, "La risurezione di Cristo non è, per la teologia occidentale nel suo complesso, che una conferma dell'opera salvifica della croce..." But this really is creating a straw man in contrast to which he can make his point on the importance of the epiclesis. The point, however, can be made effectively enough without the straw man. Does Zizioulas really believe such sweeping statements? Later, he says, "L'eucaristia è un sacrificio. La tradizione patristica, sia in oriente sia in occidente, sottolinea in modo particolare questo suo aspetto... Questo sacrificio non è altro che la morte di Cristo in croce..." *Eucaristia e Regno di Dio*, 32-33. There is a wonderful sensitivity possible to Western theology that understands that the story of the resurrection cannot be told apart from the cross. At the same time, of course, it must not be forgotten that what the cross contains cannot be known apart from the resurrection. Maintaining this delicate balance has consequences for the effectiveness with which the Church can proclaim its message to a troubled world, and I will develop that in the discussion on history and hope in the second part of this chapter. For the theological importance of this balance, see G. LAFONT, *God, Time, and Being*, 134-135. Lafont speaks of a narration of the Paschal Mystery that goes from the Resurrection to the Resurrection passing through the cross.

section. But first it will be helpful briefly to develop a fourth point on epiclesis, paralleling the fourth point on anamnesis.

4. It is enough to note here that if the epiclesis of the eucharistic liturgy is the culminating work of the Holy Spirit in the whole life of the Church, it is nonetheless important to be mindful that the other sacramental rites also have an epiclesis that is vital to understanding what each accomplishes.[285] Likewise, although there is no explicit epiclesis in The Liturgy of the Hours or in the liturgical calendar of feasts, these all have their power and force precisely through the work of the Holy Spirit. Each of the sacraments is variously ordered toward the eucharist; and in each, through an invocation of the Holy Spirit together with the particular way in which that rite expresses an anamnetic dimension, there is accomplished what the sacrament intends, among other things, bringing the Church together for the celebration of the eucharist. In each sacramental epiclesis there can be discerned its preparation in "the Holy Spirit speaking through the prophets." In each, there is some pattern which echoes the Spirit's accompanying Jesus through the course of his earthly existence. The rite is in these same forms and patterns, which, as we have said, ultimately is patterned by the form and dynamic movement of divine trinitarian love.

So far this study has taken a first step in the method I am proposing to use to bring liturgy and Fundamental Theology into closer dialogue; namely, we have looked at some particular rite or part of a rite to see what may be offered there by way of a new perspective for themes in Fundamental. We can turn now to drawing some theological conclusions from what has been said thus far.

2. *Anamnesis and Epiclesis Directed Toward Fundamental Theology*

The Good News that Christianity announces is that in Jesus of Nazareth God has revealed himself and his intentions for the world. Fundamental Theology grapples with this fact in its most

---

[285] J. Corbon speaks usefully of each of the sacraments from the point of view of their epiclesis in *The Wellspring of Worship*, 108-122.

basic dimensions. It distinguishes Revelation (that is, what can be known of God only thanks to his gracious initiative) from a natural knowledge of God left to human ingenuity. It takes account of the surprising and unexpected form of this revelation; namely, in the context of the history of a particular nation and finally in the history of one man's life, and him crucified. It describes faith as the appropriate response to the God who reveals himself, and it attempts to offer reasons that are both sound and persuasive as to why such faith is worth the risk. It identifies the means by which one has access to this revelation; namely, in the Scriptures and in Tradition as these are read and known in the communion of the one Church. It argues these positions and meets arguments that oppose them. These are some of the broad strokes that describe the discipline. As it settles down to do its work well and to engage these and similar questions at the greatest possible depth, many different theological themes are brought into its orbit.[286]

Unlike dogmatic theology, which is the effort of those who already believe to understand more deeply the content of Revelation, Fundamental Theology must always keep one eye on those who do not yet believe, addressing its discourse also to them, offering them good reason to believe, challenging them. To do this effectively one must understand well the type of person, the type of culture, being addressed. Then there can be brought to the fore those dimensions of the Christian message likely to find resonance in those addressed.[287]

Fundamental Theology is not immediately about evangelization. It is about understanding as deeply as possible all the cultural and theological dimensions that converge in a given context where the Gospel is announced. A theologian who has done this in a model way is Ghislain Lafont, especially in his

---

[286] Once again I would take the *Dictionary of Fundamental Theology* as indicative of the vast range of questions that Fundamental Theology is appropriately facing today. There are nearly 300 separate titles for entries, each providing further bibliography. Some 35 of these are identified as major articles. Its systematic index distributes the articles among 5 major headings: Revelation, credibility, faith, epistemology, and history.

[287] See the useful description of this by R. Fisichella, "Addressee," in *DFT*, 332-336, especially, 334, "Positive Elements."

important and perhaps too little known *God, Time, and Being*. In the Foreword of this book, speaking of various theological currents, he says, "These two developments, one having more to do with death and narrative, the other with Being and analogy, do not respond solely to problems internal to theology. They are also demanded by certain currents of the contemporary culture where the question of death and of time and the question of Being are beginning to reappear as of primary importance, either explicitly or more subtly."[288] This is a fine example of the necessary attention that Fundamental Theology must pay to contemporary culture. But as *theology* it is prepared to pinpoint precisely where Christian faith meets the concerns of contemporary culture. Lafont argues persuasively throughout his book that death, time, and Being are the forms in which contemporary culture is asking its most pressing religious questions. He likewise presents the way in which the Cristian message effectively meets these concerns.[289]

Time! It is an anguishing experience for human beings. But it is precisely to those who feel such anguish that the Christian Gospel can be announced, for that very Gospel proclaims not so much a being saved *from* Time but the salvation of Time itself. Fundamental Theology, not only as it articulates the unique dimensions of Christian revelation but also in its dialogue with world religions, needs to place in clear relief Christianity's unique notion of Time. Yet this cannot be adequately done without reference to the liturgy, and more specifically without reference to anamnesis and epiclesis, for these are the cultic form and the language in which the Church experiences and expresses a unique sense of Time, a saving form. Reference to the liturgy lends an indispensable "tone" to the theological discussion, without which Fundamental Theology risks presenting only a particular "content" of ideas of Time, hopefully managing to be persuasive. But ideas do not save anyone or anything. Instead, the eucharist is precisely the very experience of this saving time. From it as a foundation the form and the content of ideas about Time must,

---

[288] G. LAFONT, *God, Time, and Being*, x.

[289] In chapter 5, I summarize one part of Lafont's book which I find particularly pursuasive in this regard but also relevant to the whole relation to liturgy which I am urging. See 117-118.

at least in part, be drawn. In what follows I would like to sketch some of the ways in which what has already been said about anamnesis and epiclesis can contribute to the way Fundamental Theology might deal with the notion of Time.

2.1. *Time, The Burden of History and Freedom*

John Zizioulas asks a question that can get us immediately into the discussion: "Now if *becoming* history is the particularity of the Son in the economy, what is the contribution of the Spirit?" He answers, "Well, precisely the opposite: it is to liberate the Son and the economy from the bondage of history. If the Son dies on the cross, thus succumbing to the bondage of historical existence, it is the Spirit that raises him from the dead. (Romans 8:11) The Spirit is the *beyond* history, and when he acts in history he does so in order to bring into history the last days, the *eschaton* (Acts 2:17)." [290]

Anamnesis and epiclesis are the liturgical shape of this form of the economy, and in fact it is only in the eucharistic celebration that the Church knows and experiences this with clarity. This is because in a rite which combines and overlays anamnetic and epicletic elements, *eschatological* realities (represented by the Spirit given in "the last days") are encountered through *historical* forms (represented in the memory of Christ's Paschal Mystery). Anamnesis in the eucharist manifests this historical form of the salvific economy, remembering the life, death, and resurrection of Christ and doing so in the form of the supper, which likewise was given historically. "But," following Zizioulas again, "a eucharist founded uniquely on history and manifesting the Church as simply 'institution' is not the true eucharist. It might be said, by paraphrasing the biblical sentence, that 'history kills, it is the Spirit who gives life.'" [291] Zizioulas' biblical intuition could be expanded with other classical texts, each of which could be said to find liturgical expression in the relation between anamnesis and epiclesis. For example, "Because we no longer look on anyone according to the flesh. If at one time we knew Christ according to

---

[290] J. Zizioulas, *Being as Communion*, 130. For what follows I take many clues from this book.

[291] Ibid., 22. The biblical reference is to 2 Cor 3:6.

the flesh, we no longer know him by this standard." (2 Cor 5:16) Or, "A natural body is put down, and a spiritual body comes up." (1 Cor 15:44) Or, "The first Adam became a living being, the last Adam a life-giving spirit." (1 Cor 15:44). Or again, "He was manifested in the flesh, vindicated in the Spirit..." (1 Tim 3:16.)

Concerning history and all that is remembered in the liturgical memorial, Zizioulas uses a vivid image for what the epiclesis accomplishes in its regard: "... it dilates history and time to the infinite dimensions of the *eschata*..." [292] It is worth dwelling for a moment on the force of the word *dilate*, for this implies an expansion, a swelling, of an original something, yet without the original borders or outlines being burst. This is an excellent image both of the form of the economy and of the liturgy which echoes it. In what at first glance is but a puny slice of history — the short life of a Galilean Jew which ends in crucifixion — the entire being of God is revealed, and all the cosmos and history are taken up into a participation in this divine life. This, it could be said, is what the joint mission of the Son and Spirit accomplishes. And this joint mission, it could be said, is what is manifested in liturgical anamnesis and epiclesis. Likewise, there in the liturgy, believers enter into that saving reality in a way that dilates their own experience of history, similarly small and insignificant, to the infinite dimensions of the Spirit, of the eschata. "A natural body is put down, and a spiritual body comes up."

This interplay between the dilation of history to the infinite dimensions of the eschata both in the life of Christ and in the life of the believer, and both accomplished by the Holy Spirit, can be directed toward the particular anguish regarding Time as experienced in contemporary culture. This is an anguish both about origins and destiny, the meaning — or lack thereof — of my particular existence.[293] What is accomplished for me, a believer, by my participation in the eucharistic liturgy — participation in ritual forms both anamnetic and epicletic — is the same freedom from the burden of history which Christ crucified (i.e., Christ succumbing to history's burden) experiences in his being raised

---

[292] Ibid., 22.

[293] For a lengthy description which precisely sets the stage for the unique Christian understanding of Time, see G. LAFONT, *God, Time, and Being*, 3-109.

from the dead. By the action of the Holy Spirit in the transformation of the gifts of bread and wine — gifts which represent at one and the same time the specific history of Christ and the specific history of the community which brings the gifts[294] — the life and death that Christ underwent in history is brought into profound accord with the life in history that I am living. His particular life from a moment in history far different from my own is meant to function as the only norm and the only meaning of my time in history. Only the Spirit could bridge this otherwise impossible gap. Within one same dynamic, the Spirit who raised Jesus from the dead and who forms and fashions the vessels for the liturgy also forms and fashions from the infinite wealth hidden in the life of Christ the wonderful variety of history, giving to the Church of every age and to every believer a unique time in which to live which derives from the unique time in which Jesus of Nazareth lived.[295] But not only does it derive from this past. It derives likewise from the future in which Jesus, risen in the Spirit, already stands. It is this already existing future Jesus in whom I too find the destiny toward which my present, whose origins are in his past, is directed. I can only speak in these terms — and survive this paradoxical language — by relying on the cultic celebration which manages sucessfully to hold in tension the dialectic between history and the eschaton. This cultic celebration is anamnesis and epiclesis inextricably intertwined and overlapping.

This interplay of past, present, and future in the cultic forms is commented on further by Zizioulas: "The epiclesis means ecclesiologically that the Church *asks to receive from God what she has already received historically in Christ as if she had not received it at all...*"[296] This is an observation based on the *lex orandi,* on the simple fact that the Church repeatedly invokes the Holy Spirit in the course of her historical existence. What sense could this have if all had been posited historically? This "epicletic life of the Church shows only one thing: That there is no security for her to be found in any historical guarantee as such... Her

---

[294] On this see the previous chapter, 139-148.

[295] I rely here on the earlier discussion of von Balthasar's *A Theology of History* in chapter 5, 118-126.

[296] J. Zizioulas, *Being as Communion,* 185. Emphasis in the original.

constant dependence on the Spirit proves that her history is to be constantly eschatological."[297]

The cultic practices of anamnesis and epiclesis make it possible to overcome any Neoplatonic form of dualism, any opposing of history and the realm of the divine. In the Incarnation of Christ history has become the real bearer of the life of the divine, but, again, this incarnation is effected in the Holy Spirit. What, then, can be the meaning of my brief and limited historical existence? "History as existence in space and time offers in Christ the possibility for communion with the *eschata*."[298] And this communion is entered into precisely in the eucharistic celebration. "There is, indeed, no other experience in the Church's life in which the synthesis of the historical with the eschatological can be realized more fully than in the eucharist. The eucharist is, on the one hand, a 'tradition' (παράδοσις) and a 'remembrance' (ἀνάμνησις). As such it activates the historical consciousness of the Church in a retrospective way. At the same time, however, the eucharist is the eschatological moment of the Church *par excellence*... In and through the same experience, therefore, *at one and the same moment*, the Church unites in the eucharist the two dimensions, past and future, simultaneously as one indivisible reality."[299]

2.2. *Truth and History*

On the basis of the liturgical forms of anamnesis and epiclesis something can be said about how truth reaches us.[300] The epiclesis forces us to observe that it does not come simply as a result of

---

[297] Ibid., 185-186.

[298] Ibid., 186.

[299] Ibid., 187-188. Emphasis in the original.

[300] Here I mean "truth" in the way that Christian theology wishes to use the term, the truth about God and the world which is revealed to us in Christ. The concept as well as the means of access to it must be defined by Fundamental Theology, particularly in relationship to Revelation. For a brief discussion of this, see I. DE LA POTTERIE, "Truth," in *DFT*, 1132-1137. If such an article may be considered symptomatic of the discipline, it can be noted again that there is no reference in it to what we might call access to truth through the liturgy, specifically through anamnesis and epiclesis. For a different approach, see G. LAFONT, *God, Time, and Being*, 143-146.

a historical transmission, that is, from Christ to the apostles to their successors, the bishops, as this is described, for example, in *Dei Verbum's* discussion of Revelation and truth.[301] Certainly Christianity is founded on the historical facts of Jesus' existence, and truth comes to us from that. But we have seen that in the epiclesis this very history acquires the dimension of the future and that, indeed, without it, history could not be brought forward into the present. If history can be pictured as reaching us with its effects along a *horizontal* line of transmission from the past, the future invoked in epiclesis can be visualized as a *"vertical* dimension transforming history into charismatic-pentecostal events."[302] This pentecostal event is the liturgical celebration itself. In the celebration there is memorial of what Christ accomplished in history, but precisely through the action of the Holy Spirit that history becomes contemporaneous with the worshipping community. Yet there is more. In Christ's resurrection not only is the history he lived saved from oblivion, but he likewise already exists as that future man in whom are recapitulated all things in heaven and on earth. (Cf. Eph 1:10) In the visitation of the Holy Spirit (who is always henceforth the Spirit of this risen Christ) brought about through the epiclesis, a new Pentecostal event occurs for the assembled community; and this future becomes in that Pentecost the present event of eucharist.

It is not too difficult to imagine how it is that past events of any sort have influenced, shaped, and brought about a particular present. But what the epicletic experience of the eucharist posits is more paradoxical; namely, a future that has its effects on the present. The line that moves in a horizontal dimension from a past that flows into the present is lifted up in a vertical thrust by the epiclesis, still carried forward in a direction that can be called history's advance, but lifted nonetheless and carried forward to a future on a level it could not otherwise reach had it not already tasted in advance this future.

This truth that comes to us from past and future, this truth that is nothing less than Christ himself (John 14:6) come to full stature (Eph 4:13), this truth that is encountered in the eucharistic celebration — this can be rendered precise in its

---

[301] Cf. *Dei Verbum* II, 7-9.
[302] J. ZIZIOULAS, *Being as Communion*, 115.

content. This is done in every age of the Church according to the particular needs of the time. Such rendering precise in content is called dogma.[303] Here we see again the importance of Fundamental Theology turning to the liturgy to lay the foundations for dogmatic formulations. Without this reference, it is too easy for dogma to appear only as propositions. And as was said above in another context, propositions do not save; they cannot in themselves offer hope to those who feel anguish in the face of the terror of history. But dogmas are meant to protect a correct vision of the truth that saves and gives hope. They are principally *soteriological* declarations which maintain a correct vision of the Christ-truth in its historical and eschatological dimensions. This truth is met in the eucharistic celebration through its anamnetic and epicletic dimensions.[304] Here again we encounter the real force of the dictum *lex orandi, lex credendi.*[305]

2.3. *Hope for the Future*

What point can history have, what future? Is there anything at all like a common destiny for the human race? Is there really progress? From so many perspectives, the twentieth century which ushered in the second millenium was a terrible century: wars the likes of which have never before been seen, genocide, unnecessary famine, weapons of mass destruction, drugs destroying the minds and hearts of millions, and on and on and on. It is said that especially the young, to whom hope should

---

[303] See G. MANSINI, "Dogma," in *DFT*, 239-247, especially "The Eschatological Word Maintained Across Time," 240.

[304] This eucharistic dimension of dogmatic formulations helps us to understand why ancient councils concluded their definitions with anathemas, i.e., anyone who does not hold the correct vision of this Christ-truth cannot celebrate the rite in which it is met. And again, this is not primarily about propositions, even if the proposition plays an indispensable role. It is about being in communion with the bishop who presides at the eucharistic celebration, proclaiming the memorial, invoking the Holy Spirit. In communion with other bishops, this bishop has rendered precise some necessary understanding of what is being celebrated. This is true, *mutatis mutandis*, of course, for the eucharist presided by a priest.

[305] For more on truth in this vein, see J. ZIZIOULAS, "The Eucharist as the Locus of Truth," in *Being as Communion*, 114-122.

come so naturally, live with so little hope for the future that awaits them. In effect, their youth and its beauty has been taken from them. Thus, drugs, random acts of violence, suicide. Surely pessismism makes a certain kind of sense before situations such as these.

This is the world to which the Christian Gospel is announced. We cannot possibly expect that it be heard there unless it be announced as somehow addressing these very situations, as offering hope in what would certainly be a hopeless situation without the Gospel. Fundamental Theology, insofar as it concerns itself with the type of person and the type of culture being addressed, must develop a discourse on hope which shows the capacity of Christianity to meet in an effective way these deep concerns about the future. It must show as well the uniqueness of the Christian position before such problems. For theology, it is not a question of developing strategies for effective social programs, which surely would involve cooperation with other world religions. Theology must concern itself with understanding the deepest roots of the problems and with measuring the depth and effectiveness of the solution that has been given us in Christ.

My desire in the present chapter is to remind theologians, as they attempt this task, to turn directly to what happens to the Church and to the world when the eucharist is celebrated. The eucharist *is* the hope for which the world longs, and its very celebration secures that hope, posits the future and lets us taste it now. Theology must be able to expose just how. Here I would like to indicate some of the ways in which attention to the anamnetic and epicletic dimensions of the eucharist can help in this task.

All that we have said about anamnesis indicates the tremendous value that Christian faith assigns to particular histories. The personal history of Jesus of Nazareth was the particular vessel that carried the fullness of the revelation of God. In the resurrection, through the work of the Holy Spirit, his history and all the divine life that is contained therein is lent to all the other particular histories of those who believe in him, assigning immeasurable value and significance to every human life and every phase of world history. Here is a salvation designed to touch and move a very tender and often wounded part of the human heart. Dare we hope that our lives and the lives of those we so much love could have infinite value, that what we do now somehow matters for ever? Could the one I love live for ever? Can I hope that death does not destroy and finish our love? Every kind of horrible and hateful death — death through war, through cruel genocide, senseless acts of terrorism, death on a cross?

The Church's constant eucharistic memorial of the life, death, and resurrection of Jesus of Nazareth is not simply a proposition, a set of ideas. It is the actual experience for the Christian community of history itself being saved. The salvation that Christianity proclaims is not salvation *from* history but the salvation *of* history itself. This distinguishes Christian faith from other world religions. Said liturgically, nothing like the eucharist is accomplished in any other ritual of any other religion.

But to understand and expose the fullest dimensions of this claim, there is need to refer to the epicletic aspect of the eucharistic celebration. For a huge problem remains in the experience of the whole world, even in the world of those who celebrate eucharist; namely, the horror of the present historical situation. It is precisely for this reason that the Church has found that it has had to continually invoke the Holy Spirit, such that this has become part of its very *lex orandi*. Salvation has not been posited solely in history; it is also posited eschatologically. The epiclesis, the visit of the Spirit from the future, creates of the worshipping community not so much an icon of the community as it is in its present historical circumstances but as it shall be.

This can perhaps be grasped with the help of an image. I think of a plant or a tree whose roots stretch out to both past and future but whose head springs up in the present. Without its nourishment from the future, this plant could not survive; and yet the plant we see in the present indicates that the Church's liturgical experience of the future has its effects on the present. When they meet, the present dark historical situation and the bright future proclaimed by Christian hope certainly clash. This clash is nothing less than a clash with the demonic forces of division at work in the world.[306] What is posited historically in Christ and remembered in the anamnesis is in the Church's

---

[306] For this image and a discussion, see J. ZIZIOULAS, *Being as Communion*, 160-162.

existential experience "insufficient" to squelch the forces of division. And so the Church invokes the Holy Spirit again and again so that she may become and be revealed in history as the body of Christ in its totality.

Experience shows — and the epiclesis reveals the theological reasons for it — that the union and communion of all peoples in Christ, and indeed of the whole cosmos in him, cannot be achieved merely by human efforts historically conceived. Human attempts at togetherness, even those informed by what is known of Christ from history, can never accomplish the communion in trinitarian life to which God would bring the whole creation. The epiclesis reveals that this communion, which *is* the eschaton, must penetrate history now also from the future. This absolute need for the future shows why the Kingdom of God can never be simply identified with history as such. It is not a conquest of the world as we know it. It is the world as it is known in the eucharistic celebration.

I have spoken of the distinctiveness of Christian hope in comparison to other world religions. This distinctiveness is revealed in the eucharist. Responsible Christian theology will "always be ready to give a reason for the hope" that is ours. (1 Peter 3:15) But there is no cause for boasting here (cf. 1 Cor 1:26-31). The eucharistic community must know itself to be a kind of first fruits of humanity and creation, and the whole community exercises a priestly role on behalf of these. The glory that is given to God the Father in each eucharistic celebration through Christ, in him, with him, in the unity of the Holy Spirit, is the glory which the whole creation is destined to offer. The community which enjoys the incomparable privilege of offering that future glory already in the present moment of history exits the eucharistic assembly, exits that future, and returns to the present as it now is. But it is in this present with a leaven from the future. It is in this present as sent from God. "As the Father has sent me into the world, so do I send you into the world." (John 17:18; 20:21) This is the deepest meaning of the "Ite missa est" with which every eucharistic celebration is concluded.

Conclusion

"Only love is credible," Hans Urs von Balthasar has reminded us in so many different ways.[307] In the eucharist the Church encounters credible divine love. Every human heart longs for it, was made for it. It is satisfyingly concrete. It is as concrete as the complete historical existence of a particular man, Jesus of Nazareth; as concrete as his gruesome death in crucifixion. In the resurrection this man is shown to be also Son of God, Lord, Messiah.[308] The encounter with this risen Lord is equally concrete in the eucharist, even if filled with mystery; for he is met as risen when the gestures, signs, and words that remember his death are unfolded. The same eucharistic rite is experience for the Church of the wonderful work of the Holy Spirit, "concrete" in his own way, not as incarnate but as "the wind which blows where it wills, and you can hear the sound it makes." (John 3:8) "The Spirit of the Lord fills the world, is all-embracing." (Wisdom 1:7) The Spirit's presence lets love be known: his love for the Son, their love for the Father, the Father's love for them. His presence likewise brings us into their divine life, but again, very concretely. For we enter this love not as a place outside and beyond history but precisely within our own history. It is with the material of our lives and our world — bread and wine — that the trinitarian mystery and our participation in it is manifested. This is credible love. "God so loved the world that he gave his only Son so that everyone who believes in him might not perish but might have eternal life." (John 3:16) "I made known to them your name and I will make it known, that the love with which you loved me may be in them and I in them." (John 17:26) "No one has greater love than this, to lay down one's life for one's friends. You are my friends." (John 15:13-14) "As I have loved you, so you also should love one another." (John 13:34)

---

[307] H. Urs von Balthasar, *Glaubhaft ist nur Liebe*, Einsiedeln 1985, can be considered emblematic. On this, see R. Fisichella, *Hans Urs von Balthasar, amore e credibilità cristiana*, Rome 1981. And "Fides quaerens caritatem: ovvero l'amore come presupposto della fede," in R. Fisichella (ed.), *Noi crediamo. Per una teologia dell'atto di fede*, Rome 1993, 177-193.

[308] Peter's first preaching on the day of Pentecost in Acts 2:14-41 fills out nicely my perhaps too condensed a way of expressing myself here.

Chapter 8

THE MANIFESTATION
OF THE TRINITARIAN MYSTERY
IN THE EUCHARISTIC ASSEMBLY

"I am not you, and you are not me." That much is obvious to us all. But what is not obvious is the deeper reality, the common destiny desired for us by God, in which we would also say, "Yes, but I am not who I am without you, and you are not you without me." In this chapter, I want to explore how this deeper destiny is revealed and, indeed, actually brought about in the shape of the eucharistic celebration. Not only that. It is not merely and not even principally our deeper destiny as human beings that is revealed in the eucharistic celebration. It is the very being of God as Trinity that is revealed there. But the Trinity is never simply revealed in itself or by itself, in the abstract, as it were. It is always a part of that revelation that God's desired destiny for the human race is that it share trinitarian life.

We have already had occasion to observe that Vatican II's *Dei Verbum* begins with a statement to the effect that it pleased God to reveal both himself and the mystery of his will for the world. Thus, two objects of revelation: one about God and one about the human race. But this opening claim actually moves in a circular dynamic. The revelation of the mystery of God's will becomes in fact the revelation of himself, for his will is that we should have access to the Father, through the Son, in the Holy Spirit. "It pleased God, in his goodness and wisdom, to reveal himself and to make known the mystery of his will (cf. Eph 1:9). His will was that men should have access to the Father, through Christ, the Word made flesh, in the Holy Spirit, and thus become sharers in the divine nature (cf. Eph 2:18, 2 Pet 1:4)." [309] That God is Father, Son, and Spirit is the central content of Christian Revelation; but this is not a content grasped as one grasps abstract ideas. In other

---

[309] *Dei Verbum* 2.

words, it is not a gnosis. It is a content grasped by participation in the very reality which is revealed. As God's will unfolds, that is, when in fact there is access to the Father through the Son in the Holy Spirit, then God himself is likewise known as Father, Son, and Spirit.

This is well and fine. Nonetheless, it would not be unreasonable to ask a rather concrete set of questions; namely, where actually can I find this access to the Father? How? In what form? The answer well may be "in Christ." But, then, where actually is he? If we say that he is to be found in the Scriptures, in the history they recount, in the Church, then where are the Scriptures fruitfully and properly engaged, and where is the Church met? And if Christ opened up this access to the Father by what he once did in history, then where is that history now and how can we meet it? One of the strongest answers that we have in the Catholic tradition — one of the most fundamental — is to say, in the Liturgy, and above all in the eucharist. More than anything else and more than anywhere else, the liturgy is the actual place of God's revelation. There the mystery of his will is revealed and accomplished: we have access to the Father through the Son in the Holy Spirit.

Thus, the celebration of the eucharist is itself this participation in trinitarian life, and consequently attention to the shape of the rite can always provide a new impetus for meditating on the trinitarian mystery. The Church's trinitarian *doctrine* (in which the central content of Revelation is expressed) derives from the *action* of the Trinity in the liturgy, which itself derives from the *action* of the Trinity in the history of salvation. These are three spheres whose forms and "musics" are continually echoing each other: action of the Trinity in the world, action of the Trinity in the liturgy, doctrine of the Trinity in the understanding of the Church. The interpenetration of the spheres is necessary to keep the form and the music true and fruitful. Doctrine means to protect and advance our proper understanding of the action of the Holy Trinity in the world and in the liturgy. It is not my goal here to study trinitarian doctrine as such, but more to look at the question of foundations. Where does this doctrine come from, and in what reality is it founded? It derives from and describes a divine action, the divine action of the liturgy, which is nothing less than a continuation of the divine action in the history of salvation. And the divine action of the eucharistic celebration cannot be adequately described without arriving at an exposition of the trinitarian mystery.

The broad strokes of this action can be traced in two basic movements which define its essential form, the basic melody line, as it were. The first is a movement from God the Father to the world, while the second is a movement from the world to God the Father. However, this movement unfolds in both a trinitarian and an ecclesial shape which need to be described in order to hear the fullest resonance of what is moving. The first movement in this full trinitarian and ecclesial shape can be described as follows: the *Father* gives himself through his *Son* to the world in the Church, and the *Spirit* illumines and vivifies every dimension of this gift. It may be noted first of all that the Father is source of all this action. It is not vaguely "God" who is identified as source but specifically the Father. (This fact was important in trinitarian doctrinal struggles for determining that also within the internal life of the Trinity the Father is a source for Son and Spirit).[310] It is the Father who is addressing himself to the world; this is the God who "so loves the world that he gives the world his only Son." (John 3:16) Thus is named another, a Son; but this Son is given by the Father, given as what is most precious to him. In this way did he "so love the world." But a precise theological point in the trinitarian theology of the economy can be made on the basis of this observation about the first direction of movement: the whole liturgy proclaims not that the Father gives himself directly as Father but that the Father gives himself in giving his Son.

I have called this a trinitarian shape of movement in the liturgy, but it should also be observed that not only were the members of the Trinity named in describing this shape but also *world* and *Church*. This is the circular dynamic observed in the opening declaration of *Dei Verbum*. The Trinity is not named in the abstract as a revelation of who God is. If God is revealed, it is in relation to the mystery of his will for the world. It should

---

[310] It is often thought that this is only a concern of the Greek Fathers, but Basil Studer shows that it is very much present also in Augustine. See B. STUDER, *The Grace of Christ and the Grace of God in Augustine of Hippo, Christocentrism or Theocentrism?*, Collegeville 1997, 158-159. For the Greek view, see J. ZIZIOULAS, *Being as Communion*, 40-46.

further be noted that the Father does not give the Son directly to the world but that he places the Son in the hands of the Church. I do not want to say that the Father gives the Son simply to the Church and stop the statement there; for the movement or action does not finish with the Church. The Father gives the Son to the Church *for the sake of* the world, or put another way, he gives the Son to the world through the Church. In giving the Son, the Father gives a task; namely, gathering all into one body in the Son. It is concrete; it is historical. The Church is that: concrete, historical. The Church is the gathering in history.[311] But this concrete historical dimension is vivified by the Spirit, who accompanies and illumines every dimension of the Father's gift, enabling us to "interpret spiritual things in spiritual terms." (1 Cor 2:13) So we have named Father, Son, and Spirit in describing the first direction of the radical movement of the liturgy, but it has not been possible to do so without also naming Church and world.

The other radical movement of the liturgy is that of the world back to God; and again, to be adequately expressed, this must be done in trinitarian and ecclesial terms. The Church responds in thanksgiving by offering to the *Father* the very gift she has received: the *Son*. The *Spirit* effects the transformation of the Church's gifts into the Body and Blood of the *Son*. In doing so, the Church is not acting in her own name alone. She is intentionally representing the world and the whole cosmos in the gifts brought for transformation. This is the priestly action of the whole people. This is, as *Dei Verbum* said it, "access to the Father through the Son in the Holy Spirit." If the question of this study is about foundations for trinitarian doctrine, we are noting here in this twofold movement of the eucharistic rite the fundamental and immediate context of our encounter with Revelation, where Revelation is defined as the revelation of God himself and the mystery of his will. In the liturgy God's will for the world is accomplished and actualized.

---

[311] Earlier I tried to show how reference to the liturgy can help the fundamental theologian to discuss, even in provocative terms, one of the essential themes of the discipline; namely, the transmission of Revelation *in the Church*. See above, 145-147.

Attention is being drawn here to this intimate and inextricable connection between the central content of Revelation, with which fundamental theologians are necessarily concerned, and the manifestation of that content in the eucharistic action. It is the liturgical experience itself which impresses on our consciousness that the manifestation of the trinitarian mystery is at one and the same time participation in it. *Many* are *one*, through sharing in the death and resurrection of the Lord, in the *oneness* of Father, Son, and Holy Spirit. The kind of oneness which is achieved in the celebration of the eucharist reveals to the world a new kind of oneness, different from all human attempts at oneness or togetherness. Human attempts at oneness are often tempted to try to achieve it by uniformity and by the elimination of any who will not comply. Or, in an opposite tendency there is the attempt to achieve oneness too simply, too naively, overlooking with friendliness or liberal expansiveness the real differences which divide. But such a oneness is not destined to last. Human attempts at oneness are also either opposed by or eventually oppose those who wish to see diversity valued. Diversity crushed can never achieve real unity, but diversity raised to an absolute value divides the human community and inevitably results in warring diversities to see which can stand over against the other.

The oneness of Father, Son, and Spirit as this is manifested in the eucharistic action, is a oneness of an altogether different order, a oneness where the "diverse" members of the Trinity are constituted in their diversity precisely by their unique and wholly particular relation of unity to the others. Thus, the Father is not the Son, and the Son is not the Father, and the Spirit is neither of these; yet each is what he is in virtue of a perfect communion with the other, outside of which communion it would be impossible for any one of the three to be. This communion in difference is what is manifested in the different role of each as we have described it in the twofold movement of the liturgy. The community that participates in this trinitarian life is one and many in the same way.

This can be viewed in the whole community's relation to the whole godhead and to each member of the Trinity, as well as in the relation of the members of the community among themselves. Beginning first with the community, we can say that the bishop is not the assembly of the baptized, and the assembly of the baptized is not the bishop. The same, *mutatis mutandis*, for priests and the assembly, and, entering into details, the priests and deacons in their relation to each other and their relation to the bishop. Further, the assembly of the baptized is not the world of non-believers, and non-believers are not the baptized.

But all this is to say what they are not. Let us ask, what are they? No one in the liturgical assembly is an individual who subsists or can be defined in his own right. Each is who he is because of a precise relation, a holy order, in which he stands to the other. Thus, the bishop is not the assembly, but he is who he is only in relation to the assembly. And the assembly is only the assembly that God intends it to be in a communion with the bishop, from whom the assembly itself can be distinguished. And within the assembly, I am not you, and you are not me, but each of us is who he is only in the relationship of communion that we hold with each other and which cannot be established except through holding a same relationship of communion with the bishop. In this way, in this holy order, the many who are gathered become one, not by uniformity, not by eliminating diversity but by a divine action which constitutes each member as a particular person precisely by making that member's very being depend on unity with the other. And we cannot forget here also the constitutive relation between Church and world. The Church which is one in this way can only be what she is in a relationship with the world, a relationship which is expressed liturgically in the bringing of gifts of bread and wine — the fruits of the cosmos and of human history — and in the dismissal of the assembly for the service of the world. Every *Ite missa est* is nothing less than, "As the Father has sent me into the world, so do I send you into the world." (Cf. John 20:21; 17:18; Matt 28:19; Mk 16:15)

Is this reading of a perichoresis of relationships in the eucharistic assembly, which can be discerned by a careful penetration of the rites as they now stand, not further justified by seeing them in association with the mysterious heavenly assemblies that were the object of the Revelations given to John in the last book of the Bible? For the seer was "caught up in spirit on the Lord's day," (Rev 1:10) the day of the eucharist *par excellence*. The assemblies he saw were arrangements in a holy order of one and many. There is a throne around which others are gathered, a "throne of one whose appearance sparkled like jasper," around which are arranged "twenty-four other thrones on which twenty-four elders sat." The flaming torches that are "the seven spirits of God" surround the throne. (Rev 4:2-6) In the midst of the throne — God's throne — there appears the "Lamb that had been slain." (Rev 5:6) To him the whole assembly sings its praises. (Rev 5:8-14) God and the Lamb are distinguished but share the same throne. The rest of the heavenly court worships, not just a vague worship of God but worship of the Lamb that had been slain. (Rev 5:12-13) That is to say, this is heavenly worship based precisely on an earthly event, the paschal mystery of Jesus. "Once I was dead," he says, "but now I live forever and ever." (Rev 1:18) That "once," which includes the whole of history in it, is now united to the forever of heaven, but it also henceforth constitutes the forever. It is a different "ever" than it ever was before. The throne of God is now henceforth also the throne of the Lamb (Rev 22:1) in the midst of a new Jerusalem, a new heaven and a new earth. (Rev 21) This is no vision or knowledge of God in the abstract. It is God known in the lightning and in the roar (Rev 14:2) of the continually unfolding revelations of his unfathomable inner relations shared with the human race.

The one God, in whom the whole economy has revealed that there is mysteriously a more than one — a Father on a throne, so to speak, with the original many of Son and Spirit gathered round — is the original assembly according to which all other assemblies are patterned. With the help of the heavenly visions of the apostle, we can peer into that original one and three and discern something of the dynamic pattern of the dance of love into which "a great multitude, which no one could count, from every nation, race, people and tongue" (Rev 7:9) is invited to share. But there is no seeing the mystery apart from seeing the Lamb that was slain. The multitude "stands before the throne and before the Lamb... crying out in a loud voice, 'Salvation... is from the Lamb.'" (Rev 7:9-10)

Why this insistence upon the slain Lamb? It is first of all an insistence on a distinction, on one who is distinct from God (the Father) but shares the throne with him. So, this is in part a revelation of the trinitarian mystery. But it is revelation that is based on the historical slaying of the one who is different from the Father. That is to say, it is a revelation of the trinitarian mystery only in terms of an economy of salvation. With hindsight we can say that the eternal distinction between Father and Son is the condition within the very nature of God which makes possible the joining of "a great multitude" to the trinitarian dynamic, even if that great multitude be gathered from among those immersed in sin. There is an infinite "distance," so to speak, between the Father and Son, just in virtue of their being distinct. What they are as God they are infinitely. Thus, infinitely distinct, at the same time they are infinitely close, in love, in one nature. It is this distance that qualifies the Son for incarnation, where he transposes a distance from the Father that is holy — at once as close as it is far — and he lets it become the distance of a creature and a sinner from God. Then he, as it were, waits for awhile in this distance (the "once" of Rev 1:18), feeling all its burden and weight, letting the whole horror of sin's distance from God have its head, and then he is once again in the original closeness — the distance of creatureliness and sin being transformed into the distance of Father from Son. This is the Lamb that was slain. He leads all who will follow to the same source from which he himself derives his being. "For the Lamb who is in the center of the throne will shepherd them and lead them to springs of life-giving water." (Rev 7:17)

That this huge multitude is taken into the very glory of the relationship which the Son had with the Father from all eternity (John 17:5,22) is shown in that vision of the heavenly assembly in which "there was the Lamb standing on Mount Zion, and with him a hundred and forty-four thousand who had his name and his Father's name written on their foreheads." (Rev 14:1) This is a "new song." (Rev 14:3) It is the human race singing now that same song of love that moved among Father, Son, and Spirit from all eternity. What is new is that others join the trinitarian rhythms. This is nothing that humans could arrogate to themselves; it is not the world's song. "No one could learn this song except the hundred and forty-four thousand who had been ransomed from the earth." (Rev 14:3)

Compared with these magnificent visions given to the apostle John, our earthly assemblies for the eucharist appear at first glance disappointingly humble. But the apostolic visions are given us precisely so that we can penetrate to the deepest mystery hidden in our assemblies. The holy order of relationships among the members of the earthly assembly that I described above is nothing less than our sharing already in the heavenly assembly, the original assembly of Father, Son, and Holy Spirit. The one bishop around which the elders and the multitude gather, the bishop's "throne" and the throne of the Lamb, the altar — these are an icon of the one God in whom there is Father, Son, Spirit, and now also a huge multitude.

This unity of the one and the many that the eucharistic assembly manifests is the sign and image of a unity whose source and ground lie beyond this world. The unity of the Church is image of the eternal unity of the *"many"* of Father, Son, and Spirit in the *one* divine nature. If the Church's unity is to be a participation in this divine and transcendent unity, then it knows in what pattern it must enter into such unity. The Church comes into this trinitarian dynamic through the Son, in the Spirit. Thus, the Church is not the Son, and the Son is not the Church; the Church is not the Spirit, and the Spirit is not the Church. And yet Christ has entered into a relationship of unity with his Church — his body — such that he is henceforth constituted as the one that he is only in relationship to her. It is shocking to put it this way, but this is the shock of the Incarnation, and it is a consequence of the permanent condition of the Lord's incarnation and its permanent soteriological and theological significance. Something similar is true of the Spirit. The Spirit is completely lavished upon the Church, but the Church is not the Spirit, and the Spirit is not the Church. Yet the Spirit is who he is now only in a kenotic relation to the Church, and the Church is only that "many" upon whom the Spirit has been completely poured out and whom he binds in unity. Put another way, the Spirit who proceeds eternally from the Father and the Son proceeds henceforth and evermore as the Spirit of the risen Son, who is risen in his human body. There is no other Spirit, no separate sphere of activity. There is only the Spirit of the Son in whose risen humanity all things in heaven and on earth are being recapitulated. This recapitulation of all things in Christ is precisely "the mystery of his will" which God "has made known to us" in Revelation. (Cf. Eph 1:9-10)

This unity in distinction, which in their kenotic action constitutes the very being of the Son and the Spirit through their relationship with us, is mysteriously insinuated in that "liturgy" with which the entire biblical account reaches its conclusion and climax, and it is not insignificant that the Bible should end in precisely this way. "The Spirit and the bride say, 'Come!'"

(Revelation 22:17) Here Spirit and Church are distinguished, but they are one in what they say and how they relate to yet another. "Come, Lord Jesus," (Rev 22:20) they say, and the Church has in that moment — the Church is constituted in that moment — the same relation which the Spirit has with the Son, which is always that the Son be known and manifested as who he is. And who is the Son? In this same biblical scene he defines himself in terms of relation. "I am the Root and Offspring of David," (Rev 22:16) that is, he is who he is in relation to Israel, in relation to the world's history. "I am the Morning Star shining bright," (Rev 22:16) that is, he is who he is in relation to the whole cosmos. But this one, who in an act of sheer mercy, grace, and condescension, lets himself be constituted by relation to history and cosmos has his being in a relation which precedes all this. "I am the Alpha and the Omega, the First and the Last, the Beginning and the End." (Rev 22:13)

Thus, it is that the End, revealed here on the last page of the Bible and in the eschatological dimensions of the eucharist, is made to be like the beginning. But the end is not the beginning, and the beginning is not the end. Yet now mysteriously one constitutes the other. In the beginning there was "Glory to the Father and to the Son and to the Holy Spirit," which is to say glory in every direction from one member of the Trinity to the other and in every conceivable pair: glory from Father to Son and from Son to Father and from these to the Spirit and from the Spirit to each and both and so on-glorious perichoresis! The end is like this, but it is not this. For now Spirit, Son, and Bride are made to be one, not by being one and the same thing but by each being what he is in relation to the other. And this too is glory, the glory that the Son had with the Father before the world began and which he gave also to us. (Cf. John 17:5,22) Then, "in these last days" these three — Son, Spirit, and Bride — can turn as one to the Source and address the Source as it has been addressed from the beginning: "Father!" This is glory, as the doxology has it, "as it was in the beginning, is now, and ever shall be." That the Bride addresses the Source as the Son and the Spirit have ever addressed the Source — this is the mystery of God's will, his desired destiny for the human race.

I said above, in discussing the unique and otherworldly way in which the Church is established in unity, that the many who are gathered become one, not by uniformity, not by eliminating diversity but by a divine action which constitutes each member as a particular person precisely by making that member's very being depend on unity with the other. It is possible to speak more exactly of the divine action which accomplishes this. It is Christ's sacrifice on the cross made present in the eucharistic action. For in Christ's sacrifice a name sounds which sounded at the beginning and which sounds at the end, but in his sacrifice the name is made to sound from the middle, made to sound from the place farthest away from both beginning and end, farthest away from the nature of the one who is Alpha and Omega, made to sound from the depths of sin and death, from history and the cosmos gone farthest away from God's original intentions. In the place of Christ's sacrificial death we hear, "Father, into your hands I commend my spirit," (Luke 23:46) and all at once the place that is farthest away from God is made to be what God is. The place that is farthest away from God becomes Love, as God is Love. This love has a shape. It is a Son and a Spirit who say "Father" to the source from which they come.[312]

Precisely because the eucharist is this sacrifice made present are we able to claim all that we have claimed both about the trinitarian mystery itself and our participation in it. Completely united with the Son in the Holy Spirit, and completely united among themselves through the Son in the Holy Spirit, all the members of the assembly are able to say with one voice "Father" to the Source from which all good things come, and all are made to hear the one voice that constitutes them as the new creation that they are: "Beloved Son, in whom I am well pleased." In hearing these words, the *one* Church has attained that for which she has been given the *diverse* gifts of "apostles, prophets, evangelists, pastors and teachers to equip the saints for the work of ministry, for building up the body of Christ." (Eph 4:11-12) The eucharist has formed "that perfect man who is Christ come to full stature." (Eph 4:13)

---

[312] This reflection on the name that sounds in the beginning now sounding in the middle of time is inspired by G. Lafont's splendid and much more lengthy analysis of the Synoptic accounts of the death of the Lord in *God, Time, and Being*, 156-170, especially 164 and 168.

Chapter 9

LITURGY, SACRAMENT AND CATECHESIS
IN THE *GENERAL DIRECTORY FOR CATECHESIS*

Introduction

The first question that occurs to people interested and involved in the work of catechesis, and so required to consult the *General Directory for Catechesis,* is probably not a question about liturgy. On the occasion of the first national symposium in the United States studying the Directory, I was invited to examine the document from the point of view of what it may say about the liturgy.[313] I must confess that I did not expect to find much and rather imagined I might discover a few key ideas and have to develop them somehow. However, I was not many pages into the document before I realized that my presuppositions were mistaken. Indeed, the reference that the *Directory* makes to the liturgy can be described as very frequent, and it is sustained virtually throughout the entire document. Even so, the purpose of the *Directory* is obviously to speak about something other than liturgy; and so all that it says on the matter may not fall into clear relief or even, at first reading, be especially memorable. For this reason, I hope it might be helpful in this short chapter to summarize the nature of those references and reflect briefly on what the consequences would be for catechesis. This gives occasion to show how all that has been discussed heretofore in this book can be brought to bear in the concrete context of teaching the Church's faith.

The most obvious reference to liturgy and sacrament in the document is to the baptismal catechumenate as a fundamental inspiration and model for catechesis in the Church. This is a topic in its own right, deserving of specific treatment. What I wish to review here will be different from this, though obviously related.

---

[313] This symposium was held in San Francisco in November 1998, sponsored by the archdiocese at the initiative of Archbishop William Levada.

I propose a consideration in three steps: first, the *Directory's* understanding of ecclesial life as the broadest context for catechesis, and the foundational role of liturgy in constituting ecclesial life. Second, in the light of this, we can understand the *Directory's* repeated reference to the liturgy itself as a kind of "catechesis." In a third step, we can apply these broad frameworks of the *Directory* to some specific catechetical questions and see what the advantage is of considering these questions with their liturgical face.

1. *Ecclesial Life and the Foundational Role of Liturgy*

The *Directory* makes reference again and again to ecclesial life as a kind of frame that surrounds the catechetical effort and without which frame this effort cannot come into proper focus. This dimension is stated in a programmatic way already in the introduction. "The evangelizing activity of the Church, catechesis included, must tend all the more decisively toward solid ecclesial cohesion. To this end it is urgent that an authentic ecclesiology of communion be promoted and deepened in order to arouse in Christians a deep ecclesial spirituality." [314] This ecclesial life has a liturgical face. Indeed, in the sacraments, and especially in the eucharist, the Church comes into being as a communion. It will be necessary to return to this point in the third part, but let this be a guiding idea for what follows.

Liturgy is constitutive of the ecclesial community, which is the principle protagonist of all catechesis. The Church that catechizes comes into being through the liturgy. She is what she is especially in the celebration of the eucharist, "a source and a summit" of ecclesial life, to use the oft quoted phrase from *Sacrosanctum Concilium*. [315] The Directory reminds us that this constitutive role tells us something about how the protagonist appropriately operates in the catechetical task. For example, it says, citing the conciliar document *Ad Gentes*, that the Church always operates "by slow stages," among which can be named "the formation of the Christian communities through and by

---

[314] N. 28.
[315] *Sacrosanctum Concilium* 7.

means of the sacraments and their ministers." This is, it says, "the dynamic for establishing and building up the Church." Thus, the slow and patient building up of the Church through, among other things, the regular celebration of the sacraments, becomes a kind of pattern of a slow and comprehensive plan of evangelization and catechesis.[316]

Not surprisingly, the *Directory* makes repeated reference to *The Catechism of the Catholic Church*. Indeed, the *Directory* is a major step in the process for developing strategies of delivering the contents of the *Catechism* to vastly diverse populations and age groups. In this light it is worth pausing to remark, as the *Directory* does, on the structure of the *Catechism* around the four fundamental dimensions of the Christian life: the profession of faith, the celebration of the liturgy, the morality of the Gospel, and prayer. Here we see liturgy in the context of all that the Church believes. What the Church believes — and thus what will be communicated in catechesis — is celebrated and communicated in liturgical actions. So, the liturgy has an absolutely foundational role in understanding the task of catechesis. Citing the Apostolic Constitution *Fidei Depositum* which introduces the *Catechism*, the *Directory* reminds us, "The Liturgy itself is prayer; the confession of faith finds its proper place in the celebration of worship. Grace, the fruit of the sacraments, is the irreplaceable condition for Christian living, just as participation in the Church's liturgy requires faith."[317] In short, the Church's life and belief cannot go forward without what the liturgy and sacraments communicate. In fact, so important is this that as one of the pillars of the *Catechism*, catechesis about the liturgy is nothing less than one of the basic tasks of the entire catechetical enterprise. This point is made at the outset of Chapter 2, Part 2, which discusses the relation between the *Catechism* and the *Directory*.

I think of these kinds of references as the *Directory's* drawing a larger frame around catechesis so that its "text" may always be determined by its ecclesial "con-text" and draw its inspiration from this. Another example of such framing would be the

---

[316] Nn. 48, 49.
[317] N. 122.

following consideration: apart from the obvious need for different kinds of catechetical training for individuals at various stages of their lives, the *Directory* reminds us that the Christian community as a whole requires an ongoing formation that must be more broadly conceived than a program of catechesis. Thus, we read, "In the Christian community the disciples of Jesus Christ are nourished at a twofold table: 'that of the word of God and that of the Body of Christ.' (DV 21) The Gospel and the eucharist are the constant food for the journey to the Father's House."[318] At this twofold table the Church is built up in unity so that, according to the Lord's own prayer, "The world may believe that thou hast sent me." (John 17:21) The *Directory* makes a profound point here, and we must perhaps pause to catch its significance. A deep unity is established among the Christian faithful at the table of the word and the eucharist, a unity whose origin and depth are within the unity of the Father and the Son. This unity, this visible unity — it must be visible! — is envisioned as that which will provoke belief in others and thus, by implication, require their catechesis. Approaching the ideal of this unity requires, the *Directory* insists, "the constant nourishment of the Body and Blood of Christ."[319]

The references to the liturgy in the *Directory* are cumulative in their effect. Liturgy is rarely a point discussed in its own right, but referring to it as part of the discussion of other topics is the significant point. There are frequent reminders to attend to the liturgical face of the catechetical question under consideration. A document on catechesis is, of course, going to make frequent reference to the word of God as the source of the message of catechesis. The *Directory*, following *Dei Verbum*, understands the word of God as being contained not only in Sacred Scripture but also in Sacred Tradition. It then notes that this word "is celebrated in the Sacred Liturgy, where it is constantly proclaimed, heard, interiorized and explained."[320] This is the kind of remark that deserves development beyond what could be expected in the *Directory* itself because the liturgical proclamation of the Word is not just one encounter with the Word among so

---

[318] N. 70.
[319] N. 70.
[320] N. 95.

many others that could be listed. Something of a very profound nature happens for the Church in this proclamation. It is nothing less than a real presence of Christ in his Word for the community, creating an event in the worshipping assembly that is nothing less than the same action of God to which the Sacred Scriptures bear witness. So, a sentence like this in the *Directory* is a sleeper; and we need to awaken it with our further theological reflection. If this reference to the liturgy is made in the context of a discussion on the source of the message of catechesis, it means that we shall not understand the message unless we tap into this source that is the event character of the word of God.[321]

These references are, I hope, sufficient to establish a sense of what I would consider a major idea about liturgy and the sacraments in the *Directory;* namely, that these in a foundational way bring into being the ecclesial life which is the context for the task of catechesis. I think it would be a fair summary of all of the references in this regard to say that they want to remind us that Christianity is not fundamentally a message. To think so could be a risk in focusing on catechesis, which obviously must be done at some point and which is done in the *Directory.* But first we must be clear that Christianity is more than a message. It is the reality of a new creation accomplished in the celebration of the sacraments. This, then, has a "message" dimension, *internal* to the Church in understanding this new creation; *external* in evangelization, an evangelization that aims ultimately at bringing others to the eucharistic banquet.[322]

2. *Liturgy as Catechesis*

In light of what has been said so far, perhaps the significance of the *Directory's* repeated references to the liturgy as a kind of catechesis can be better understood. Mark well: this is a different

---

[321] Nn. 95 and 96 repeat *Dei Verbum's* insistence on the intimate relation among Scripture, Tradition, and Magisterium. The balance among these three is in fact what the very shape of the liturgy expresses; for there the Scripture is read in the context of the Tradition and in the presence of the bishop or one whom the bishop has ordained.

[322] For this internal dimension, see nn. 27, 28. For external see nn. 46, 47, 48. For the eucharist as goal, see nn. 46, 79. For still other references to the foundational role of liturgy, see nn. 30, 50, 59, 87, 150.

idea from catechesis about the liturgy, which is perhaps more obvious and which also receives attention. (I do not intend to go into the latter here. The sense is that the meaning of the liturgy must also be considered part of the content of catechesis).[323] Liturgy considered as a kind of catechesis means that liturgical celebrations teach something, even if this is not their main point. The main point is simply communicating the divine realities that are signified. Nonetheless, in the context of catechesis it would make little sense to overlook how much in fact is implicitly taught in the very celebration of the sacraments. Catechesis, then, would want to build on and deepen "a something learned" in the ecclesial, liturgical context.

In the regular life of a community this point is most firmly established in reference to the eucharist. The homily is the most obvious catechetical moment of the eucharistic celebration, but this is a unique catechetical moment to be distinguished from a classroom setting or other extra-liturgical settings. It is unique and finds its force precisely from its context, which is, as the *Directory* says, "celebrations of the word," and "above all the participation of the faithful in the eucharist, as a primary means of education in the faith."[324] Participation itself is what teaches the faith. And this is because participation in the eucharist is nothing less than an experienced knowledge of the mysteries of faith, of Christ in his Paschal Sacrifice, of the Holy Trinity as mediated to us through this sacrifice.

It is because of what in fact is imparted through participation in the liturgy that the Directory speaks against what it calls a "presumed neutrality between method and content." In this context the document identifies what it calls "the method of liturgical and ecclesial signs" and calls this "a process of transmission which is adequate to the nature of the message."[325] What does this mean? I think it means that the nature of the message is that it is more than a message. "Liturgical and ecclesial signs" accomplish what they signify, and they signify our participation in trinitarian life. Thus these signs are a process of

---

[323] See, for example, nn. 51, 71, 85, 87, 117, 174, 227.
[324] N. 51. See also n. 159.
[325] N. 149.

transmission adequate — and it takes something huge like the liturgy to be adequate to this! — to the nature of the Christian mysteries.

Some specific considerations of methodology and approach are discussed within this larger frame of liturgy as catechesis. One example would be the reflections on the role of memorization in catechesis. Memorizing something risks being a mechanical and impersonal process, but conceiving the liturgical role of memorization aids in overcoming this. The Church has a memory, and this memory is maintained, among other ways, in "the major formulae... of the liturgy..." Some of these can be memorized — or even without people realizing it, become memorized through constant repetition. Such a personally acquired capacity to recite such "syntheses" of the faith increases the interior capacity for participation. In this regard the *Directory* suggestively draws our attention to understanding memorization within the ancient liturgical context of the *traditio* and the *redditio:* "the handing on of the faith in catechesis *(traditio)* corresponds to the response of the subject during the catechetical journey and subsequently in life *(redditio)*." This pattern, rooted in an ancient liturgy of the catechumenate, can be extended to any consideration of memorization. The *Directory* draws this conclusion: "This process encourages a greater participation in the received truth. That personal response is correct and mature which fully respects the datum of faith and shows an understanding of the language used to express it *(biblical, liturgical, doctrinal)*." [326]

It is also possible to encounter the *Directory's* idea about liturgy itself as catechesis coming from the other direction as well, that is, in the context of concrete consideration of a particular kind of catechetical setting. For example, "When given in the context of the Catholic school, religious instruction is part of and completed by other forms of the ministry of the word (catechesis, homilies, liturgical celebration, etc.) It is indispensable to their pedagogical function and the basis for their existence." [327] The wording here is useful for making the point:

---

[326] Nn. 154, 155.
[327] N. 74.

instruction is "part of and completed by" something larger, a something larger which includes liturgical celebration, a something larger which is ultimately ecclesial life.

A measure of how deeply the experience of liturgy is considered to contribute to the profound formation of those who celebrate it is found in the *Directory's* discussion of liturgy among what it calls "the forms most apt to inculturate the faith." About inculturation it says, "A privileged means of this is liturgical catechesis with its richness of signs in expressing the Gospel message and its accessibility to so great a part of the people of God. The Sunday homily, the content of the Lectionary and the structure of the liturgical year should be valued afresh..." [328]

Developing just briefly only this last point, think for a moment about the catechetical possibilities in a greater attention to the liturgical year. (Such a consideration can serve as an emblem that summarizes all that has been said in this second major part about liturgy as catechesis.) The liturgical year is a reality larger than the catechetical task of the Church. Its round of seasons and feasts is nothing less than the whole history and mystery of Christ delivered to the Christian people in the "today" of their lives in which the feasts and seasons intervene. To live this year, to live the "today" of any feast, is itself already hugely instructive. It is a catechesis in its own right. Catechesis — using the term more strictly now — would want to build on this and return those instructed to ever deeper and more personal participation in the feasts.

Here we see the point at which liturgy as catechesis and catechesis about the liturgy touch each other and overlap. But we can relate this as well to what was established in the first part of this presentation about the foundation role of the liturgy in ecclesial life. We are in position now to make three interrelated claims. (1) Liturgy is foundational to the content to be delivered in catechesis. (2) Its celebration is itself instructive. (3) For these very reasons catechesis about the liturgy is nothing less than one of the basic tasks of the entire catechetical enterprise.

---

[328] N. 207.

3. *The Liturgical Face of the Catechetical Task*

In the third part of this chapter I would like to apply some of these basic positions about the foundational role of the liturgy to specific dimensions of catechesis, hoping thereby to demonstrate the usefulness of considering the liturgical face of the catechetical task.

From the point of view of theological interest, one of the most suggestive sections of the *Directory* is that which considers the "criteria for the presentation of the message." (Numbers 97-118) The way to this discussion is prepared very carefully in the preceding paragraphs. The general context is the word of God as *the* source of catechesis, by which it means not only the Scripture but also Tradition together with the Magisterium, as classically defined for our times by *Dei Verbum*. Listing a number of different contexts where this full sense of the word of God is encountered, the Sacred Liturgy is, of course, mentioned.[329] In this section if the word of God is considered as *the* source, other sources of the message derive from this, among which are included "liturgical texts." [330] These sources are said to do nothing less than express the word of God and to provide catechesis with those criteria for the transmission of its message.[331] It is these criteria that I find so stimulating for considering the catechetical task.

At the top of the list — and certainly because they are the most important — are christocentricity and the trinitarian dimension into which this unfolds. No one can read the *General Directory for Catechesis*, much less *The Catechism of the Catholic Church*, without being firmly impressed by the clarity with which christocentricity in its trinitarian dimensions defines the very core of our Catholic faith.[332] This is clearly the central content that catechesis must deliver. And yet put like that to the average catechist it can seem a daunting if not impossible task. If the

---

[329] Nn. 94, 95.

[330] Note: it is not the liturgy itself which derives from this but liturgical texts. The liturgy itself is the place where the word of God "is constantly proclaimed, heard, interiorized and explained." N. 95.

[331] N. 96.

[332] N. 99 citing *The Catechism of the Catholic Church*, n. 234: "The mystery of the Most Holy Trinity is the central mystery of Christian faith and life."

catechist considers the mystery of the Trinity as a content to
be somehow explained, one might well despair, claiming that it
is beyond one's capacities. However, if one looks at it as a
dimension of the liturgy to be opened up and unfolded, then
possibly the task might be more calmly considered.

Let me explain how this might work, focusing on what is our
most intense encounter with the mystery of faith, the celebration
of the eucharist.[333] This is, after all, a familiar experience. And if
there is any truth at all in the contention that participation in the
liturgy is already a kind of catechesis, it means that we have
something to build on, something constantly to refer to. In this
way we can gain a much more concrete sense of terms which
may otherwise seem abstract — christocentricity, trinitarian
dimension — by considering at depth the thoroughgoing
christocentric and trinitarian shape of the eucharistic rite. First
I will gather a few key remarks from what the *Directory* says
about these two criteria, and then I will indicate how the rite
helps us to consider these more concretely.

Concerning christocentricity, we read that "at the heart of
catechesis we find, in essence, a person, the Person of Jesus of
Nazareth, the only Son of the Father, full of grace and truth."[334]
This says in christological terms what I stressed in the first part
of this chapter; namely, that Christianity is not fundamentally a
message but an encounter with a reality, here the reality of Jesus
Christ. Being sensitive to the Beatitudes or the rest of the ethical
message of Jesus in the Sermon on the Mount does not constitute
Christian faith. Belief in the resurrection constitutes it, a belief
which yields an encounter with his person. Thus, catechesis
"promotes the following of Jesus and communion with him; every
element of the message tends to this... all that is transmitted by
catechesis is the teaching of Jesus Christ, the truth that he
communicates, or more precisely, the Truth that he is."[335] The
fundamental issue here is communion with Jesus, with the Truth

---

[333] Cf. *The Catechism of the Catholic Church*, 1327, quoting St. Irenaeus:
"In brief, the eucharist is the sum and summary of our faith: 'Our way of
thinking is attuned to the eucharist, and the eucharist in turn confirms our
way of thinking.'"

[334] N. 98, citing *Catechesi Tradendae* 5.

[335] N. 98, citing *Catechesi Tradendae* 6.

— not conceived as a message to be mastered — with the Truth that he himself is. I will indicate in a moment how the eucharistic rite intends precisely this communion with Jesus, but first let us gather several key ideas from what the *Directory* says about the trinitarian dimensions of this christocentricity.

"The christocentricity of catechesis, in order of its internal dynamic, leads to confession of faith in God, Father, Son and Holy Spirit... [In] the internal structure of catechesis... every mode of presentation must always be christocentric-trinitarian: 'Through Christ to the Father in the Holy Spirit...' Following the pedagogy of Jesus in revelation of the Father, of himself as the Son, and of the Holy Spirit, catechesis shows the most intimate life of God..."[336] This is wonderful, of course, at least to theologians who like to talk like this. But what is to keep this from seeming a hopelessly abstract way of conceiving catechesis? Furthermore, this trinitarian dimension is said to have "vital implications for the lives of human beings," "immense" in their scope. "It... implies that humanity, made in the image and likeness of God who is a 'communion of persons,' is called to be a fraternal society, comprised of sons and daughters of the same Father, and equal in personal dignity... The Church [is] 'a people gathered together in the unity of the Father, Son and Holy Spirit.'"[337] This is saying an awful lot, and those involved in catechesis must simply grapple with it. It will not do to pass on to something more easily understood, for the *Directory* considers these thoughts nothing less than the criteria by which an adequate catechesis is to be measured. My suggestion is that attention to the ecclesial celebration of the eucharist, so common a dimension of our experience together, can offer considerable guidance in rendering these criteria more concrete.

Here I can offer only a few suggestions in this regard, but it is worth remembering that the eucharist is a treasure in which an infinite wealth is hidden. Therefore, it can continually be mined for direction in considering these criteria. The phrase already cited is again relevant: "the constant nourishment of the Body and Blood of Christ."[338] If here I take but one pass at the mystery,

---

[336] Nn. 99, 100.
[337] N. 100.
[338] N. 70.

it must be remembered that we all pass it again and again. This constant nourishment provides, among other things, directions for catechesis.

Put in summary fashion, it could be said that the eucharist establishes believers in communion with Jesus (the christological dimension). Such communion unfolds as communion with the one whom he calls Father, and this is both accomplished and grasped in the power of the Holy Spirit (the trinitarian dimension). Entering into this communion *is* the Church, "a people gathered together in the unity of the Father, Son and Holy Spirit" (the ecclesial dimension). In what follows I will look at four different parts of the rite, attempting to discern there these christocentric, trinitarian, and indeed ecclesial dimensions. These four are the liturgy of the word, the bringing of the gifts to the altar, the transformation of the gifts, and the communion.[339]

In the liturgy of the word the Scriptures are read in a certain order, an order that follows the order of salvation history; that is, the liturgy begins with a text from the Old Testament and moves toward the climax of the proclamation of the Gospel. The Gospel is the christocentric climax of all the Scriptures. The history of Israel — and so of the world — is understood only with Christ at its center. So, Jesus may be said to be a new center of the history of Israel, but his own life itself has a center; namely, his life-giving death and resurrection. Any given liturgy of the word must be understood in the context of its position within the liturgical year. Thus, the most complete example of it and indeed its central climax is the long liturgy of the word at the Easter Vigil. Seven long readings of the Old Testament climax in the Gospel which announces Christ risen. Any other readings in the course of the year are meant to be understood as leading to or deriving from this christological and historical center.

So much for the structure. But a theological understanding of what is actually happening when the word is proclaimed in a believing assembly can suggest much about the catechetical task. Every proclamation of the word in the liturgy is a moment irreducibly new: the event of Christ — and all the events of

---

[339] Here I condense and transpose into a catechetical key what I developed at greater length above in chapter 6.

Scripture are the event of Christ, for he is their center — becomes the event of a particular assembly that here and now hears this word. The word proclaimed in liturgy is not some pale reflection or residue of the event proclaimed there. It is the whole reality to which the words bear testimony made present. In this way the person of Jesus of Nazareth is met. What he said and what he did at one moment in history he now does again in the "today" of the assembly that gathers round his word, for he is risen and so brings from his past to our present all that he accomplished in that past. This is Truth: not a message, but a divine person. Everything centers on him.

Meeting Christ and entering into communion with him is an astonishingly concrete experience. He may be invisible — that is part of being risen and glorified — but this does not mean that he is some sort of vague free floating version of divinity to be defined variously by whoever might wish to claim him. Christ has done something on this earth, and he wishes to associate all his disciples with this work. He has offered his body on the cross for the redemption of the world and as a perfect act of obedience and adoration of his Father. It is profound association with his Paschal sacrifice that is accomplished in what follows in the eucharistic rite, and by entering into this sacrifice the trinitarian dimensions of the divine life are unveiled. But note: we still are remaining very christocentric, indeed very historical. The rite is fundamentally a memorial that points to the utterly concrete action of his death. It is there that the Trinity is to be revealed.

Our association with Christ in his sacrifice is revealed by the action of bringing gifts of bread and wine to the altar. The significance of these gifts should be dwelt on in catechesis. These are not purely natural symbols, as is, say, water in baptism. They are the fruits of creation combined with human history, the fruits of nature combined with human ingenuity. That is, they represent our whole lives. And the faithful who bring the gifts are doing a priestly work, representing the whole created order and representing the whole of humanity in its history. So creation and humanity are placed in the hands of Christ when these gifts are presented to the bishop or to one whom he has ordained. Still, in one sense the gift is a poor one if with them we would offer a suitable and worthy thanksgiving to the Father. Nonetheless, it is precisely in this condition of poverty before God that Christ comes to meet us and reveal his solidarity with us in this poverty.

Christ takes our gifts into his hands and in the course of the eucharistic prayer transforms them into his very body and blood, transforms them into his Paschal sacrifice. Our attention should be directed here to the very stuff, to the material out of which an event of Revelation is made to occur in our midst. God's Word to us, his Revelation, is Jesus Christ, and not just vaguely Jesus Christ but Jesus Christ above all in the action of his Paschal Mystery.[340] And this Word is articulated to us in the syllables and words and phrases of bread and wine transformed. They become a language. The name of this language is flesh. They become the Word made flesh. Thereby the whole cosmos and the whole of history are rendered capable of something which by definition would be impossible to them. They are rendered capable of being God's adequate expression of himself. More: they are rendered capable of being an offering to God the Father, of being the thanksgiving and adoration that Christ's very sacrifice on the cross was and is.

The transformation of the gifts reveals and actualizes God's intentions for the world, and we can understand this in the terms provided by *Dei Verbum;* namely, participation in the divine nature which gives access to the Father, through the Son, in the Spirit.[341] In every celebration there is a radical twofold movement, of the Father toward the world, of the world toward the Father.[342] In the first direction, the Father gives himself through the Son in the Holy Spirit. It is necessary to pause and to try carefully to grasp the depth and mystery of what this means. Without attention to this dimension of the eucharist, such trinitarian formulations are perhaps just pious and habitually uttered phrases. Yet what we are dealing with here is the form, the dynamic, the very shape of Revelation; namely, that the Father gives himself *by* giving his Son. This is "the Father who so loved the world that he gave his only Son." (John 3:16) But there is more. The shape of the liturgy here — with its dimension of

---

[340] Cf. *Dei Verbum* 4.

[341] *Dei Verbum* 2.

[342] On this see J. CORBON, *The Wellspring of Worship,* 94-97.

memorial and invocation of the Holy Spirit — reveals that the Father gives his Son in and by the Spirit who is Spirit of the Father; and the Father gives his Spirit an assignment, as it were; namely, to effect and illumine and clarify and arrange everything in such a way that the Son be known and that all who believe in him might live their lives entirely from the Son's life.[343] It is this precise trinitarian form that the transformation of the gifts reveals, that is, not merely or vaguely that the Father gives himself to the world; but concretely and specifically that the Father gives himself to the world in the giving of his Son, a Son at every moment accompanied by the action and work of the Holy Spirit.

An opposite direction also forms part of the radical movement of every liturgy; namely, that of the world toward the Father. This too has a trinitarian and ecclesial shape within which it must be described. The eucharistic action at the time of the transformation of the gifts reveals this shape. When the Father places his Son into the hands of the Church, he does so in order that the Church may do something with this gift; namely, offer it as its own back to the Father. Or the same mystery can be described from a different angle. When the Word assumes our flesh, he does so in order that he may offer it to the Father as what he is and has always been.

All this is accomplished in the Holy Spirit. The Spirit who molded a body for the Word in the womb of the virgin Mary, the Spirit who raised the body of Jesus from the dead — this same Spirit now fills the gifts which the Church has brought and makes them to be one same thing: the body formed from Mary's body, the body raised from the dead.[344] And this is not some static body. It is the body crucified and risen which, standing at the right hand of the Father, forever offers itself to him in an hour which does not pass away. In the Spirit death disappears, and the body of Christ, formed from the whole cosmos and the whole of history,

---

[343] On this particular formulation of the Spirit's role, see H. URS VON BALTHASAR, "The Word, Scripture, and Tradition," 11-12.

[344] Cf. Rom 8:11: "If the Spirit of him who raised Jesus from the dead dwells in you, then he who raised Christ from the dead will bring your mortal bodies to life also, through his Spirit dwelling in you."

rises alive from the tomb and passes over to the right hand of the Father.

To return for a moment to the language of the *Directory:* we read that "[in] the internal structure of catechesis... every mode of presentation must always be christocentric-trinitarian: through Christ to the Father in the Holy Spirit."[345] Understanding this moment of the eucharistic prayer is perhaps the most concrete instance of the christocentric-trinitarian pattern that the Church knows. At the end of the eucharistic prayer, the bishop or the priest lifts the signs that represent the cosmos and history, but these signs have been transformed into the body and blood of Christ's sacrifice. Through Christ all this is presented to the Father in the Holy Spirit.

This is the place, this is the moment, this is the shape in which the Church knows God as Trinity, here where, centered on Christ and in communion with him, she turns in the power of the Holy Spirit and says with her whole being, together with Spirit and Son, "Our Father!" to the source from which not only the creation comes but even the being of the Son and the Spirit. To eat the body of the Lord and to drink his blood is, as the third eucharistic prayer has it, to "be filled with his Holy Spirit, and become one body, one spirit in Christ." It is to be placed into the same relationship with the Father that the Son has had with him from all eternity. "Just as I have life because of the Father, so the one who feeds on me will have life because of me." (John 6:57)

At the beginning of this chapter I quoted the *Directory's* introduction, where it said that "... it is urgent that an authentic ecclesiology of communion be promoted and deepened in order to arouse in Christians a deep ecclesial spirituality."[346] Here in the eucharist this ecclesiology of communion is established. The reception of communion is not merely the coincidental juxtaposition of so many individual believers, each of whom is sacramentally united with the Lord in his body and blood. It is all those individuals being constituted as one body and as one body — *only* as one body! — united with the body's head, Christ, and animated by the one Spirit who has raised this body, the Church,

---

[345] N. 100.
[346] N. 28.

from the dead. In this oneness which is accomplished by the reception of communion by all and in the sign which is thus made, we can then see in the Church the sign, the image, of the Holy Trinity, that is, many who are one, "a people gathered together in the unity of the Father, Son and Holy Spirit."

Arriving here at the Church conceived in its trinitarian dimensions, we have come full circle from where I began my remarks. I suggested at the outset that ecclesial life is a kind of frame that surrounds the catechetical effort and without which frame this effort cannot come into proper focus. This ecclesial frame is established in a preeminent way in liturgical celebrations, above all in the celebration of the eucharist. In the eucharist we have the form and the proportions in which an icon of the Holy Trinity is constructed, with Christ crucified and risen at its center, and the reality of the Church emerging from it as from an inexhaustible wellspring. It is the context for catechesis. It is its text. It is its goal and source.

Chapter 10

PREACHING IN THE CONTEXT OF THE EUCHARIST: A PATRISTIC PERSPECTIVE

Introduction

In this chapter I would like to reflect on the opportunities that liturgical preaching provides for sharing the theological contents that have been the major subject of this book to this point. I find special inspiration in the tradition of patristic preaching. The earliest testimony we have of preaching at the eucharist is from the Acts of the Apostles, and the account reports considerable excitement. "On the first day of the week when we gathered to break bread, Paul spoke to them because he was going to leave on the next day, and he kept on speaking until midnight. There were many lamps in the upstairs room where we were gathered, and a young man named Eutychus who was sitting on the window sill was sinking into a deep sleep as Paul talked on and on. Once overcome by sleep, he fell down from the third story and when he was picked up, he was dead." The rest is known. Paul brings him back to life, and then we read, "Then he returned upstairs, broke the bread, and ate; after a long conversation that lasted until daybreak, he departed." (Acts 20:7-12) There are lessons about preaching in this — for example, going on and on can kill a man — but I cite it not for that reason but more as a primitive account of the same topic I wish to address in this chapter; namely, that the celebration of the community's eucharist is both preceded and followed by talk. Here we will ask what kind of talk? What kind of preaching? [347]

Classic is the account of Justin Martyr at least a hundred years later, where he describes the practice of the community's

---

[347] The first answer to this is given, together with its context in Acts 2:42: "They devoted themselves to the teaching of the apostles and to the communal life, to the breaking of the bread and to the prayers."

Sunday eucharist. Describing the first part, he says, "On the day called Sunday all who live in cities or in the country gather together in one place, and the memoirs of the Apostles or the writings of the prophets are read, as long as time permits. Then when the reader has finished, the Ruler in a discourse instructs and exhorts to the imitation of these good things."[348] Then he goes on to describe the celebration of the eucharist. So, once again: eucharist with preaching. We are given only a small clue of the content of the preaching, though it is a suggestive one. The preacher gives an exhortation to imitate the "beautiful things" read in the Apostles and prophets. Certainly there is something here that all preaching must accomplish: the application of ancient texts to our own lives, an indication of how we might live today in conformity with the sacred texts that are read when the community assembles.

In the liturgical reforms stemming from Vatican II, we have been blessed with a new lectionary which over time exposes both the Sunday and weekday eucharistic assemblies to a wide range of scriptural texts. And through all sorts of insistence and training, it seems that most of the bishops, priests, and deacons who preach at these eucharistic celebrations feel themselves responsible for exposing the meaning of the scriptural texts read. This is certainly a gain and one of the fruits of the reform: more Scripture for the Catholic people and more preaching about Scripture.

Nonetheless, few preachers, it seems, have learned to make any sort of connection between the Scriptures on which they are preaching and the eucharist which the community is about to celebrate. Furthermore, concentrating preaching on the Scriptures is usually done to the loss of much preaching of doctrine, doctrine on the eucharist or doctrine of any sort. Indeed, some ways of preaching Scripture have just turned out to be exegetical lectures, a treatment of the sacred text that can raise all sorts of doubts and problems about doctrine for those without theological training, that is, for the majority of those to whom preaching is addressed.

---

[348] Justin Martyr, *Apology* I, 67. PG 6, 429B-C. Translation by L.S. Barnard, *ACW*, 56, 71.

What can be done to improve this situation? That is, how can we preserve the gains of our more scripturally based preaching and at the same time make clearer the relation between the proclaimed Scriptures and the eucharist to be celebrated, between the Scriptures and the doctrines of the Church? I propose to offer suggestions by thinking through four basic areas. First, I will offer a theological description of the *foundations* for preaching. Second, I will try to describe a theological *framework* in which preaching can unfold. Thirdly, I will speak about specific theological *content* in preaching and finally, *style* and *tone*. In developing these I will be thinking about the eucharist. But there are at least two ways of doing this. "Preaching and the eucharist," suggests both preaching about the eucharist and preaching during the eucharist about other things. I will speak about both of these.

1. A Theological Description of the Foundations of Preaching

Even though Christian preaching relied on rabbinical and Hellenistic precedents, in its essence it is a new phenomenon in the ancient world. Its newness corresponds to the newness of the Christian message. In the same way that the Gospels are a new literary genre conformed to the need of professing faith by telling the story of Jesus, so Christian preaching becomes a new way of public speaking precisely because its message was altogether new: the incarnation of the Son of God, his death and his resurrection.[349]

Christian preaching derives from the Lord himself, more precisely, from his resurrection. "Go, therefore, and make disciples of all nations... teaching them to observe all that I have commanded you." (Matt 28:19-20) Making disciples, teaching what comes from the Lord — this is the task of preaching. Theologically this is important. Preaching is not the initiative of

---

[349] For the theological significance of the newness of the gospel genre, see R. LATOURELLE, "Gospel as Literary Genre," in *Dictionary of Fundamental Theology*, 368-371. The newness of Christian preaching is something that emerges again and again in the exhaustive study of patristic preaching by A. OLIVAR, *La predicación cristiana antigua*, Barcelona 1991. To my knowledge this is the best single work on patristic preaching.

the Church but of the risen Lord, who said in this same context, "And behold, I am with you always, until the end of the age." In Mark's gospel we are told that this presence of the risen Lord confirms preaching: "They went forth and preached everywhere, while the Lord worked with them and confirmed the word through accompanying signs."

This commission to preach, which the apostles received from the Lord, parallels the Lord's own receiving of his mission from the Father: the risen Lord says to his disciples, "As the Father has sent me, so I send you." (John 20:21) This "as" and "so" express a huge mystery; indeed, nothing less than an echo of the trinitarian mystery in which the Son comes forth from the Father. In that same way, from those same mysterious depths, the apostolic preacher comes forth from the risen Lord. Thus, the pattern according to which the Lord preached must become the pattern of every Christian preacher. Jesus expressed that pattern precisely: "My teaching is not my own but is from the one who sent me." (John 7:16)

Even so, there is a difference in kind between the preaching of Jesus and the preaching of the apostles. Jesus, though bearing testimony to the Father, also bears testimony to himself.[350] The apostles for their part bear testimony not to themselves but to Jesus. He indeed becomes the principal content of their preaching. Beginning with the preaching ascribed to Peter in the Acts of the Apostles, the texts of the Old Testament are referred to Jesus, to his death and resurrection. This use of the scriptural text in reference to the Lord's paschal mystery becomes the basis of all preaching. Explaining the text in this way becomes the preacher's task. The exegetical methods and the apologetic scope of the sermons of Peter and Paul in the Acts are followed up and developed by the Fathers. To understand why the Fathers preached the way they did, one must realize that they themselves saw what they were doing to be a continuation of the apostolic preaching. What will develop in patristic preaching is all based on decisions made in the apostolic preaching. Peter's sermon on Pentecost can summarize the method. To explain the

---

[350] Luke 4:21; John 3:11; 5:31-47; 8:14-18; 10:25; 15:26; 1 Tim 6:13; 1 John 5:7-8.

extraordinary things that had just happened, Peter begins by saying, "This is that which was spoken by the prophet Joel." (Acts 2:16)[351]

That this kind of preaching begins on Pentecost is no accident. If from one angle it can be said that Christian preaching derives from the risen Lord, from a different angle it can be said to be the fruit of Pentecost, the gift of the Spirit. A solid theological principle to employ in seeking to discern what the Spirit is doing in the Church is to remember what Paul himself learned from the Spirit: "No one can say, 'Jesus is Lord,' except by the Holy Spirit." (1 Cor 12:3) And further, "God sent the Spirit of his Son into our hearts, crying out, 'Abba, Father!'" (Gal 4:6) This defines the preacher's task: enabling the whole community and each individual believer to say with one's whole being, "Jesus is Lord," and to cry out "Abba, Father!" to God. This is a task of infinite proportions and inexhaustible wealth. To preach Christ is to preach, "the mystery of God," to preach the one, "in whom are hidden all the treasures of wisdom and knowledge." (Col 2:2-3) This infinite wealth begins to unfold in the Church in the patristic centuries. Preaching in our own times should be marked by continuity with this apostolic and patristic unfolding.

2. *A Theological Framework within which Preaching Unfolds*

Good preaching must derive from an awareness of what wonderful mysteries are taking place in the celebration of the liturgy. These wonders begin with the proclamation of the Word. The Word of God recalls the wonderful deeds of God in the history of salvation. But this is not a question of mere memory. Whenever it is proclaimed, the Word of God becomes a new communication of salvation for those who hear it. The event proclaimed becomes the event of the listening assembly, and ultimately all the events of Scripture are reducible to one event which encompasses them all; namely, Christ in the hour of his Paschal Mystery. The moment of listening to the Word — the Word which proclaims ultimately the Lord's death and

---

[351] The basic sermons are Acts 2:14-36; 3:12-26; 4:8-12; 5:29-32; 10:34-43; 13:16-41; 14:14-17; 17:22-31. Jesus himself set this pattern in Luke 4:16-22; 24:25-27; 44-47.

resurrection — becomes in the very hearing an event of salvation, nothing less than the same event which the words proclaim.

But that is not all, for in some mysterious sense the eucharistic liturgy echoes the pattern of the Word becoming flesh in the mystery of the Incarnation. The scriptural words proclaimed in the liturgy become sacrament; that is, the ritual actions and words performed around the community's gifts of bread and wine proclaim in their own way at an even deeper level the one and only event of salvation: the Lord's death and resurrection. And they proclaim that event as the very event of the community's celebration. The bread and cup are a "communion," as St. Paul says, in the body of Christ, in the blood of Christ. (1 Cor 10:16) That is, the bread and cup put the celebrating community into participatory relation with *the* event of salvation history, an hour which does not pass away.[352]

Preaching during the eucharist must speak of these things. The preacher must be capable of explaining them, proclaiming them, lifting the community's minds and hearts up toward them. The Scriptures must be expounded in this way, and not left at the

---

[352] For justification of the expression "an hour which does not pass away" as a way of describing the presence of the historical Paschal Mystery in every celebration of the liturgy, see *The Catechism of the Catholic Church*, n. 1085. What I have said in this paragraph condenses, I believe, some of the major issues in sacramental theology that various Fathers tried to confront. For example, in his mystagogical catechesis, Cyril of Jerusalem sees the sacraments as an ontological imitation of the events of salvation. See, for example, *Mystagogical Catechesis* III, 4-5, where he attempts both to distinguish and unite. Basing himself on Rom 6:5, he observes that Christ really died, but that in Baptism we have a death "like his." Nonetheless, the salvation for us is as real as his death. For more, see E. MAZZA, "Les raisons et la méthode des catècheses mystagogiques de la fin du quatrième siècle," in A.M. TRIACCA - A. PISTOIA (eds.), *La prédication liturgique et les commentaires de la liturgie*, Bibliotheca Ephemerides liturgicae. Subsidia 65, Rome 1992. 153-176. In his concluding remarks, Mazza says on 174, "Le but de cette méthode, dans sa totalité, est d'assurer un lien ontologique entre le rite et l'évenement du salut, et, en même temps, de garder la supériorité ontologique de celui-ci." The same emerges in Ambrose. See the fine study by G. FRANCESCONI, *Storia e simbolo*, Brescia 1981. On 25, he says, "... che la predicazione e la teologia di Ambrogio si fondino sulla convinzione di una profonda unità (pur attraverso modalità diverse) e quindi di una continuità tra la 'storia-di-salvezza' proclamata nella Scrittura e la esperienza liturgica della Chiesa."

level of an exegetical exercise which explains the text only in its original historical context. All the texts must be brought to the event that encompasses them: the Lord's death and resurrection. That through the eucharist about to be celebrated we have communion in the very same death and resurrection — this too must be proclaimed and explained.

The practice of biblical typology as developed by the Fathers is what enabled such a claim about the liturgy to emerge. No one can preach in this way without understanding the logic of that development. I think that logic is still valid today, and indeed necessary, but considerably under-employed. Let me try to outline its main features.[353]

Typology, as a biblical hermeneutic, is concerned with the ontological relationship of participation between the principle event of salvation history — the death and resurrection of Christ — and the prior announcements of that event. Ancient events are found to be speaking in their deepest sense of the Paschal Mystery. They already participate in it; they are part of the one and only story, the hour of Christ. So this is not a placing of the New Testament in priority over the Old, so much as a hermeneutical requirement that one be continually referred to the other. It is from this dynamic relationship that the mystery of the text emerges. These relationships are the subject of patristic preaching. In order to express them a technical vocabulary emerged, drawn from the New Testament itself. In the Latin tradition it is words like the following which express this dynamic between preceding announcements and definitive event: *mysterium, sacramentum, imago, similitudo, species, umbra, typus, figura.*[354] One of the most influential New Testament guides was in Paul's summary of the exodus events, where he concludes, "These

---

[353] There is, of course, a vast bibliography on this question. Here I can only summarize briefly, offering my own digestion of the material and referring to several works which will offer further bibliography.

[354] Francesconi's entire book on Ambrose, *Storia e simbolo*, is an examination of all this vocabulary and its tradition. For a useful summary of typology and its bearing on eucharist, see E. MAZZA, *The Celebration of the Eucharist, The Origin of the Rite and the Development of Its Interpretation*, translated by Matthew J. O'Connell, Collegeville 1999, XIII-XVII. Basic bibliography for the question is discussed in these pages.

things happened as types for us." (1 Cor 10:6; cf. 1 Cor 10:11) (In Greek, *tupos*, in Latin *exemplum*.) Also influential from the letter to the Hebrews was the phrase, "The law has only a shadow of the good things to come." (Heb 10:1; see also Col 2:17)[355]

What is significant for our purposes here is that this exegetical terminology was taken over and applied also to the liturgy. In the same way that there was something hidden in the biblical text (called, for example, the *mystery* of the text), so too there was something hidden in the liturgy, in the bread and the wine and the actions around them. For the same reason, then, these too were called mysteries, or sacraments, or figures. Something very profound is expressed in this transfer of terminology. It is not simply a question of seeing that interpretive tools in one field will also work in another. Rather, some deep relation is intuited between the biblical events attested to in Scripture and the signs and actions of the liturgy. A theology is achieved in the biblical text as a whole when read with the eyes of Christian faith and in a typological key. From this whole biblical world there emerge also symbols and ritual actions which correspond to the same theological understanding. Every type — biblical or liturgical — points to Christ in his Paschal Mystery; and so every type — biblical or liturgical — precisely because it is a type, ontologically participates in the one event which encompasses them all.

The Fathers were keen to strike a balance between identity and difference in their talk about these things. The mighty action of God in the concrete historical death of Christ is a unique reality which happened once and for all.[356] But in virtue of the resurrection, what happened once in one place is made available in every time and place through figures, sacraments, types. These correspond on the deepest ontological level to the central event; they are for that reason "communion" in that event. (Again, 1 Cor 10:16) We have thus a middle term between ourselves and the events of the Paschal Mystery. We have a *sacrament* between ourselves and that. A sacrament is a sacrament *of:* a sacrament of

---

[355] The exegetical procedures in the entire Letter to the Hebrews were influential in shaping and authorizing the patristic hermeneutic. Also strongly influential was the use of the word "allegory" in Gal 4:21-31.

[356] Rom 6:10; Heb 7:27; 9:12.

the Paschal Mystery. In preaching, explaining how events of the Old Testament are sacraments of Christ (or call them also figures, shadows, types) becomes the basis for explaining in preaching how bread and wine and the assembly that communes in these are also sacraments of Christ.[357]

The way I am putting this is perhaps complicated, or at least somewhat dense. But I am trying to offer here a theological understanding of preaching the eucharist and not merely a how-to-preach workshop. Nonetheless, once understood theologically, preaching these things is not as difficult as following the theological discussion as to why it works; for the sacraments or figures — biblical and liturgical — have their own power to work on the mind and heart. It is enough for the preacher to put them into relief, to draw the mysterious connections with confidence, to proclaim the presence of the Lord in the types which announce or figure him. Then the celebration takes care of the rest. The Scriptures and the symbols have been set free to work in the interior of the believers' minds and hearts.

3. *Specific Theological Content*

From this general framework of preaching it is possible to pass on to a consideration of the specific theological content of preaching. First of all, it is worth noting that what I have just described here — namely, the connecting of types, bringing every text toward Christ's Paschal Mystery, and doing the same with the symbols of the liturgy — is the original context in which sacramental theology was defined, refined, and practiced. This is different from the way sacramental theology is done in a speculative school or in learned writing. These latter are also

---

[357] For further discussion of this, see E. MAZZA, *The Celebration of the Eucharist. The Origin of the Rite and the Development of Its Interpretation,* tr. M. O'Connell, Collegeville 1999, 120. Mazza is speaking of the Latin tradition as represented in Tertullian. For the same as unfolding in the Alexandrian tradition, see B. STUDER, "Die doppelte Exegese bei Origenes," in *Mysterium Caritatis, Studien zur Exegese und zur Trinitätslehre in der Alten Kirche,* Roma 1999, 37-66. For useful summaries of Tertullian and Cyprian on these questions, see J.D. LAURANCE, *'Priest' as Type of Christ, The Leader of the Eucharist in Salvation History according to Cyprian of Carthage,* New York 1984, 63-72, 75-86.

necessary, but it cannot be what is conceived as needed when one speaks of preaching more doctrine.

Of course, sacramental theology is not the only kind of doctrine or teaching that needs to be the subject of preaching. The Fathers very often had heresy in mind when they were preaching, and their pastoral concern urged them to articulate correct doctrine in opposition to this. The golden age of patristic preaching was between Nicea and Chalcedon precisely because doctrine was known to be important and comes into most of the sermons. Again, this was not academic talk. The Fathers used the Scriptures and the celebration of the sacraments as an occasion to develop this or that necessary emphasis to oppose clearly some false idea.[358]

Our doctrinal situation and concerns cannot be reduced to those of the Fathers. Our eucharistic theology is more developed than that of the patristic age. So, if in part we rely on the Fathers for major clues, they are not sufficient.[359] But they are splendid models of how to preach doctrine in the very exposition of scriptural texts and in the explanation of the Scripture's relation to liturgical symbols. The most important doctrines remain the same through the ages and need to be approached again and again in preaching; namely, the divine and human natures of Christ and the mystery of the Trinity which Christ reveals in his Paschal Mystery. I am not suggesting that preachers ought simply to stand up and talk more about these things. Rather, I am claiming that these doctrines are the deepest sense of the Scriptures and that this deepest sense was discovered precisely when the Scriptures were proclaimed in the liturgical assembly

---

[358] For example, as A. Olivar notes, the obligatory proclamation of the divinity of Christ and of the Holy Spirit gave to patristic preaching a sublime tone, and did the same for the liturgy as well. A. OLIVAR, *La predicación cristiana antigua*, 966.

[359] F. Van der Meer makes a legitimate observation, clearly written from our perspective, on the eucharistic preaching of Augustine, for example, when he says, "It does not enter his [Augustine's] mind that under the forms of bread and wine the Lord, in his human nature, is, though hidden, directly present, that he can approach him and throw himself in adoration at his feet, and in the intimacy of that meeting overlook, indeed, ignore, the sacramental veil which hides the inwardness of the sacrament." *Augustine the Bishop*, New York 1961, 313.

and when the Scriptures became sacrament in the eucharistic rite. The preacher who understands this dynamic will be in a position to expound the Scriptures and the liturgy in such a way that these doctrines sink more and more deeply into the consciousness of the worshipping assembly.

Let me offer examples of two different possible approaches to the more doctrinally aware kind of preaching that I am proposing here. Both focus on the eucharist, not because this is the only topic of preaching but simply because I have concentrated the central point of this book around that theme. The first approach could be described as explicitly applying the Scriptures of the day to the eucharist about to be celebrated. Every Gospel passage of the liturgy is a special and unique door of entry into the eucharistic mystery. The preacher can bring the assembly to the eucharist precisely in the terms provided by the Gospel text, and, of course, in terms of the other texts which are there as supports of the Gospel. If we hear in the Gospel of a centurion who says to Jesus, "Lord, I am not worthy that you should come under my roof," (Matt 8:8) it is surely not too difficult to see that the eucharist is a *figure* of this same encounter, a *sacrament* of it, a *type* of it, and that *we* can just as well say in the course of the coming celebration, "Lord, I am not worthy that you should come under my roof."

Peter Chrysologus was a master of this kind of preaching. The banquet given for the Prodigal Son's return is the eucharist about to be celebrated.[360] Jesus dining in the house of a Pharisee is occasion for Chrysologus to pass from that scene (the Jewish people) to the Gentiles, whom Christ feeds with his "heavenly flesh."[361] In explaining Jesus' words, "Don't worry about what you are to eat or drink," (Matt 6:31) Chrysologus launches into a summary of the whole of salvation history conceived as the preparation of the food and drink of the eucharistic table spread for the Church every day.[362] The woman who only wants to touch the hem of Christ's garment (Matt 9:20) is an example of the reverence with which one ought to approach Christ in the

---

[360] Sermon 5:6.
[361] Sermon 95:3.
[362] Sermon 71:8.

eucharist.[363] In a very natural use of typology which knows how to connect one part of the Scripture with another and bring it all to the Paschal Mystery, Chrysologus comments on Jesus' words, "I am the bread come down from heaven." (John 6:51) He says, "He is the bread that was sown in the virgin, leavened in the flesh, readied in the passion, baked in the oven of the tomb, seasoned in the churches, and given over every day as heavenly food to the faithful."[364]

The examples from the whole patristic tradition are innumerable. Ambrose finds many Old Testament types of the eucharist.[365] When any of these texts is proclaimed in the liturgy of the day, they can be led to the eucharist, which is to say, they can be explained in terms of the Lord's death and resurrection. I think virtually every Sunday homily should make this connection, not necessarily at length, but Sunday after Sunday. This is not the context to offer more examples, but I do think the hermeneutical key can be summarized briefly and simply. Certainly, a skill with the Scriptures is required for this, but the Christian people have the right to expect such skill from their preachers. The key could be expressed like this: the climax of each of the four Gospels is the death and resurrection of Christ. Everything else in the Gospel is connected to that. The preacher finds that connection in the passage at hand and exposes it. Then its terms and images are used as a means of understanding the memorial of the Lord's death that is about to be celebrated.

A second kind of approach, different from this, is actual eucharistic mystagogy, that is, an explanation of the eucharist as subject of preaching.[366] I can mention here only some of the features of this rich tradition which seem to be relevant to us in

---

[363] Sermon 34:3.

[364] Sermon 67:7. *CCL* 24A, 404-405. Translation mine.

[365] This list come from G. Francesconi, *Storia e simbolo*, 311-312. Types of the eucharist from the Old Testament include the bread and wine offered by Melchizedek; the paschal lamb; manna; water from the rock; the showbread; the flour replenished by Elijah; Wisdom's banquet; many festive meals as in Cant 5:1-2, Pss 22; 42:4; 33:9; 103:15; Joseph's meal with his brothers; the ancient sacrifices; the meal offered by Abraham to his guests.

[366] Mazza, in his extensive study of this kind of preaching, notes that it was not really a very widespread phenomenon. See E. Mazza, "Les raisons et la méthode," 153. Nonetheless, it needs to be done.

our own day. Mystagogy in the strict sense is preaching to the newly baptized, explaining to them after the experience of baptism, confirmation, and first eucharist the meaning of these rites. Five steps can be discerned in this kind of preaching: (1) a description of the rite, (2) citation of Scripture of which the rite is an imitation, (3) theological explanation, (4) coming back again to the rite after the Scripture and theological explanation, (5) elaboration of sacramental terminology: mystery, sacrament, figure, image, symbol, image-truth, type-antitype, resemblance, and so forth.[367] Basically what is happening in mystagogy is an application of the biblical event to the event of the rite.[368]

Mystagogy in an extended sense would be continuing to explain these rites to those who have long been baptized. For our purposes, it would mean preaching on the meaning of the rites and words of the eucharistic celebration. It should first be noticed how scriptural is this kind of preaching. It is not a scholastic explanation of eucharistic doctrine, but rather a connecting of the rite to its biblical images and building up doctrine from that. Of course, scholastic doctrine can guide the preacher in this task, ensuring correct interpretation.

One of the especially effective features of mystagogical preaching is that it deals directly with the tension between the visible and invisible in the ritual celebration. Something is seen, but it points to an invisible working of the divine Spirit. This is the most common use of the word *mystery* for the sacraments. The *mystery* of the eucharist is what the bread and wine and euchology and action of the assembly all point to. Bread and wine and an assembly are seen, but the *mystery* is that all these figures, all these "sacraments," effect a "communion" of the assembly in the death and resurrection of the Lord. "Let us proclaim the Mystery of Faith," that is, "When we eat this bread and drink this cup [visible actions], we proclaim the death of the Lord until he comes [the invisible mystery]."

---

[367] E. MAZZA, "Les raisons et la méthode," 156, 172. For a more extended discussion, see E. MAZZA, *Mystagogy, A Theology of Liturgy in the Patristic Age*, translated by Matthew J. O'Connell, New York 1989.

[368] E. MAZZA, "Les raisons et la méthode," 162: "Pour conclure: on s'aperçoit que la théologie du rite n'est rien d'autre que la théologie de l'évenement biblique appliquée au rite."

In their mystagogical preaching on the eucharist both Ambrose and Theodore of Mopsuestia give us examples of dealing directly with the question of eucharistic consecration. "How is it," they ask and answer, "that the bread and wine become the body and blood of Christ?" [369] These are fair questions. No one can celebrate the eucharist without eventually wondering about this. The assembly has the right and the need to hear preaching on these kinds of questions. There is not time here to follow the arguments of Ambrose and Theodore in this regard; and in any case, though what they say is certainly a contribution to the question, they are not entirely satisfying. [370] My point is simply that the question needs to be taken on directly in preaching and that there is precedent for it.

Explanation of the eucharist in preaching should certainly not be limited to clarification of the consecration. This is a Western tendency, traceable to the influence of Ambrose. Cyril of Jerusalem shows another method. [371] In his second mystagogy on the eucharist he moves step by step through the anaphora. Again, my suggestion here is not that a preacher simply say what Cyril said. I only mean to draw attention to a promising method. This would be a splendid opportunity to teach about the Trinity. One could comment on the prayer addressed to the Father through Christ in the Spirit. One could speak of epiclesis in relation to

---

[369] See AMBROSE, *On the Sacraments*, IV, 13-14, 21-24. THEODORE, *Homily* 16, 12.

[370] Ambrose concentrates everything on the power of the words of Christ spoken by the priest. This has been too restrictive in the West, as if in itself it explained all that needs explaining. Theodore at least explains the work of the Holy Spirit in the consecration. This certainly needs more emphasis in our own preaching. Theodore parallels the Spirit raising Christ from the dead and the Spirit transforming bread and wine. This is a tremendous theological reality that should be opened up for the Christian people. Augustine, in his sermons to the newly baptized, also attempts to explain how bread can be the body of Christ and wine his blood. See especially Sermons 229, 272.

[371] For our purposes here there is no need to solve the controversy over the disputed authorship of "Cyril's" mystagogical homilies. For a recent discussion summarizing the *status questionis*, see, K.J. BURRESON, "The Anaphora of the Mystagogical Catecheses of Cyril of Jerusalem," in P. BRADSHAW (ed.), *Essays on Early Eastern Eucharistic Prayers*, Collegeville 1997, 131-151, here 131-133. For a convenient edition of Cyril's works, see F.L. CROSS, *St. Cyril of Jerusalem's Lectures on the Sacraments*, Crestwood 1977.

consecration and thus discourse on the intimate relation between the mission of the Son and that of the Spirit. In fact, the language of the various anaphoras is deeply scriptural. The images and phrases of the eucharistic prayers in use in the Roman rite are by now very familiar to the people. And so it would not be too difficult to take some image or phrase, expose its biblical background, and then clarify its effect in the eucharistic prayer. Again, this requires knowledge and skill on the part of the preacher, but we would not be wrong to expect precisely that from those who preach. Certainly one of the contributions of a Society for Catholic Liturgy could be to identify the need for such skills and promote their acquisition.

A model exercise in developing such a capacity to preach is offered in E. Mazza's study of the influence of second century Paschal homilies on the formation of the text of the eucharistic anaphora found in the *Apostolic Tradition of Hippolytus*.[372] He shows how the typological preaching employed in Paschal homilies developed into stock phrases and key concepts that appear again in the anaphora. The preaching prepares for the anaphora and supports its sense. All of the eucharistic prayers used in the Roman rite would be susceptible to such study, yielding much concrete material for preaching.[373]

In our day it is said that Catholics no longer understand the eucharist correctly. Probably so, but, of course, there is no generation in which the eucharist is understood adequately. If a pastor perceives the community's understanding to be weak, incorrect, capable of expansion in this or that direction, then

---

[372] E. MAZZA, *The Origins of the Eucharistic Prayer*, translated by Roland E. Lane, Collegeville 1995, 98-176. Mazza's thesis has not won universal acceptance among scholars. Nonetheless, his extended examination of the language of the homilies and of the anaphora offers a deep exposure to the interface between biblical, homiletical and euchological language. For cautions about Mazza's thesis, see P. BRADSHAW, "Introduction," in P. BRADSHAW (ed.), *Essays on Early Eastern Eucharistic Prayers*, Collegeville 1997, 10-14. Also see, V. RAFFA, *Liturgia eucaristica, mistagogia della Messa: dalla storia e dalla teologia alla pastorale pratica*, Bibliotheca Ephemerides liturgicae. Subsidia 100, Rome 1998, 512-523.

[373] For a study of the prayers in use in the Roman rite, see E. MAZZA, *The Eucharistic Prayers of the Roman Rite*, translated by Matthew J. O'Connell, New York 1986.

those concerns should find their way into preaching. I have spoken about some of the broad theological frameworks within which particular concerns can be dealt with. Elucidating the difference between invisible and visible, explaining the consecration, commenting on various parts of the eucharistic prayer, urging and teaching concrete ways of receiving the eucharist with reverence and awe [374] — surely, Catholics would grow to understand the eucharist "correctly" in our generation if these were more often the subject of preaching.

What we should be concerned about in the eucharistic understanding of the Catholic people cuts in different directions. I am troubled, for example, by often strident opposition from some quarters to any talk or emphasis about the importance of the eucharistic assembly. It is as if any emphasis on the assembly would necessarily be had to the detriment of our reverence for Christ present in the eucharistic species. Of course, that is an unacceptable outcome, and there should be preaching which prevents such an outcome. On the other hand, not to speak of what happens to the assembly through the eucharistic celebration — namely, that it is transformed itself into the body of Christ — would be to foreshorten a full Catholic understanding of the eucharist. [375] Indeed, I would suggest that insufficient understanding of this dimension is one of the saddest deficiencies in current Catholic understanding of the eucharist. The way in which St. Augustine speaks of this theme can give us the measure of what we have lost, as well an indicate a way of recovery: "So, if you want to understand the body of Christ, listen to the apostle telling the faithful, *You, though, are the body of Christ and its members* (1 Cor 12:27). So if it's you that are the body of Christ and its members, it's the mystery meaning you that has been placed on the Lord's table; what you receive is the mystery that means you." [376] Or, "So receive the sacrament in such a way that

---

[374] I did not speak of this last point above, but this is also traditionally done in mystagogical preaching. See CYRIL OF JERUSALEM, *Mystagogy* 5, 21-22.

[375] Helpful for understanding the process of a shift in language and so of theological perception on this question is the classic study by H. DE LUBAC, *Corpus Mysticum, l'eucharistie et l'église au moyen âge*, Paris 1949.

[376] AUGUSTINE, *Sermon* 272, PL 38, 1247. English translation from *The Works of Saint Augustine, Sermons III/7 (230-272B) on the Liturgical Seasons, translations and notes*, Edmund Hill, O.P., New Rochelle 1993, 300.

you think about yourselves, that you retain unity in your hearts, that you always fix your hearts up above." [377] Or, "This sacrament, after all, doesn't present you with the body of Christ in such a way as to divide you from it. This, as the apostle reminds us, was foretold in holy scripture: *they shall be two in one flesh* (Gn 2:24). *This*, he says, *is a great sacrament; but I mean in Christ and in the Church* (Eph 5:31-32). And in another place he says about this eucharist itself, *We, though many, are one loaf, one body* (1 Cor 10:17). So you are beginning to receive what you have also begun to be, provided you do not receive unworthily..." [378] "What you receive is what you yourselves are, thanks to the grace by which you have been redeemed; you add your signature to this, when you answer *Amen*. What you see here is the sacrament of unity." [379]

4. *Style and Tone*

I must at least name it here and treat briefly another important question, lest it be lost: the question of style and tone in preaching at the eucharist. What is believed about the eucharist by the Church logically requires a certain style and tone for preaching in that context. It can be achieved in many ways. Again, I am not offering a how-to workshop on preaching. I want instead to indicate in theological terms what is required.

First of all, there is a dimension of the ineffable in the liturgy, which should somehow be reflected also in preaching. It is not possible to say all, and no preacher should pretend to have done so. Indeed, the very opposite impression should be created. Preaching should lead the assembly into a sense of an ever expanding mystery, an encounter with the mystery that is, at least in part, met with silence; an encounter that is greeted not so much with words as with the upcoming ritual gestures reverently performed. I like the suggestive description of a

---

[377] AUGUSTINE, *Sermon 227*, PL 38, 1100. English, E. Hill, *Sermons* III/6 (184-229Z), 255.

[378] AUGUSTINE, *Sermon 228B*. *MA* [= *Miscellanea Agostiniana*] 1, 18-20. English, E. Hill, *Sermons* III/6 (184-229Z), 262.

[379] AUGUSTINE, *Sermon 229A: 1. MA* I, 462-464 or *PLS* 2, 554-556. English, E. Hill, *Sermons* III/6 (184-229Z), 270.

scholar of Ambrose's mystagogy, when he describes Ambrose's language as speaking prophetically of prophetic realities, imaginatively of imaginative realities, heroically of heroic realities, poetically of poetic realities, and mysteriously of mysterious realities.[380] This style characterizes the realities of Scripture and liturgy, which correspond so deeply to each other. They are prophetic, imaginative, mysterious. Their correspondence is the same. The language that names them must move in the same stream.

This is not simply a question of rhetorical skill. The history of preaching shows that rhetoric and eloquence can be employed either to the benefit or the detriment of preaching. What seems to make the crucial difference is the spiritual experience itself of the preacher. The secret of good preaching lies ultimately in the secret life of the preacher with Christ and the way in which the very task of preaching conforms him to the mystery of the cross. St. Paul set down a perennially valid pattern when he reflected on his own experience of preaching to the Corinthians. (1 Cor 1:18-4:13) When he came among them to proclaim "the mystery of God," he resolved not to come with "sublimity of words," but with his own "weakness and fear and trembling" as the frame and support of his message which was itself the "weakness and foolishness of the cross."

Origen, who learned so much from Paul and extended in detail what Paul had begun both exegetically and spiritually,[381] felt his own weakness keenly and preached first to and for himself. He confesses his own sins before his listeners.[382] Origen is so spiritual in tone because he searched and struggled in a prayerful way for the meaning of the Word in the presence of his hearers, just as

---

[380] This is P. Duployé as cited by, P.-M. GY, "La mystagogie dans la liturgie ancienne et dans la pensée liturgique d'aujourd'hui," in A.M. TRIACCA - A. PISTOIA (eds.), *Mystagogie: pensée liturgique d'aujourd'hui et liturgie ancienne*, Bibliotheca Ephemerides liturgicae. Subsidia 70, Rome 1993, 137-143, here 139.

[381] On Origen and Paul, see H. DE LUBAC, *Histoire et Esprit, l'intelligence de l'Écriture d'après Origène*, Paris 1950, 69-77. See also F. COCCHINI, *Il Paolo di Origene*, Rome 1992.

[382] P. NAUTIN in SCh 232, 152-157 collects many examples of Origen reflecting on his own preaching.

he did in his studies.[383] Augustine is another model of a way of giving oneself to the congregation. Among the things that make him such an effective preacher is his complete familiarity over years with his congregation, his being totally at ease with them and they with him- not the ease of a friendly chat about nothing, but the ease of exchange for the sake of love on matters that bear on salvation and eternal life.[384]

If there is a spiritual work that the preacher must undertake and dare to reflect in his preaching, there is also a spiritual work to be done among the listeners; and, indeed, the preacher must call them to it. The following is an especially effective example by Augustine: "Behold, brothers and sisters, a great mystery: the sound of my words hits your ears, but the teacher is within! Don't think that you can learn something from a mere mortal. I can exhort you with the sound of my voice, but if there be not one within who teaches, all my noise achieves nothing. Do you need a proof of this? Well, you've all heard this sermon, haven't you? But how many will go out of here having learned nothing? I've done my part; I've spoken to you all. But those in whom the interior anointing has not spoken, those whom the Holy Spirit has not instructed interiorly, they will go out of here having learned nothing. The exterior teaching is a certain kind of help; it acts as a spur. But the one who teaches hearts has his pulpit in heaven. This is why he himself said, 'Call no one on earth teacher; one only is your teacher: Christ.' (Matt 23:10)"[385]

---

[383] For good summary accounts of Origen as a preacher, see A. OLIVAR, *La predicación cristiana antigua*, 62-69; P. NAUTIN, SCh 232, 101-191; D. SHEERIN, "The Role of Prayer in Origen's Homilies," in *Origen of Alexandria, His World and His Legacy*, edd. C. Kannengiesser and W.L. Petersen, University of Notre Dame Press, 1988, 200-214; T.K. CARROLL, *Preaching the Word, Message of the Fathers of the Church*, Wilmington 1984, 42-47.

[384] See F. VAN DER MEER, "Augustine the Preacher," in *Augustine, Bishop of Hippo*, 412-452.

[385] AUGUSTINE, *Tractates on the First Epistle of John 3:13*, SCh 75, 210. Translation mine.

Conclusion

I would like briefly to offer by way of conclusion four practical recommendations which are suggested to me by all of the foregoing and for which the foregoing has been the argument.

First, preachers need to become again masters of the tradition of typology. Some will think me nostalgic in this, but in my defense I think it appropriate to share a concrete experience I have had with its success. Several years ago I found myself involved in preparing a seven year old boy for baptism. He had heard from other children that he was going to somehow or other become amply wet during the course of the ceremony. He asked me with considerable anxiety if this were true and what was it about. Relying on our having already read many Bible stories together, I asked him if he remembered the day when God created the waters and gathered them into the sea. He did. I asked him to tell me the story of Noah's flood, and he was able to do so. Then we spoke of the water of Exodus, and he knew that story well. We remembered Christ's baptism in the Jordan, and he was able to remember the detail of the appearance of the Holy Spirit in the form of a dove as well as the voice of the Father. I spoke to him also of the blood and water which flowed from Christ's pierced side. At the end of this conversation, which took perhaps five minutes, I simply told him that this was the water that would be poured all over him in his baptism, that the Spirit would hover over him and the Father's voice speak within him. His little body gave an involuntary shudder; his eyes widened and brightened; the expression on his face passed in an instant from the anxiety that had been there to an excited smile. He said nothing, and he clearly understood. Then I went through with him some of the types of the eucharist, finishing, of course, with the Lord's Supper and the gift of his body and blood. I told him simply that this same body and blood would be given to him. He understood.

At a party after these sacraments of initiation, Nicholas was running on the lawn and playing with other children. I called him over and asked how he felt. He said, "I feel like I have a new body." "Oh!" I exclaimed; "and what does it feel like?" "It feels like it's filled with light!" he said. I thought only to add a promise to the theological understanding he had achieved. I told him that if he ever felt the light go out, anytime in the rest of his life, he could come again to Sunday eucharist and fill his body again with this same light. Typology will work if we would but give it to the Christian people.

My other recommendations will be offered without examples and thus more briefly. My second recommendation is that preachers practice regularly connecting the Scriptures of the day to the celebration of the eucharist which follows them. I have suggested that every Gospel and every other biblical text which supports the Gospel is a unique door of entry into the eucharistic mystery. Preachers should lead the assembly through such doors.

Thirdly, we should not shy from preaching doctrine. This should not be conceived as preaching something other than Scripture. Doctrine is Scripture's deepest sense in a way that exactly parallels the liturgy itself as Scripture's deepest sense. I have not entered into detail here about doctrinal questions, but I hope to have shown that the liturgical celebration itself is the context in which doctrine first emerges and the foundation on which it rests. Consequently, it is there that it can be expounded and continually refreshed. The center is clear: in the eucharist we have communion in the death and resurrection of Jesus, true God and true man, in whom God is revealed as Trinity.

Finally, as has been often suggested in recent decades, we should work to promote again a well developed eucharistic preaching during the season of Easter. Everything in the season cries out for this and is in place for it: the Lectionary, both for weekdays and Sundays, is full of passages that without much effort can be expounded in the ways I have been suggesting here.[386] But more: of this whole season, it can be said with theological precision, "This is the day that the Lord has made."[387]

---

[386] In the context of the Lectionary, mention should be made of the opportunity for a special series of preaching on the eucharist provided from the 17th to the 21st Sundays of the Year in cycle B, where the Gospels are taken from the Bread of Life discourse in the Gospel of John with Old Testament and apostolic readings which support their sense.

[387] See Augustine's delightful Easter homily on this Psalm verse which was repeated again and again throughout the Easter season. The sermon is a fine example of the Fathers' capacity to unite many scriptural texts around just one key word, in this case, the theme of *day*. "So what is this day which the Lord has made? Live good lives, and you will be this day yourselves."

This means that the Lord himself through his Spirit is very much at work in the Church during this time. The Church that celebrates eucharist during the Easter season knows itself to be in communion with the Apostles, who described themselves as those "who ate and drank with Jesus after he rose from the dead." (Acts 2:10-41) This is the Lord who still will open our minds to the understanding of the Scriptures,[388] showing from Moses and the prophets and the psalms what refers to him, showing that the Messiah had to suffer so to enter into glory; that is, showing the mystery of the text as converging on his death and resurrection. And this is the Lord whom we will recognize precisely in the breaking of the bread, whereupon he vanishes from our sight. Visible sacraments, invisible Mystery!

AUGUSTINE, *Sermon* 229B. *MA* 1, 464-466 or *PLS* 2, 556-558. English, E. Hill, *Sermons* III/6 (184-229Z), 273.

[388] For the phrasing of what follows, see Lk 24:25-47.

Chapter 11

ADORATION OF THE BLESSED SACRAMENT

Introduction

It is not possible to love Christ without adoring him. Indeed, one of the greatest joys of our loving him is to adore him. Of course, he is loved in other ways also: by keeping his commandments, by our love for one another, by sharing with him in prayer the joys and sorrows of each day. If there are many ways of loving him, there are also different ways of adoring. One of the privileged ways is to adore him in the Blessed Sacrament. But what is the meaning of this? How is it done? What actually are we doing when we come in prayer before the Blessed Sacrament in the tabernacle or when the Sacrament is exposed to our view for veneration? These reflections will try to give some answer to such questions.

It is important to find the right starting point for an answer, and in this regard the tradition and teaching of the Church are completely clear. Adoration of Christ in the Blessed Sacrament is always to be understood as deriving from the presence of Christ in the actual celebration of the eucharist; adoration is meant to bring us again to the celebration of the eucharist with greater fervor and understanding. So, adoration begins in the celebration of Mass itself. However, in the Mass adoration is primarily directed to God the Father. It is adoration "in spirit and truth," (John 4:23) that is, adoration of the Father through Christ, the Truth, and in the Holy Spirit. Nonetheless, there are different moments in the course of the eucharistic celebration where Christ himself is adored in the very elements of the Sacrament, that is, in the bread and in the wine which have been transformed into his body and blood.

The celebration of the eucharist, the Mass, is an unfathomable mystery. It is the Church's greatest treasure, indeed, her essence. It is an inexhaustible fountain, yielding in every generation and in the heart of every believer ever fresh knowledge of God-Father, Son, and Holy Spirit. Often, however, the actual celebration seems to pass us by too quickly, even when we have managed to participate with attention and understanding. So, I want to suggest here that adoration of Christ in the Blessed Sacrament outside of Mass can be best conceived as a meditative contemplation of what is too difficult to grasp and digest all at once during Mass. In prayer before the Blessed Sacrament I am continuing in quiet reflection my communion with Christ from Mass, and I am preparing for the next communion. A little history and some theological reflection can help in understanding why I suggest viewing things in this way.

Historical Notes

Adoration of the Blessed Sacrament outside of Mass is a practice peculiar to the Latin church, and it developed there only in its second millennium. Such a fact requires some caution and raises some questions. We should be cautious, for example, of thinking that such adoration is a practice to be required of all. In fact, it is a gift found in some parts of the Church, given to some to practice, while others are blessed with other gifts and different ways of prayer. Naturally, concerning a practice that was virtually not present in the Church's first thousand years, we will want to ask how it came about.

Reservation of the Blessed Sacrament outside of Mass seems to have been a part of the Church's eucharistic practice almost from the beginning. But this is different from adoration. In the patristic era, the purpose of reservation was so that the sick and others who could not attend the actual celebration of the eucharist would also be able to communicate.[389] In the second century Justin Martyr tells of deacons carrying the sacrament directly from the Sunday eucharist to those who could not attend. Towards the end of the same century Tertullian speaks of the faithful carrying the sacrament from the eucharistic celebration so that they could communicate later in their homes. In the early third century *The Apostolic Tradition*, a church order which

---

[389] The earliest witnesses for this question are JUSTIN MARTYR, *Apology* I, 65-67; TERTULLIAN, *On Prayer*, 19; *The Apostolic Tradition of Hippolytus*, nn. 36-38; CYPRIAN OF CARTHAGE, *On the Lapsed*, n. 25. What follows summarizes what is found in these texts.

describes various liturgical practices, speaks of the same custom, as well as of taking special care of the particles of the eucharist.

When I say that this is to be distinguished from adoration, I simply mean that the purpose of reserving the eucharist was not so that Christians could be before it in prayerful adoration. It was rather that they might receive it. But these very early practices of the Church show us at least two essential things about the eucharist that we will want to retain for our own understanding of prayer before the Sacrament. First, the ancient practices show that reservation is done primarily with a view toward receiving the sacrament. It comes from the actual celebration and extends that celebration to those who cannot be present at it. The scope of eucharistic *reservation* is that people might *receive* the eucharist. A second thing that the ancient practices show is that there was an implicit, instinctive understanding that the presence of Christ perdured in the consecrated bread beyond the time of the actual celebration. The practice of actually adoring Christ present in the bread develops slowly as a logical unfolding of this implicit understanding.

In drawing attention to these practices, I am speaking not about the heart of the eucharistic celebration but rather about something derivative from it. The heart of the celebration from the patristic era to the present has always been what the name eucharist means: thanksgiving. Thanksgiving for our salvation is offered to God the Father through Jesus his Son in the Holy Spirit. To speak of our thanking the Father "through Christ" is not a throwaway phrase. The Church's thanks to the Father could never be worthy of the divine majesty were her gifts of bread and wine not transformed into the body and blood of Christ offered for the world's salvation on Calvary. This pouring out of the life of Jesus for the sake of the world was his act of adoration of the Father, and it is this that the Church likewise holds up in thanksgiving to the Father. This is why the eucharist is called a memorial of the Lord's death, and the very same is our thanksgiving to the Father. This is thanking him "through Christ," adoring him "through Christ:" "Through him, with him, in him, in the unity of the Holy Spirit, all glory and honor is yours, Almighty Father, forever and ever."

So, in the heart of the eucharistic celebration it is primarily the Father, not Christ, to whom worship is directed. And yet this does not say it all, for from the beginning there was also a sense of Christ himself being hymned and adored in the community's gathering for prayer.[390] The Council of Nicea in 325 faced really only one specific question about Christ: was Christ to be considered a creature, however highly exalted, or was he to be considered as divine, existing from all eternity? It was this latter that was deemed to express the apostolic faith of the Church. Such clarity about the divinity of Christ was useful for the Christian community, even if it raised other problems; [391] and it inevitably had its influence on how Christians understood their eucharistic experience. A sense of the presence of the crucified and now glorified Christ always pervaded the community which assembled to give thanks to the Father through him. Now, with the language of Nicea, the community could understand that the Christ who was present and active in the eucharistic assembly was none less than "God from God, Light from Light, true God from true God." Inevitably — and quite rightly — liturgical practice expanded to include gestures and words which were appropriate to this belief; namely, an adoration also of Christ through whom the Father was being adored.

If we ask what the patristic Church understood about the bread and wine of the eucharistic rite, we could respond by saying that there was at this time an almost instinctive sense of the nature of a sacrament. The bread and wine were a *sacrament* of the Lord's body and blood.[392] That is, by means of bread and wine we come into contact with something that now would otherwise be beyond reach; namely, the risen and glorified body

---

[390] This is a long and complex story, for there was a kind of tension in preserving a clear and coherent monotheism while at the same time adoring both the one whom Christ called God and Father and Christ himself. For more on this see L.W. HURTADO, *One God, One Lord, Early Christian Devotion and Ancient Jewish Monotheism*, London 1988.

[391] For example, if Christ is God and the one whom he calls Father is God, how many gods are there? Any answer other than "one God" was impossible, and yet Christ and the Father are not the same thing, so how many gods are there? It will be subsequent councils that are able to give solid answers to these questions.

[392] Other terms were also used: *figure* of his body and blood, *type* of, *image of*, the *mystery* of..., etc. For examples, see TERTULLIAN, *Against Marcion*, 4:40; AMBROSE, *On the Sacraments*, 4:5; AUGUSTINE, *Exposition on the Psalms*, Ps 3:1.

of Christ, no longer confined to space and time. So, by means of a sacrament we come into contact in space and time with that which transcends space and time. The sacrament is a middle term between us and the transcendent body of the Lord. I can touch and hold another person in my hands, make contact with another through touch. It is not quite the same with Christ, though it is like this. With Christ I touch the *sacrament* of his body and thereby make contact with his body through my body. The sacramental experience is at one and the same time concrete and transcendent, just as Christ is concrete and transcendent.

The delicacy and precision of this kind of thinking was in part lost in the Latin West during the early Middle Ages. In the ninth century complicated controversies about how to understand the presence of Christ in the eucharist swung between two poles. Was Christ to be understood as being truly present *(in veritate)* or only symbolically present *(in figura)?* These poles could not have been considered opposites in the patristic Church, where symbolic presence — presence by means of a sacrament — was not a less real presence, but one appropriate to both the transcendent and concrete reality of Christ. Now, in these controversies, a symbolic presence seemed to mean a less real, a less concrete presence. The alternatives hardened into extreme positions, on the one hand describing the presence of Christ in crudely realistic terms, on the other hand describing it as a presence not belonging to the physical world but something entirely symbolic and spiritual. Neither of these alternatives is correct, though each carries a partial truth. It took several centuries to establish the view that the eucharist can be real without being crudely realistic, and symbolic without being unreal.[393]

This was the context in which adoration of the Blessed Sacrament outside of Mass seems to have arisen. We first have

---

[393] I have summarized here very briefly complex theological questions which stretch over three or four centuries. There is an immense literature studying all this. Two useful summaries would be the following: E. Mazza, *The Celebration of the Eucharist, The Origin of the Rite and the Development of Its Interpretation,* translated by Matthew J. O'Connell, Collegeville 1999, 161-224. N. Mitchell, *Cult and Controversy: the Worship of the Eucharist Outside Mass,* New York 1982, 66-195.

evidence of it in the late twelfth or early thirteenth centuries. A fruit of the controversies was — despite all the wrangling — a stronger sense of the intense presence of Christ in the eucharist, a sense of wonder in the manner of his presence. From this arose an even greater desire to adore Christ so present, to contemplate the mystery, to gaze on it with awe.[394]

Theological Reflections

With some of the relevant history thus summarized, a few theological reflections can help us to step beyond the controversies and to understand the value of eucharistic adoration in our own time. Most important of all is that adoration be linked to the actual celebration of the eucharist and to the reception of communion. This has always been at the heart of the reason for reservation and at the heart of the practice of adoration, even if this focus was sometimes lost in the midst of controversies. In our own times the Church reiterates this teaching with clarity: "When the faithful honor Christ present in the sacrament, they should remember that this presence is derived from the sacrifice and is directed toward sacramental and spiritual communion." [395]

Where the Blessed Sacrament is present, either in a tabernacle or exposed on the altar for adoration, this is evidence that a community has celebrated the eucharist, with all that this means and implies. We can never adequately grasp how much is accomplished in the community every time the eucharist is celebrated. It is this that we are seeking to understand the more

---

[394] This is the best fruit of the controversies, a fruit which shows itself in deep eucharistic devotion in the lives of many saints through the coming centuries. See É. LONGPRÉ, "Eucharistie et expérience mystique," in *Dictionnaire de spiritualité* IV/2, 1590-1621. There could also be a polemic edge to various practices of adoration, i.e., against those who claim the presence is "merely symbolic" one asserts realism by adoring the very bread and wine. This will be true later also in response to the position of some Protestant Reformers, who held either a soft symbolic presence or that the presence of Christ in the bread and wine did not outlast the actual celebration. Being on one's knees before the tabernacle or the exposed sacrament obviously expresses a different faith.

[395] *Holy Communion and Worship of the Eucharist Outside Mass*, n. 80 in *The Rites of the Catholic Church*, New York 1976, 484.

and contemplate in a continued adoration of Christ in the sacrament. When I am present before Christ in the tabernacle, it is a time of intimate communion with him simply because I am concentrated on him. I can deepen in a very personal way the communion with him that I have experienced in the communal celebration, a communion which, as I suggested in the beginning, is perhaps too difficult to grasp and digest all at once during Mass. The Sacrament exposed on the altar concentrates my attention on the very place where the community has celebrated the memorial of the Lord's death. Generally the exposition of the Blessed Sacrament is done for the sake of a more communal adoration. Even if I am in silent prayer alone, I am alongside others who adore with me. We adore because we have celebrated. Our adoration increases not only communion with Christ but with one another, expressing one same faith together.

Whether it is a question of private prayer before the tabernacle or communal prayer before the sacrament exposed, the adoration of Christ during the course of the Mass can indicate a proper and fruitful approach to these devotions. It remains true and must not be forgotten, as we have said, that in the Mass it is primarily the Father who is adored, through Christ and in the Holy Spirit. But there are moments in the celebration where the ritual act is an act of adoration directed to Christ. Already in the liturgy of the Word, apart from the general sense of the presence of the risen Lord "who opens our minds to the understanding of the Scriptures" thus causing "our hearts to burn within us," (Luke 24:32) there are prayers like "Lord, have mercy; Christ, have mercy," or "Praise to you, Lord Jesus Christ," together with all the signs of respect and joy that greet the reading of the Gospel. All these are ways in which I can also pray before the Blessed Sacrament.

Nonetheless, it is especially the eucharistic prayer and communion that indicate the sense of adoration outside of Mass. After the priest has pronounced the words of Christ over the bread, he holds it up for our view that we may seek somehow to penetrate the mystery of its transformation into the body of Christ. Then he genuflects in adoration before it, with all in the community following his gesture in their hearts and with gestures of their own. He does the same with the cup of wine. Exposition of the Blessed Sacrament is like a freezing of this moment for our continued contemplation. Prayer before the tabernacle is much the same. Such contemplation will help me in the next celebration to be present to the moment with even greater awe and love.

Again, just before communion the priest holds up the body of Christ for the view of all, proclaiming, "Behold the Lamb of God!" Already in the liturgies of patristic times this was a strong moment of adoration of Christ present in the Sacrament. I approach communion knowing that "I am not worthy" but trusting in his mercy. And just before receiving communion each communicant is directed to render a sign of reverence, a bow or genuflection, before the Sacrament. Above all in the reception of communion I adore Christ. It is the fundamental attitude with which I receive him. Either in the silent prayer of the whole community which follows immediately or in that silent prayer extended later before the Blessed Sacrament, I hear his words echoing within me: "Behold, I stand at the door and knock. If anyone hears my voice and opens the door, I will enter his house and dine with him, and he with me." (Rev 3:20) But there is more. For through this wondrous intimacy with Christ, I am taken by him to know another; namely, his Father. My knowledge of Christ becomes knowledge of the Father: "Just as the living Father sent me and I have life because of the Father, so also the one who feeds on me will have life because of me." (John 6:57) I want to hold myself before this mystery. I want to penetrate it more and more. I want Jesus' words to be fulfilled in me and in the whole Church: "On that day you will realize that I am in my Father and you are in me and I in you." (John 14:20)

I cannot love Christ without adoring him. Love of him promises me trinitarian communion and eternal life: "Whoever loves me will keep my word, and my Father will love him, and we will come to him and make our dwelling with him." (John 14:23)

REFERENCE TO ORIGINAL PUBLICATIONS

As mentioned in the Introduction, the studies contained in this volume collect and reformulate into a whole, articles previously published elsewhere. Below the references are given to the original place of publication of each chapter. They are published here with permission.

CHAPTER ONE:

"Theology at the Eucharistic Table, Master Themes in the Theological Tradition," in *Pro Ecclesia*, 11:4 (Fall 2002): 389-401.

CHAPTER TWO:

"Deepening the Theological Dimensions of Liturgical Studies," *Communio* 23 (1996): 508-523.

CHAPTER THREE:

"Uncovering the Dynamic *Lex Orandi-Lex Credendi* in the Anaphora of *The Apostolic Tradition of Hippolytus*," in *Ecclesia Orans* 18 (2001): 327-364.

CHAPTER FOUR:

"Uncovering the Dynamic *Lex Orandi-Lex Credendi* in the Trinitarian Theology of Origen," in *Ecclesia Orans* 19 (2002): 85-100.

CHAPTER FIVE:

"Liturgy and Fundamental Theology, Frameworks for a Dialogue," *Ecclesia Orans* 11 (1994): 69-99.

CHAPTER SIX:

"The Eucharist and Fundamental Theology," *Ecclesia Orans* 13 (1996): 407-437.

CHAPTER SEVEN:

"Anamnesis, Epiclesis and Fundamental Theology," in *Ecclesia Orans* 15 (1998): 211-238.

CHAPTER EIGHT:

"The Manifestation of the Trinitarian Mystery in the Eucharistic Assembly," in *Imaginer la théologie catholique, Mélanges offerts à Ghislain Lafont, édités par Jeremy Driscoll*, Rome (2000): 501-512.

CHAPTER NINE:

"Liturgy, Formation, and the General Directory for Catechesis," in *Antiphon, A Journal for Liturgical Renewal* 4:1 (1999): 14-21.

CHAPTER TEN:

"The Fathers and Eucharistic Preaching," in *Antiphon, A Journal for Liturgical Renewal* 5:3 (2000): 29-38.

"The Fathers and Eucharistic Preaching," in *Pro Ecclesia*, 11:1 (Winter 2002): 24-40.

CHAPTER ELEVEN:

"Eucharistic Adoration," in *A Book of Readings on the Eucharist, A Eucharistic Jubilee*, ed. National Conference of Catholic Bishops, Subcommittee on the Third Millennium, Washington (2000): 79-87.

INDEX OF NAMES

Ambrose of Milan, 220 221 226 228 232 240
Apollinaire of Laodicea, 75 76
Athanasius of Alexandria, 67
Augustine of Hippo, 47 187 224 228 230 231 233 235 236 240
Azevedo M.C., 124

Baldovin J., 49
Balthasar H.U. von, 24 41 101 114 118-124 127 132 137 138 144 176 183 211
Barkley G.W., 93-96 98
Barnard L.S., 216
Beauduin, 100
Boethius, 34
Bonaccorso G., 158 159 164
Botte B., 46 62 63 65 71 73-75 77 79 80
Bradshaw P., 48-50 69 228 229
Burreson K.J., 228
Buschmann G., 72

Camelot P., 72
Cantalamessa R., 53 59 66 67 75 76
Capelle B., 63
Carrier H., 124
Carroll T.K., 233
Casel O., 100
Castagno A.C., 83
Celsus, 83
Chadwick H., 34 83-85 88 89
Chupungco A., 46 47
Cocchini F., 232
Connollly R.H., 61 63 68 77 79
Corbon J., 134 137 144 171 210

Cross F.L., 228
Cuming G.J., 61
Cummings O., 14
Cyprian of Carthage, 16 60 68 223 238
Cyril of Jerusalem, 220 228 230

Daly R., 84-88
Daniélou J., 58
De Clerck P., 45 142
De Soos B., 165
Dix G., 49
Dotti G., 142
Duployé P., 232
Dupuis J., 124

Eutychus, 215

Fisichella R., 99-103 105-111 114 115 117 126 127 129 148 150 172 183
Flannery A., 131 133
Foley E., 142
Francesconi G., 220 221 226

Gilbert M., 136
Giraudo C., 51
Granfield P., 47
Greer R.A., 88-92
Gregory the Great, 153
Grillo A., 130 132 158
Guardini R., 101
Gy P.-M., 232

Hänggi A., 46
Hamman A., 47
Hannah D.D., 58
Heraclides, 84-87 92 96 98

Hill E., 230 231 236
Hippolytus of Rome, 45 63 67
Hippolytus Ps., 48 49 51 52 58 59 66
  69 75 76
Hughes K., 142
Hurtado L.W., 240

Ignatius of Antioch, 73
Irenaeus of Lyons, 13 50 51 60 62 65
  68 69 77 78 206
Irwin K., 45 101

Jasper R.C.D., 61
John Chrysostom, 75
John Chrysostom Ps., 75
Jungmann J., 47
Justin Martyr, 49 50 58 60 62 65 66
  79 85 215 216 238

Kannengiesser C., 233
Kasper W., 166
Kavanagh A., 153

Lafont G., 41 101 111-115 117 118
  121 125 127 143 170 172 173 175
  177 195
Lane R.E., 87 229
Latourelle R., 99 102 105 136 217
Laurance J.D., 68 223
Lebreton J., 46
Leo the Great, 23 144
Levada W., 197
Lies L., 83
Littledate A.V., 132
Lonergan B., 29-31
Longpré E., 242
Lubac H. de, 230 232

McPartlan P., 44 134 151
Maluf L., 112
Mansini G., 179
Marsili S., 42 100-104 107 108 119
  126 127 132 133 137

Martín J.P., 79
Mazza E., 48-54 56-60 63 64 66-70
  72 74-78 87 220 221 223 226 227
  229 241
Mazzucco C., 83
Meer F. van der, 224 233
Melito of Sardis, 48 49 51 52 59 64 67
Metzger M., 46 49
Mitchell N., 49 241

Nautin P., 80 84 88 92 233
Neunheuser B., 159 161

O'Collins G., 148
O'Connell M.J., 221 223 227 229 241
Olivar A., 217 224 233
Origen, 51 54 83-97 223 232
Ostdiek G., 142

Pahl I., 46
Pavlidou E., 166
Pazzini D., 85
Perler O., 67
Peter Chrysologus, 225 226
Petersen W.L., 233
Philo of Alexandria, 75
Pistoia A., 220 232
Polycarp of Smyrna, 72
Potterie I. de la, 117 177
Pozzo G., 105
Prosper of Aquitaine, 36 45 47

Rad G. von, 161
Raffa V., 51 62 229
Ratcliff E.C., 69
Rocchetta C., 105

Scherer J., 84 85 88
Schilson A., 45
Schütz W., 83
Sheerin D., 233
Skublics E., 14
Studer B., 46 47 54 60 187 223

Taft R., 71
Terrin A.N., 158
Tertullian, 54 60 223 238 240
Theodore of Mopsuestia, 228
Triacca A.M., 220 232

Vagaggini C., 102

Wicks J., 113

Zizioulas J., 44 134 139 141 150 152
    164 166 168 170 174-176 178 179
    181 187

Printed in the United Kingdom
by Lightning Source UK Ltd.
126567UK00001B/112-291/A